Prologue to Revolution

Studies in Cuban History
Series Editor: Louis A. Pérez Jr.

Politics of Illusion: The Bay of Pigs Invasion Reexamined,
edited by James G. Blight and Peter Kornbluh

Insurrection and Revolution: Armed Struggle in Cuba, 1952–1959,
Gladys Marel García-Pérez

Prologue to Revolution: Cuba, 1898–1958,
Jorge Ibarra

PROLOGUE TO REVOLUTION

Cuba, 1898–1958

Jorge Ibarra

translated by Marjorie Moore

LYNNE
RIENNER
PUBLISHERS

BOULDER
LONDON

14434

30 JUL 2001

Published in the United States of America in 1998 by
Lynne Rienner Publishers, Inc.
1800 30th Street, Boulder, Colorado 80301

and in the United Kingdom by
Lynne Rienner Publishers, Inc.
3 Henrietta Street, Covent Garden, London WC2E 8LU

Library of Congress Cataloging-in-Publication Data
Ibarra, Jorge.
     Prologue to revolution :   Cuba, 1898–1958   /   by Jorge Ibarra   ;
translated by Marjorie Moore.
          p.   cm. — (Studies in Cuban history)
     Includes bibliographical references and index.
     ISBN 1-55587-791-5 (alk. paper). — ISBN 1-55587-792-3 (pbk.   :
alk. paper)
     1. Social structure—Cuba—History—20th century.   2. Cuba—Social
conditions.   3. Cuba—Social conditions—1918–1959.   4. Cuba—
Economic conditions.   5. Cuba—Economic conditions—1918–1959.
6. Cuba—History—1895–   I. Title.   II. Series.
HN203.I23   1998
306'.097291—dc21   97-49324
                                                                              CIP

British Cataloguing in Publication Data
A Cataloguing in Publication record for this book
is available from the British Library.

Printed and bound in the United States of America

     The paper used in this publication meets the requirements
∞   of the American National Standard for Permanence of
     Paper for Printed Library Materials Z39.48-1984.

     5 4 3 2 1

Contents

Tables

Introduction

Louis A. Pérez Jr.

Cuba inaugurated its national existence compromised by North American interests, the defense of which was incorporated directly into the institutional structures of the new republic. Under the terms of the Platt amendment, Cuba was forced to acquiesce to limitations on national sovereignty, agreed to U.S. intervention, and was obliged to cede national territory to the United States for a naval station. These were the concessions that the United States demanded in exchange for ending the military occupation (1899–1902) and that were later negotiated into the Permanent Treaty of 1903. In that same year, Cuba and the United States signed a reciprocity trade treaty, whereby the island was directly and formally integrated into the North American economic system. The reciprocity treaty not only bound Cuba's principal export commodity—sugar—to a single market, the United States, but also opened key sectors of the Cuban economy—agriculture (especially sugar and tobacco), ranching, mining (especially iron), transportation (especially railways), utilities (gas, electricity, water, telephone), and banking—to foreign, mainly North American, control.

These developments had broad implications. The Platt amendment served to institutionalize U.S. hegemony in Cuba. The United States developed early into a power contender in the Cuban political system, with interests to defend and allies to support. The exercise of North American hegemony on this scale, for such sustained periods of time, acted insidiously on the principal institutions of the republic. North American intervention, in virtually all spheres of public life, was the dominant element of the Cuban republic.

In the decades that followed, U.S. control over the Cuban economy expanded, virtually unchecked, in almost all spheres. North American capital expanded in all key sectors. Under the reciprocity

1

treaty, preferential access to U.S. markets for Cuban agricultural products acted to promote Cuban dependency on sugar and facilitated foreign control over vital sectors of the economy. Reciprocity also discouraged economic diversification by fostering the consolidation of land from small units into the latifundia and concentration of ownership from local families to foreign corporations. The United States dominated Cuban trade and provided Cubans with most of their capital goods and consumer durables. North American manufactured goods saturated the Cuban market and hindered the development of local competition.

These were years, too, during which the island filled with North Americans. Merchants, traders, and retailers organized local distributorships of U.S. products. Technicians arrived to service the machine imports, operate the refineries, and work the mills. Tourists descended upon the island by the hundreds of thousands.

A thorough study of republican social structures in Cuba rests on an understanding of the forces that acted to shape the institutions and value systems of the postcolonial period. Two distinct phases were central to this process. The first spanned the years between 1898 and 1928, a time of expansion of North American economic forms and political structures that acted in decisive ways to shape the character of the nation. The second phase developed between 1929 and 1958, a period of economic contraction and structural readjustment to a diminishing role of North American capital, even as U.S. cultural forms and normative systems continued to play a dominant role within the national system. Both phases had as their point of departure—and end—economic crisis, political tumult, and social unrest; both culminated in upheavals of far-reaching consequences.

In this complex process, North American capital investment exercised a decisive impact on the formation—and deformation—of national institutions, as well as on forces related to class structures, gender roles, race relations, and demographic change. The North American presence of this magnitude, could not but contribute to the distortion of national institutions in both form and function. Social relationships, economic development, political structures, and cultural forms took definitive shape around the North American presence.

The failure of the Cuban economy to sustain both expansion and the expectation of the middle and working classes had significant repercussions. In many ways, Cubans were worse off in the 1950s than they had been in the 1920s. The island's share of the vital U.S. sugar market had decreased. In real terms, Cuban incomes had increased little. The purchasing power of Cuban exports between 1952 and

1956 was no more than it had been thirty years earlier. Unemployment and underemployment continued to cast a dark cloud over all social classes and took a serious toll on the morale and material condition of almost all Cubans.

This study by Jorge Ibarra examines the transformations in the social structures of the republic occasioned by economic developments. Class structures that were in utter disarray at the end of the war in 1898 had hardly been reconstituted and stabilized when the crisis of the 1920s, climaxed by the Great Depression, plunged the island into a new round of economic dislocation and political turmoil. After the 1930s, the new middle classes experienced a process of proletarianization and inevitably downward mobility in the face of contracting purchasing power and expanding uncertainty. At the same time, demographic pressure—most notably population growth within the context of a stagnant economy—had overtaken the capacity of production to sustain growth, contributing to what appeared as a permanent crisis. By the late 1940s and through the early 1950s, the economy underwent increasing stress. Sugar continued to dominate developmental strategies, to the detriment of all other potential growth sectors. Cubans continued to depend on an export product in which worldwide competition was especially intense.

All sectors of the Cuban economy remained vulnerable to the effects of price fluctuations in the international sugar market. The decline in sugar prices between 1952 and 1954 precipitated the first in a series of recessions in that decade. The effects of reciprocity were taking their toll, impeding in Cuba the type of industrial development characteristic of other Latin American countries at mid-century. Local industry that did exist had to face strong foreign competition with little or no tariff protection. Little incentive existed to expand manufactures beyond light consumer goods, largely food and textiles. With the Cuban population expanding at an annual rate of 2.5%, and 50,000 young men alone reaching working age every year, only 8,000 new jobs were created in industry between 1955 and 1958.

Into these circumstances, the deepening political crisis served further to polarize large sectors of the population. The illegal seizure of power by Fulgencio Batista in 1952 was under serious and direct challenge from a variety of sources: from students in the high schools and universities to workers in the provinces, from peasants in the countryside to armed insurgents in the mountains. As the political crisis deepened and economic conditions deteriorated, the island edged closer to social upheaval.

Batista's continued presence in power through the late 1950s compounded the crisis by creating political conditions that made economic growth almost impossible. Graft, corruption, and administrative malfeasance had a deleterious effect on economic confidence. As political opposition increased and armed struggle expanded, prospects for economic development grew bleak indeed. It was in this context that the process of disintegration, characterized by uncertainty about the present and loss of confidence in the future, fused with the political crisis of the 1950s to give the rationale for radical change a force of almost irresistible momentum.

As Ibarra argues persuasively, the antecedents of the Cuban revolution, what can properly be understood as "prologue," reached deeply into the final years of the nineteenth century as forces and circumstances that formed the basis of virtually every facet of republic institutions. They appeared in many forms: in gender hierarchies and state structures, as social formations and generational tensions, in reformist tendencies and revolutionary impluses. Ibarra's ranging analysis sheds insight on complex interrelationships that gave decisive definition to twentieth-century Cuba.

1

Finance Capital
and Economic Structures
of the Republic

The predominant role of U.S. financial capital in Cuban neocolonial society was determined by the key positions it held in the economic and social structure of the island and by its tendency to decapitalize and denationalize the dependent domestic bourgeoisie. For the purposes of this study, it is essential to elucidate the mechanisms by which U.S. financial capital was able to take possession of a considerable part of Cuba's economic surplus. Only an empirical study of these mechanisms can provide evidence of the diverse methods financial interests adopted to attain this end. At the same time, to demonstrate the dependence of the domestic bourgeoisie on foreign financial capital, it is not enough to enunciate this as a matter of principle; it is necessary to analyze it as a historical reality, corroborating by which expedients and in what way the national economic surplus was siphoned off.

A brief overview of the principal economic mechanisms of domination should give us an idea of how the Cuban social structure was distorted and how the autonomous evolution of its classes and strata was frustrated by U.S. financial capital.

Tariffs and Economic Development

The most common sociological generalizations have characterized the penetration of Latin America by U.S. financial capital solely in terms of the extraction of raw materials destined for use by U.S. manufacturing industries. In that schema the export of unrefined natural resources has been the logical result of the backwardness of Latin American productive forces, the scarcity of domestic capital, and the absence of an entrepreneurial spirit that would engage in transformational rather than merely extractive industrial activities. U.S. capital investments thus were made in branches of agriculture or in the creation of extractive agrarian or mining industries with the aim of supplying the U.S. market with raw materials or finished products. In reality, transformational agrarian industries capable of supplying the world market with finished goods in high demand did not exist in practically any Latin American country. In Cuba, however—where an exporting transformational agroindustry had processed finished products from sugar and tobacco in great demand on the world market since the end of the eighteenth century—the penetration of financial capital was forced to follow a totally different path. In the early nineteenth century, the United States began to purchase a considerable part of Cuban products derived from sugar and tobacco. But as it came to realize that its own industry could manufacture those products, the United States modified its customs tariffs, raising them considerably on finished products (refined sugar and Cuban cigars) and lowering them on raw materials and semiprocessed products (leaf tobacco and raw sugar). In the case of sugar, the U.S. tariff law of 1842 and the Sugar Act of 1861 made it virtually impossible for sugar refined in Cuba to enter the U.S. market, favoring instead the purchase of semiprocessed molasses and raw sugar (Moreno Fraginals, 1978, vol. 2: 180–189, 191–208).

The process of monopolistic concentration that ensued ended with the creation of the Havemeyer sugar trust. Havemeyer wrote that "the tariff was the mother of the trusts." By mutilating the Cuban sugar industry, U.S. tariff policy encouraged the creation of refineries in the United States based on the alliance of bank and industrial capital. In brief, the final phase of manufacture in Cuba's industrial process was chopped off at the base, with the aim of creating an artificial industry in the United States using raw or semiprocessed sugar. At the beginning of the twentieth century, following Cuba's wars of independence from Spain, capital linked to the sugar-refining industry on the Atlantic and Gulf coasts was finally able to make direct investments on the island that enabled U.S. investors to acquire dozens of sugar mills and create a vertical monopoly comprising production, refining, and marketing of the finished product for the U.S. market.

A similar fate had overtaken the Cuban tobacco industry in the nineteenth century. A decline in cigar manufacturing occurred when the industrialized countries of Europe and the United States began to establish cigar factories with the purpose of working leaf tobacco directly into cigars, leaving the dependent country to specialize only in production of the raw material. Thus, in July 1852 and again in October 1890 with promulgation of the McKinley Bill, tariffs were raised on Cuban cigars destined for the U.S. market, with the result that the island's sales of cigars were reduced by 50%, while purchases of leaf tobacco by the nascent U.S. cigar industry were stepped up (Rivero Muñiz, 1965: 280–286, 314).

The exact significance of U.S. tariff policy is apparent in some of the economic estimates of the epoch. According to the most accredited U.S. specialists in sugar production and marketing, more than one-fourth of the profits of Cuban sugar mill owners was absorbed by the refineries of the United States (Dalton, 1937: 256; Linski, 1939). Leland Jenks later estimated that 38% of the total value of the Cuban harvest in 1918 went into the coffers of the U.S. sugar-refining trust, U.S. shipping companies, and the U.S. Treasury (Jenks, 1966: 195–197). The historian Ramiro Guerra believed that 51.3% of the value of Cuban sugar in 1938 was appropriated by the same entities (Torras, 1984, vol. 1: 144).

A legislative error in the U.S. Congress opened the possibility in 1930 for the establishment of sugar refineries in Cuba. Important U.S. and Cuban interests immediately invested in the refining industry, making subsequent rectification of the erroneous legislation very difficult. Thus, in 1934 a quota was established for sugar refined in Cuba, equivalent to 22% of the basic quota assigned to Cuban raw sugar. This quota was systematically reduced year after year until it reached a low in 1958 of 10.8% of the quota for raw sugar (Ibarra, 1995: 12–13).

The Cuban refining industry, which in conditions of free competition could have processed all the raw sugar sold to the U.S. market, helping considerably to diminish the catastrophic effects of unemployment in Cuba from 1928 to 1958, was notably held back by the iron hand of U.S. tariffs (Ibarra, 1995: 13–14).

U.S. tariff policy regarding Cuban cigars likewise was unvarying in its impact throughout the first half of the twentieth century. Table 1.1

Table 1.1   Leaf Tobacco and Cigar Exports, 1909–1933 and 1934–1958

	Exports of Leaf Tobacco		Exports of Cigars	
	(thousands of pounds)	(thousands of pesos)	(thousands of units)	(thousands of pesos)
1909–1933	914,482	552,024	2,847,085	258,085
1934–1958	857,514	626,458	1,262,787	162,102

Source: Cuba, Ministerio de Agricultura, 1947.

illustrates the movement of leaf tobacco and cigar exports over a span
of forty-eight years.

As shown in Table 1.1, the value of exported leaf tobacco compared to cigars was 2:1 in the first period, whereas this value was
almost 4:1 in the second period. At the same time, the value of
exported cigars declined by 37%. The progressive displacement of
the finished product in favor of the raw material in the foreign market testified to the acute process of deindustrialization that took place
on the island. Not only were cigars displaced by leaf tobacco, but
Cuban leaf tobacco was gradually replaced by tobacco grown in the
southern United States.

This process of deindustrialization led to a reduction in the number of workers in Cuban cigar factories. Thus, whereas 15,000 cigar
makers were employed in the cigar industry in Havana and 20,000 in
the rest of the country in 1860, by 1899 these numbers had been
reduced to 10,000 in the capital, although a total of 20,000 still existed in the country as a whole. Two decades later, the 1919 census registered only 3,500 in Havana and 6,000 in the entire country.
According to the 1943 census, cigar makers numbered 5,000 in
Havana and some 12,000 throughout the nation (Stubbs, 1985: 67).
In the meantime, the number of workers in the U.S. cigar industry in
Florida increased from 10,000 at the beginning of the twentieth century to more than 100,000 in 1923. In this way, the dependent country was deindustrialized and left with a permanent situation of unemployment as the northern neighbor's industry grew, accelerating its
process of industrialization and attenuating the effects of its own
unemployment (Perdomo and Posse, 1945: 118–125).

Finance Capital and Transportation

The progressive displacement of Cuban and Spanish capital from
maritime and railway transportation by U.S. and British financial capital beginning in 1910 reveals the delicate situation in which domestic
interests were placed vis-à-vis U.S. tariff policy. Until 1892, the year in
which English capital made its first important investments in Cuban
railways, Spanish and Cuban interests had controlled railway property
on the island. Table 1.2 shows the correlation between domestic and
foreign capital in Cuban railways from 1900 to 1920.

Similarly, at the opening of the century some fifty Spanish-Cuban-
owned ships, weighing between 500 and 2,000 tons, carried out a
large part of the maritime commerce between Cuba and Spain. By
the middle of the century, only four ships of this tonnage remained in
the possession of domestic capital (Riccardi, 1966: 296–297).

Table 1.2   Capital Invested in Cuban Railways, 1900–1920 (in millions of pesos)

	British	U.S.	Spanish-Cuban
1900	.926	.246	.888
1911	1.926	1.140	.495
1920	1.824	1.880	.640

Sources: Carlson, 1901; Lloyd, 1913: 333; Santamaría, 1995: 500.

Confronting the evident fact of the growing penetration of U.S. financial capital during the first two decades of the twentieth century, those inspired by the counterfactual current of the school of new economic history might ask, "What would have happened if Cuban sugar and tobacco had enjoyed conditions of free competition, without a tariff barrier protecting the U.S. market? Would the Cuban agroexporter bourgeoisie have become a class sufficiently powerful to broaden or maintain its position at least in the country's railways and maritime transportation?" The answers to these questions could be found in a series of statistics on the amount of the agroexporting bourgeoisie's surplus that was appropriated by the U.S. government and U.S. refineries. Nevertheless, it is unnecessary to quantify the plundering to which that bourgeoisie was subjected in order to accept the idea of the inevitability of its defeat. A correlation had existed between the predominant position of the domestic bourgeoisie as a producer class and the dominant position it held in the economic infrastructure. The progressive decline of its role in transportation stemmed from the following realities: (1) the fragile condition in which this class was left by the war of 1895, which destroyed or seriously deteriorated the greater part of its properties; (2) the damage and severe loss inflicted on it by the U.S. tariff policy on refined sugar and cigars; and (3) the further weakening it suffered under the rigid control of sugar prices exerted by U.S. refineries. This set of circumstances contributed heavily to the loss by the domestic bourgeoisie of absolute control of transportation of its products that it had held since the nineteenth century. The loss of its position in the country's infrastructure in turn weakened still further its position as a producing class.

The exact significance for the domestic sugar bourgeoisie of the high railway tariffs imposed by successive Cuban governments to benefit the railroad companies was repeatedly stated by its most outstanding representatives of the epoch. According to the estimates presented by the Cuban hacendados, the freight rates paid by sugar mills to the railways ranged between 16% and 20% of sugar production costs. These rates affected Cuban mills primarily, since they, in contrast to U.S.-owned mills, lacked railway lines of their own (Ibarra, 1995: 19–20). At the same time, U.S.- and British-owned railways took advantage of their dominant influence on the Cuban government to impose on the rural propertied classes freight rates on agricultural products far higher than those charged by railroad companies in the United States and Europe. According to the railroad expert Alberto de Ximeno, producers of agricultural products in the western provinces of Cuba were obliged to pay 1.3 times more per metric ton of merchandise than producers in Switzerland, 1.8 times more than in England, 2.6 times more than in France, 2.7 times more than in Germany, 3 times more than in Belgium, and 5.1 times more than in the United States (Ximeno, 1912). It is extremely difficult to imagine how the Cuban agrarian bourgeoisie, constrained as it was by the mechanisms of foreign financial capital, could have become independent. Only the construction of the island's central highway by the Machado government finally put an end to the transportation monopoly of the U.S.- and British-owned railways. As a result of competition from highway transportation companies and the economic stagnation that characterized the country from 1928 to 1958, railroad earnings fell sharply. Between 1906 and 1928, net profits of railroads were 293,264 pesos; between 1928 and 1950 they amounted to only 127,599 pesos (Zanetti and García, 1987: 402). (Throughout the twentieth century, the peso and the dollar were equivalent in value.)

Nevertheless, the sugar industry and agricultural production in general were not exempt from excessive railway charges. Thus, by government stipulation, railway freight rates increased from $0.89 per ton/kilometer in 1928 to $1.03 in 1952 (U.S. Department of Commerce, *Investments in Cuba*, 1956: 109). Referring to the transportation of agricultural products in general, the Truslow Report recognized that "discriminatory freight rates still favored sugar against other agricultural products transported by railway" (Truslow, 1951: 96).

At the same time, the virtual monopoly of the island's maritime transportation attained by U.S. shipping companies was likewise unchallenged by legislative measures favoring expansion of the Cuban merchant marine. The interminable river of foreign exchange extracted from the country in the form of freight rates was at no time detained. The Cuban government that dared to establish preferential flag rights ran the risk of provoking direct U.S. intervention in the country. The large remittances of foreign exchange absorbed by foreign shipping companies amounted to $110 million annually between 1935 and 1945 (Valmaña, 1945: 71). The National Bank of Cuba reported a drain of $177 million from the national economy for the years 1952 to 1954.

Finance Capital and Banking Structures

At a very early stage, foreign financial capital acquired control of bank loans for economic activities on the island and loans to successive Cuban governments. The first U.S.-owned banking institutions established themselves in the country during the first U.S. intervention. By 1925 the majority of banks on the island were in U.S. hands. Beginning in 1910, the greater part of banking operations to finance the country's harvests were carried out by U.S.-owned banks. These institutions extended credit only to those domestic investments able to offer guarantees equivalent to those existing in their country of origin. That is, access to credits from U.S. banks was limited to those who could offer the same guarantees as those provided in the United States by firms with considerable capitalist development. In Cuba the only economic activity able to extend such guarantees was the sugar harvest.

Additionally, from the beginning U.S.-owned banks had a decisive advantage over Spanish-owned banks. The backing the home banks in New York provided to their Cuban branches impeded their ruin in times of crisis.

Deposits in Cuban banks in 1926 totaled $61.3 million, whereas those in U.S. banks amounted to some $106 million. U.S. banks' dominance of loans was even more decisive: Loans made by Cuban banks reached only $26.5 million in 1921; those by U.S. banks totaled $201 million. Nevertheless, from 1925 to 1955 Cuban banks progressively increased their importance in the financial field, as indicated in Table 1.3.

Table 1.3   Deposits Made to Cuban Versus Foreign Banks, 1925–1955 (in millions of pesos)

	1925	1951	1955
Cuban banks	61.3	431.5	561.5
Foreign banks	106.2	389.5	387.8

Source: U.S. Department of Commerce, *Investments in Cuba,* 1956: 124–125.

Although the capital of national banks was derived fundamentally from the island's large Spanish merchant class, this class did not control the financing of harvests. Meanwhile, by putting into practice a more flexible and more liberal policy, Cuban credit institutions began to control the majority of commercial and industrial activities on the island. The factors that determined the growing importance of Cuban banking in 1950 were: (1) the creation of the National Bank, (2) the adoption of a monetary system based on the Cuban peso, (3) the growing diversification of short-term operations, and (4) a more liberal approach to loans than that of U.S. banks.

The National Bank, however, did not vary greatly from the methods for granting loans typically employed by Spanish and U.S. credit institutions. The structure of loans according to their recipients in 1957 shows that although the amount of credit considerably surpassed that of the 1940s, its distribution remained unaltered in its general lines. Thus, the proportion of total credit granted to the sugar industry in 1957 (40.4%) was very close to that in 1940 (43.3%). Nevertheless, credits destined for the importation of products in 1957 (34.8%) diminished in relation to 1940 (45.1%). Agricultural loans for food products in 1957 (18.2%) increased over agricultural loans in 1940 (16%). A considerable increase also took place in the tobacco and textile industries in 1957 (8.6%), compared to 1940, when total loans to all industries was almost insignificant (0.3%) (Collazo, 1989).

Taking into account that in 1957 75.2% of bank credit was destined to the sugar industry and the importing sector, we reach the conclusion that credit continued to be concentrated in the sectors offering absolutely safe guarantees to banks. Under such conditions, Cuban credit institutions could not encourage industrial and agricultural diversification in the country. The financial bases of economic activity continued in the 1950s as before despite the creation of the National Bank of Cuba.

Loans between the neocolonial Cuban state and U.S. financial capital revealed the same inflexible and exclusive practices. From 1902 to 1927, the neocolonial state obtained loans from large U.S. banking houses in the amount of more than $262 million. The grant of these loans depended invariably on the dominant financial interests of the various presidential administrations in the United States. The impossibility of the Cuban state's arranging loans with European banking institutions had been made clear from the beginning, even though those institutions offered more favorable interest rates. The first loans were granted to Cuba by the Spayer Bank, by virtue of the influence of that bank in the administrations of Theodore Roosevelt and William Taft. The loans the governments of Mario García

Menocal and Gerardo Machado obtained from the house of Morgan were the result of the prominent role of J. P. Morgan in the State Department until 1930.

Between 1928 and 1958, the structural dependence of Cuban governments was reinforced by credits granted by U.S. financial capital, with the difference that almost all credit was at that time assigned directly by U.S. government financial entities. Loans no longer came through private financial capital influential in the successive administrations but had to be arranged directly with federal financial agencies. Loans granted from 1928 to 1958 reached more than $541 million, doubling the amount obtained in the first three decades of the republic. With the introduction of the good neighbor policy of Franklin Roosevelt, the Export and Import Bank (EXIMBANK), a U.S. financial agency founded in 1934 to facilitate U.S. exports and investments in Latin America, was given the exclusive right to grant loans to the governments of Fulgencio Batista, Ramón Grau San Martín, and Carlos Prío Socarrás (Mikesell, 1955: 121–122; Espinosa García, 1971: 117).

Growing unemployment and the intensity of the depressive cycle between 1928 and 1958, as well as the institutional instability that characterized the period, strengthened the country's financial dependence on the United States. Successive loans helped to shore up governments that used the state budget to broaden their political clientele base to combat the growing sociopolitical opposition derived from the economic recession. The Machado and Batista dictatorships (1928–1933 and 1952–1958, respectively) arranged the most onerous and largest loans of the republican period. With the end of the expansive stage of the sugar industry (1898–1927) and the onset of the recessive economic cycle (1928–1958), the ties binding the Cuban neocolonial state to U.S. financial capital were tightened.

The denial or retention of authorization for loans was the means employed by the Department of State to control the objectives and plans traced by the Cuban governments. It was also a highly efficacious way to set forth, in the most peremptory terms, a series of demands on the Cuban governments. In this context, the EXIMBANK proved to be the most direct and suitable instrument for U.S. political interference.

Finance Capital, Sugar, and Utilities

Among the investments of U.S. financial capital on the island, the U.S.-owned sugar plantations and the Electric Bond and Share

Company were notable for their appropriation of a gigantic portion of the national economic surplus. The strategic position held by these investments in the sugar industry and in the island's electric power stations enabled them to dominate the domestic social classes. Their organic insertion in the productive forces of the country constituted one of the factors that determined the subordination and dependent character of the sugar bourgeoisie and domestic industry.

The heavy investments of U.S. financial corporations in the sugar industry contributed objectively to an accentuation of the process of *denationalization* of the island's productive forces and to the *decapitalization* of its sugar bourgeoisie. This dual process tended to paralyze development and impede the consolidation of a Cuban-Spanish domestic sugar bourgeoisie.

The movement to denationalize the country's wealth followed two directions: (1) At the end of the war of 1895 and in the first two decades of republican life, financial corporations of the northern neighbor rushed in to buy up dozens of Cuban- and Spanish-owned sugar mills and plantations that had been seriously damaged during the war. In view of the sustained rise in sugar prices during that period, those mills could have been rebuilt had it not been for the U.S. offers to purchase them. (2) With the establishment of U.S. financial capital in the sugar industry—for the most part in large mills capable of absorbing all the production of vast regions of cane plantations— many factories, technologically deteriorated and lacking capital, were transformed into large and medium-sized cane *colonias* dependent on the new foreign owners. In this way dozens of Cuban- and Spanish-owned sugar mills disappeared.

The process of decapitalization of the domestic productive forces followed three different directions: (1) The large-scale appropriation by U.S. plantations of the best lands, from the point of view of both their quality and their geographical proximity to ports for the export of sugar, left the plantations of the domestic bourgeoisie in the former provinces of Las Villas, Camagüey, and Oriente with severe structural limitations for their development. According to the Foreign Policy Association, of 250,000 *caballerías* (1 *caballería* = 33.3 acres, or 13.4 hectares) of cultivated land, 175,000 were the property of or were leased by U.S. owners in 1930. (2) Because large U.S. plantations typically had their own railway system whereas the Cuban sugar mills were obliged to depend on public railroads to transport their cane and its derivatives, the U.S. companies were better able to regulate the commercial value of sugar. (3) Accounting for 55% of sugar production by the 1930s, the U.S. plantations were able to lower their costs of production, allowing them to fix the commercial value of

sugar. At the same time, the plantations of the domestic sugar bourgeoisie, with a very low organic composition of capital and whose production of sugar amounted to only 27% of the total, were severely
affected by the unequal competition with U.S.-owned plantations.
Thus, the Truslow Report stated that in 1949 U.S.-owned sugar companies controlled almost two dozen sugar mills with production costs
of $8.39 per 325-pound bag, whereas Cuban-owned mills had produc-
tion costs ranging between $9.63 and $10.78 per bag of the same
weight (Truslow, 1951: 807–808).

Another factor that intervened indirectly in production costs was
the presence of investments by U.S. refineries in the island's sugar
industry. Thus, a part of the U.S. plantations were organically linked,
by belonging to the same trust or cartel, to Atlantic coast and Gulf of
Mexico refineries in the United States. In this way the cost of refining
their raw sugar was considerably reduced, whereas the Cuban- and
Spanish-owned mills were submitted to prices imposed by the refineries for refining their raw sugar. It was conservatively estimated in 1928
that 20% of the sugar produced in Cuba was directly controlled by
mills belonging to U.S. sugar refineries (Mondéjar, 1976: 80).

The withdrawal of a sector of U.S. financial capital from the sugar
industry in the 1930s, inspired by fear of a repetition of the economic
crisis and of the revolutionary events of 1933, did not signify a fundamental change in the existing power relations. U.S. financial capital
continued to play a leading role in the Cuban class structure.
Although the number of U.S.-owned mills diminished from sixty-six
to forty-one between 1939 and 1952, this represented a drop of only
10%, from 55% to 45%, of the total production of sugar these mills
controlled on the island. From 1940 to 1953, yearly accumulations of
sugar surpluses by the U.S. companies tended to grow uninterruptedly. These surpluses as well as agricultural and industrial salaries in the
sugar industry began to decline only in 1953. Nevertheless, the sugar
restriction that year did not bring losses but only a reduction in the
profit rates of the sugar companies linked to U.S. financial capital;
the weight of the crisis fell mainly on the sugar proletariat and the
small cane growers (colonos). Some small mills as well as medium-sized
and large cane growers who did not benefit by the policies of the
Sugar Stabilization Institute also suffered losses (Cepero Bonilla,
1958: 191–219).

Recent studies of the situation of the sugar industry in the 1950s
suggest that the large U.S. financial corporations owning dozens of
sugar mills in Cuba were in full retreat. Another sector of financial
capital that seriously affected the production costs of national industries and small manufacturers was the Electric Bond and Share

Company. In Cuba alone this electric power trust earned 25% of its total world profits. The profits from its operations on the island in the 1940s surpassed those it obtained in other Latin American and Asian countries where it also owned properties. Eduardo Chibás, the leader of the Ortodoxos, the Cuban People's Party (Orthodox), a populist reformist party, declared that the appropriation by the electric trust of the economic surplus of the Cuban industrial and agrarian bourgeoisie helped keep the country in a situation of dependence and backwardness. Chibás affirmed that "high electricity rates . . . constitute the main obstacle to industrial and agricultural progress in our country, devoid of coal and petroleum. It is true that operational costs of the so-called Cuban Electric Company have increased 60% in recent years, but the number of consumers has grown from 150,000 to 408,000, which represents an increase of 180%. Although its profits are more fabulous each year, it has not even renovated its equipment, so that its service is highly deficient. Because of the lack of modern equipment, one town in the interior of the country is left without electricity every day. Not even in African colonies do the electric companies maintain a situation as exploitative as this" (Chibás, 1949: 46, 47, 75).

Of course, despite the justice of Chibás's denunciation, the Electric Bond and Share Company, the proprietor of the Cuban Electric Company, was far from being the principal mechanism of appropriation of the national economic surplus—that is, of the decapitalization and deindustrialization of the country.

The earnings from operations of that company grew steadily from $24.1 million in 1946 to $59.9 million in 1955, an increase of 244.55%. Yearly per capita earnings of Cubans, in contrast, grew scarcely 1.9% between 1933 and 1958 (Brundenius, 1984: 140). In fact, from 1951 to 1954 the annual per capita income of Cubans diminished by 21% (Baudi, 1973: 103). Meanwhile, the number of industrial clients of the company grew only slightly between 1946 and 1955, from 1,290 in 1948 to 1,456 in 1956. In the four years between 1952 and 1956, the industrial clients of the company went from 1,323 to 1,383, an addition of only sixty new clients. It is worth emphasizing that the majority of that clientele was composed of small manufacturing plants and small equipment repair shops (Baudi, 1973: 94).

It is evident that the profits of the electric company during those years resulted primarily from increases in electricity rates and not from a growth in the number of industrial clients. The decline in the electric company's sales of kilowatt hours was counteracted only by new investments of U.S. financial capital in industrial installations. The monopoly of the Cuban Electric Company, therefore, functioned as another economic mechanism of neocolonial domination oriented toward subordinating the development of the domestic bourgeoisie to the expropriation of its surplus along with the earnings of the working population.

Finance Capital and National Industry

The signing by the United States and Cuba of reciprocal trade treaties in 1902 and 1934 opened the doors of the Cuban market to merchandise produced by U.S. industry. The latter treaty, however, not only made possible a considerable increase in the volume of goods introduced into the country but also paved the way for the progressive domination of the Cuban market by industrial investments of financial capital.

The treaty of 1934 was far harsher than that of 1902 and constituted a settling of accounts by the large importing interests of the United States in response to the nationalist tariff legislation dictated by the Machado government in 1927 and the revolutionary process of 1933. The treaty of 1902 had conceded a preferential tariff of 20% for sugar and tobacco in exchange for tariff privileges ranging from 20% to 40% for 497 groups of U.S. products. The treaty of 1934 granted to the United States preferential tariffs between 20% and 60% for 480 categories of products and reduced the participation of Cuban sugar, tobacco, and rum in the U.S. market. The reduction in sugar amounted to 26%; in tobacco, 12%; and in rum, 23%. The most significant change was that whereas in the 1902 treaty only 241 groups of merchandise (52%) were favored with preferential treatment ranging between 25% and 40%, in the 1934 treaty some 406 groups of merchandise (63% of the total) were given tariff privileges of between 25% and 60%. Thus, from 1934 on, the margin of domination by a majority group of U.S. products was extended over the goods of other nations and those produced in Cuba.

Table 1.4 illustrates the growing control of the Cuban market by U.S. exports following the reciprocal trade treaty of 1934.

From 1934 on, agricultural and industrial production on the island had to face not only the competition of goods imported from the United States but also the rivalry of the new industries founded by U.S. financial capital in Cuba. As sugar ceased to be a highly profitable business in comparison to other possible investment fields, U.S. financial capital turned to other branches of the national economy in which it could obtain a higher rate of profit, such as industry, mining, and oil refining. Since U.S. imports to Cuba, although favored by the

Table 1.4 Total Value of U.S. Imports and Their Proportion of the Cuban Market, 1900–1934 and 1935–1958 (in thousands of pesos)

	U.S. Imports	Proportion of the Cuban Market (%)
1900–1934	3,755,057	62.8
1935–1958	6,746,410	76.5

Source: Zanetti, 1975.

treaty of 1934, could not entirely eradicate competition from domestic products, many U.S. consortia decided to buy up the rival domestic firms or obtain a majority control of shares in given industries. When control of domestic industries by this means was impossible, new industries were founded that, thanks to their technological level and high productivity, were able to displace national competitors from the market. Between 1936 and 1958, U.S. investments in industries and manufacturing plants rose from $27 million to $80 million, and investments in oil refineries in that period grew from $6 million to $90 million. The aim of these latter investments was to displace British gasoline and other petroleum by-products from the Cuban market. U.S. investments in mining also grew from $15 million to $180 million. In this way the capital withdrawn from the sugar industry was relocated.

In many cases the U.S. industrial investments were not competing with products of national industry but with merchandise from Europe or other countries. Investments of this type were aimed at displacing such rivals by taking advantage of the lower salaries paid in Cuba and the possibility of avoiding payment of import duties on U.S. products going through the country's customs.

The manufacture of tires and inner tubes was concentrated in three large monopolies: Firestone, Goodyear, and U.S. Rubber. The flour mill in Regla, which belonged to the Burroughs Flour Mill, supplied 65% of national consumption of flour from 1952 to 1956; the remaining 35% was imported from the United States. The American Agricultural Chemicals Company manufactured practically all the fertilizers produced in the country, and the Ariguanabo Textile Company, with a capital base of $1.5 million, controlled nearly all the production of rayon. Of 87,000 weaving looms on the island in 1949, the Hedges Company owned 72,000, and 80% of the production of detergents, 67% of laundry soap, 41% of toothpastes, and 31% of bath soap were manufactured by two U.S. monopolies, Procter and Gamble and Colgate-Palmolive. The remaining production of these goods was in the control of independent U.S., European, and Cuban manufacturers. The Portland Cement Company, a branch of the Lone Star Cement Company, accounted for almost all of cement production until 1957. Three oil-refining companies, Esso Standard Oil, Texaco, and Shell, controlled the production of gasoline in the country, and the Owens-Illinois Company made most of the glass used in Cuba. From 1928 on, the Cuban Electric Company produced more than 90% of the island's electricity, and from 1913 on, the Cuban Telephone Company monopolized its telephone service. The Sherwin-Williams Company of Cuba and the National Paint Company, a property of the Glidden Company, shared control of paint manufacturing. Three pharmaceutical firms, Abbott, Parke Davis, and Squibb, controlled 69% of the production of pharmaceuticals in the mid-1950s.

At the end the 1950s, approximately 150,000 Cubans were employed by U.S. firms on the island, many at salaries higher than those paid by Cuban industries. Nevertheless, these industrial investments represented only a slight proportional increment of the working class in the active workforce, and their higher salaries served to create but a thin social layer, the so-called worker aristocracy.

2

Social Formations
in the Republic

The Dual Character of the Commercial Bourgeoisie

My study of the commercial importing and exporting bourgeoisie has led me to rethink traditional notions about this sector of Cuban bourgeois power, considered one of the fundamental pillars of U.S. neocolonialism. The large importing sector benefited from substantial sales of products received from the United States by virtue of its function as intermediary between the small Cuban retail establishments that directly served consumers and the great industrial monopolies that exported their surplus production to Cuba. These intermediaries imported from $100 million to $200 million annually in rice, lard, shoes, flour, potatoes, textiles, cereals, and so on. Of course, if the economic role of the large merchants had been limited to the importation of these products, defining them would have been a simple matter. They would necessarily have been the principal enemies of all internal industrial development, whose production might compete with the merchandise they imported under the preferential treatment conceded by the reciprocal trade treaty with the United States.

In reality, the economic role of the importing bourgeois merchants was much more complex and contradictory than it might appear at first sight. During the first fifty years of republican life, the most important commercial importers were frequently the country's leading industrialists. In its beginnings the island's industrial capital, whose production was destined for the domestic market, had its source in merchant capital. The Chamber of Commerce and Industry of Cuba did not have that name by chance or caprice but because the most important industrialists and merchants were often the same persons. The same can be said of the magazine *Cuba Importadora e Industrial*, the organ of the country's major merchants and industrial-

21

ists. This duality gave the merchant-industrialists a certain progressive coloring at the same time that it impregnated them with a reactionary scent. What is needed, of course, is to determine at what moment of their historical evolution the merchants or the industrialists prevailed. What cannot be denied is that it was a fraction of this class that set forth on the path to industrialization.

The merchant-industrialists, in keeping with their dual character, always had one foot in the past and another in the present. The names of some of the most prominent merchants and industrialists of the 1930s and 1940s show us the nature of this tendency. Among them were Rafael Palacios, president of the National Association of Industrialists of Cuba, proprietor of paper and textile mills, and one of Cuba's leading importers; José F. Barraqué, president of the Shipping Enterprise of Cuba and a large foodstuff wholesaler; José Balcell, president of the Cuban Institute of Coffee Stabilization and the Commercial Exchange; Segundo Casteleiro, large-scale importer and textile industrialist; Alfredo A. Cebeiro, secretary of the National Association of Industrialists and a major wholesaler; José Ignacio de la Cámara, president of the Bank of Commerce and co-owner of the firms New Cuban Paper Mill and the Fiber and Cordage Company. Many tobacco factories, even those that changed hands during the early years of the republic, continued to have backing from Spanish commercial capital following Cuba's independence from Spain. Thus, Ramón Cifuentes Llano, who bought the Partagás factory in 1900; Ramón Arguelles y Busto, who took over the cigar company Romeo y Julieta in 1903; and Eustaquio Alonso, who became managing director of Por Larrañaga, were originally Spanish merchants who rebuilt their tobacco concerns over the first two decades of the twentieth century. Most new Spanish capital fused with important leaf tobacco companies set up during these years, such as Menéndez and Company (1910), which later bought up the cigar factories H. Upmann and Díaz (1913), Junco (1921), and Toraño (1919) (Stubbs, 1985: 33). Many of these factories, dating back to the nineteenth century, had also arisen from commercial capital.

Some members of another group of merchants with important investments in the sugar industry carried out large-scale sales abroad. According to Alejandro García, in the early decades of the republic nine merchants owned twenty-five sugar mills (García, A., 1990: 47–51, 75–119, and 120.) The large exporter merchants owned sugar refineries, warehouses, and mills. Between 1930 and 1958, the most outstanding were Julio Lobo, proprietor of sugar refineries and warehouses of sugar and foodstuffs in general as well as eleven sugar mills; Francisco Blanco Calás, proprietor of sugar warehouses and three sugar mills; García Beltrán, owner of refineries, warehouses, and three mills; the descendants of Falla Gutiérrez, with sugar warehouses and five sugar mills; Nicolás Castaño, importer and exporter and owner of three sugar mills; and the Arechabala family, refiners and warehousers. Other sugar mill owners—Pedro Gómez Mena, José Ignacio Lezama, Esteban Cacicedo, Ignacio Nazábal, Aspuru, and Gamba and Company—had similar commercial origins.

Also present were U.S. corporations, owners of cane plantations and sugar refineries, devoted to large-scale sugar marketing. The most important were Cuban Trading, a branch of Czarnikovski y Rionda, the proprietor of ten sugar mills, refineries, and warehouses, and the Cuban American Sugar Company. Also outstanding were Arechabala and Company; Bea, Bellido, and Company; and Caragol and Company, all of them refiners and exporters.

Obviously, for the large sugar exporters who were as well owners of sugar mills there was no contradiction in their position as producers and merchants. This was not the situation, however, for large importers who were at the same time industrialists. As importers of foreign merchandise, they benefited by the tariffs that favored these products over those made in Cuba or impeded national production, but as industrialists, they were affected by the competition of the foreign merchandise aided by the tariff. In this way, the prevailing attitude toward the tariffs among importer-industrialists was one of particularity, of individual advantage, not of class. Their aspiration was merely that the tariffs that benefited them as industrialists remain invariable and that those that favored them as importers did not suffer variations, even if they were prejudicial for other industrialists.

This did not mean that the importers held a negative position with respect to a revision of the reciprocal trade treaty signed by the U.S. and Cuban governments. Since 1924, the Association of Commission Agents of foreign firms had indicated its support for modification of the existing tariffs. This attitude was based on a desire to obtain better treatment for Cuban sugar in the U.S. market, which would help increase the purchasing power of the Cuban consumer, thus expanding consumption of the goods they imported. The tariff reform dictated by the Machado government provoked an angry protest from *Cuba Importadora e Industrial*, whose interests were more closely tied to commercial than to industrial activities. The treaty of 1934 aroused stronger objections from the large importers than from any other sector of the dependent bourgeoisie. The director of the magazine *Cuba Económica y Financiera*, who had backed revision of the treaty since the 1920s, opposed the terms in which the new relations between Cuba and the United States had been conceived and criticized the representatives of the sugar industry for not having demanded a larger quota in the U.S. market. The importing bourgeoisie had seen its earnings reduced even more than those of the sugar bourgeoisie as a result of the economic crisis and the 1927 tariff reform. Thus it affirmed more peremptorily its need to recover economically by means of a normalization of sugar sales to the United States. To this end, the large importing firms demanded from the government a much more aggressive policy than that posed by the sugar industry, whose most notable representatives in those years— among whom was Ramiro Guerra, a leading Cuban intellectual— decidedly approved the signing of that treaty.

Acting on behalf of the importers of U.S. products, González Rodríguez, director of *Cuba Importadora e Industrial*, severely criticized the attitude of the representatives of the sugar industry in the negotiations that culminated with the treaty of 1934, since "Cuba . . . could very well . . . have objected to such reduced import quotas for sugar and tobacco . . . or at least, in accepting them, established at the same time limitations on importations from the U.S., with the aim of reserving part of its internal consumption as a weapon for the negotiation of other RTTs [reciprocal trade treaties] that would provide the United States with the outlets it claimed for its products" (*Cuba Importadora e Industrial*, April 1935: 23–26).

Of course, the U.S. goods that the merchant importers who were at the same time industrialists were willing to sacrifice were those that competed with their own industries, not those that they imported to compete with the production of other industrialists. These were the limits of the positions maintained by the merchant importer-industrialists from 1930 to 1958. They aspired to raise the duties on U.S. goods that competed with already established national industries but did not propose a general tariff revision aimed at raising duties on all foreign products able to compete with Cuban goods. Such a measure would have been a longer-range policy in defense of national interests, directed toward facilitating the development of Cuban industry, but the merchant importer-industrialist sector of the domestic bourgeoisie had an economic-corporate, not a national, character.

The commercial-industrial sector of the domestic bourgeoisie was not disposed to sacrifice its interests as importers of essential consumer products for the sake of stimulating an increase in national production of those goods. The president of the National Association of Industrialists, Rafael Palacios, and the secretary of that institution, Alfredo Cebeiro, at no time agreed to depriving themselves of the enormous profits that they obtained as speculators in lard and foodstuffs during World War II in behalf of helping the country develop its agricultural and industrial food production. Neither did the executives of the association speak out for tariff measures that might have provoked reprisals by the U.S. Department of State against Cuban sugar. Thus Palacios suggested the possibility "of reaching a high development of the domestic economy without, because of this, creating any economically dangerous tension for the consolidated position of the export economy," something that could be carried out "without friction or harm to what exists and that we should all be concerned with attending to and ensuring." Naturally, these possibilities of industrial development were severely limited in that they had to face the competition of U.S. products, which had preferential treatment. As we will see in studying the industrial bourgeoisie in more detail, this sector was able to survive such unfavorable competition in the 1940s and achieve relative growth because a great part of surplus U.S. industrial and agricultural production, traditionally destined to Cuba, was diverted to satisfy needs created by World War I (*Cuba Económica y Financiera*, 1948, no. 227: 19–21).

With respect to expansion of the internal market, the directors of the magazine *Cuba Económica y Financiera* insisted on the need to augment the minimum wage in the sugar industry in order to increase the demand for imported goods. To compensate the sugar industry for this rise in wages, the magazine said, the state should cancel the taxes imposed on that industry since the 1920s. The representatives of importing firms further solicited the suppression of all taxes on articles of basic consumption. In this way the increases in wages in the sugar industry and the improvement in the living standard of the working class were to be borne by the state, not by the commercial and sugar bourgeoisie.

In turn, the leaders of the sugar plantation owners made no effort to disguise their hostility to all domestic industrial development. José Manuel Casanova, president of the Association of Hacendados for many years, freely proclaimed that "Cuba can obtain more in terms of meat, cereals, vegetables and textiles by the production of sugar and its exchange for such articles than by producing them itself" (*Carteles*, February 6, 1936: 16). This attitude was still maintained by the leaders of the association in the 1940s and 1950s. The demands of the large merchants and industrialists were ignored by the Cuban state, which had to satisfy the demands of its political clients, avid for posts and sinecures. As usual, the workers were left to carry the brunt of the economic crisis.

At the end of the 1930s, the industrial bourgeoisie, together with the sugar bourgeoisie, insisted on the need to create a corporate chamber in which their interests were directly represented (*Carteles*,

September 8 and 29, 1936). At the same time, the Association of Industrialists proposed the creation of a consultative council of state (Tabares del Real, 1973). Inclined during the first dictatorship of Batista to adopt fascist formulas that would give their interests direct representation in the bourgeois state, the large merchant-industrialists ended by accepting the democratic-bourgeois orientations personified by Grau San Martín, in view of the strong rise in worker demands from 1940 to 1944. Support for this charismatic leader of the revolution of 1933 was conditioned by his promise to oppose the organized worker movement and defend the neocolonial status quo. Following his coup d'état of March 10, 1952, Batista recalled the ideological tendencies that had animated the industrial and commercial bourgeoisie at the end of the 1930s, and as a means of winning them over, he established a consultative council and several constitutional statutes conferring on direct representatives of that class attributes and powers in the direction of the state.

The Dual Character of the Industrial Bourgeoisie

No industrial censuses or statistics exist for the nineteenth century or the first twenty-five years of the twentieth century that permit an exact evaluation of the evolution of domestic manufactures. Departing from the limited information available, nevertheless, it is possible to formulate some valid generalizations in this respect. The most interesting facet of this development is, without doubt, the process of industrial concentration advocated by the Spanish financial bourgeoisie.

The greater part of the island's industries in the first years of republican life were the property of Spanish merchants. As time went on, many of them were taken over by the Spanish financial bourgeoisie. The Nation Bank of the Island, owned by José Marimón and Falla Gutiérrez, held the majority of shares in the Territorial Bank of Cuba, Shipping Enterprise of Cuba, Hispanic-American Insurance Union, National Manufacturing Company, Park Planning and Mariano Beach Company, Port of Havana Docks, Cienfuegos and Palmira and Cruces Electric Railway Company, Electric and Traction Company of Santiago de Cuba, Cuban Company of Fishing and Navigation, Cuban Paper Company, and Industrial Glasswork Company. Hermann Upmann and Armando Godoy were associated with Marimón and Falla Gutiérrez.

At the beginning of 1919, the Spanish Bank controlled five new industrial enterprises with a capital of $19 million. These new enterprises were the Headwear Industry, the National Shoe Company, United States and Cuban Allied Work Engineering, Cordage Company, and the Cienfuegos and Palmira and Cruces Electric Railway and Power Company. Marimón further controlled National Manufacturing Company, *Manufacturera Nacional*, made up of factories of pastries and salted crackers, which employed some 2,855 workers and had a capital of $11 million. Marimón also held the majority of shares in the Cuban Liquor Producers, a company that earned him profits of $250,871 around 1920. Serving as front men for Marimón were the well-known politicians Senator Manuel A. Suárez; Antonio Sánchez de Bustamente y Montoro, a supporter of the Platt amendment; and the liberal cacique from Las Villas Province, Marcelino Díaz de Villegas.

An important Havana industrialist was the Spanish entrepreneur José López Rodríguez, widely known as "Pote," who controlled the National Bank of Cuba, National Finance Company, Labor Accidents Company, Miramar Zone, Cienfuegos Paving, Industrial Slaughterhouse, Almendares Cement Company, Stamp Printing House, and the España, Reglita, and Nombre de Dios sugar mills (*El Mercurio,* November 5, 1920).

Around 1917 another outstanding capitalist, Ramón Crusellas Faura, had merged a series of industries owned by his family since the beginning of the century with the factories of other Spanish producers and merchants into an organization with authorized capital of $3.25 million. In the same industrial line, the partnership in commendam Sabatés y Boada was developed, which had capital of $250,000 around 1916.

As I have pointed out, these industries were originally the property of Spanish merchants, many of whom were forced by the competition of imported U.S. goods to sell their shares to the National Bank of the Island. Of course, the process of centralization of these industries in the hands of the major Spanish financiers made them more vulnerable to economic competition from the United States. Around 1920 the banking interests of Marimón and Pote provided financial backing to the sales committee of the plantation owners and large Cuban *colonos* who decided to hold back their sugar in a strategy aimed at breaking the stranglehold of the principal U.S. sugar refineries. This maneuver had a dramatic denouement when the refineries, with the aim of forcing down the prices of Cuban producers, bought their sugar at extraordinarily high prices from countries whose production was destined primarily for domestic consumption.

The final result was the bankruptcy of the main Spanish banks and dozens of Cuban sugar mills. The crisis led to the escape of Marimón abroad to evade his creditors and to the suicide of Pote. Shortly afterward, Crusellas y Sabatés were obliged to sell their properties to U.S. monopolists. The bankruptcy of these interests testifies to the difficult conditions under which the domestic industrial bourgeoisie had to confront the neocolonial mechanisms of U.S. financial capital.

In contrast to the domestic industries whose production was destined fundamentally for the internal market, the Spanish tobacco bourgeoisie encountered no great obstacles in monopolizing the national market. Cuban tobacco, which had no rival in the world, could not be displaced in its own territory. This did not mean that the Spanish tobacco bourgeoisie could always evade the difficulties presented by U.S. neocolonial domination in Cuba. At the end of the war of 1895, a part of the Spanish bourgeoisie, opposed to the establishment of a republic governed by Cubans, decided to sell its properties and return to Spain.

Nevertheless, in 1904 52% of the total exportation of tobacco was in the hands of the American Tobacco Company. This meant that 48% was still controlled by Spaniards. According to Martín Duarte, in 1902 forty-seven factories and fifty-eight brands of tobacco were "not controlled" by the U.S. monopolies (Duarte, 1973). In 1927, however, the factories of the U.S. tobacco trust produced more than 55 million Havana cigars. The total Cuban production reached more than 332 million, signifying that at that time the trust controlled only 16.5% of national production. This decline in the production of the monopoly was due in part, without doubt, to the fact that many of its factories were transferred to the United States, where the tobacco acquired in Cuba could be manufactured into cigars more cheaply. But it is worth pointing out that the 16.5% of national production the trust controlled amounted to only 30% to 40% of the total value of Cuban production. Of a total of 570,471 cigarettes manufactured in 1927, the factories of the trust produced 131,856, which represented 15.76% of the total. That is, 83.5% of cigars and 84.2% of cigarettes were produced by domestic capital.

In 1927 Cuban capital invested in the tobacco industry amounted to $23.8 million, Spanish capital $13.8 million, and unidentified capital catalogued as "foreign" $3.4 million. Unlike sugar production, which from 1920 on was controlled almost totally by the U.S. financial oligarchy, the tobacco industry was in the hands of Spanish industrial capital on the way to becoming Cuban. Unfortunately, the decision of the U.S. trust to move its investments to the United States with the

aim of manufacturing cigars there under U.S. tariff protection limited the possibilities for development of this sector of the domestic
bourgeoisie.

The drop in a series of imports from the United States during
World War II stimulated the development of national production destined for the domestic market. Thus, from 1935 to 1947 the manufacture of alcohol grew eightfold, and that of beer, textiles, and footwear
doubled; that of cigars and cigarettes increased 1.5 times.

The statistics of 1927 and 1945 allow us to appreciate the process
of industrial concentration and the tendency of capital per enterprise
to grow. Thus, the $52,607 invested in equipment per enterprise in
1925 had risen to $107,278 by 1945. The average number of workers
per enterprise grew from 19.5 to 28.8. The number of industries with
fewer than twenty-five workers, which represented 92.7% of the total
in 1925, was 80.5% in 1954, showing a reduction in the number of
small factories. At the same time, the number of industries with more
than twenty-six workers grew from 7.2% in 1925 to 19.4% in 1954.

In spite of this, the predominance of manual production was still
irrefutable in 1954. A total of 45.1% of the country's factories had
fewer than five workers. Domestic industry fell so far short of meeting
internal market demand that Cuba relied on foreign imports. Thirty-
five war industries employing 1,194 workers were created between
1939 and 1944. From August 1945 to June 1948, twenty-three factories were opened with a total workforce of 2,094. The capital of the
industries reached $7.7 million in the first period, and the declared
capital of the industries founded in the second period was $13.2 mil-
lion. Many of these industries created to substitute importations during the war were unable to survive the 1940s, since their raw materials
were not produced in the country and had to be imported. Once U.S.
exports were again oriented toward Latin American markets, the new
industries that had arisen in this stage were largely displaced by foreign competition. Industrial growth, constrained by the country's
dependent neocolonial structure, led the domestic bourgeoisie to
oscillate between what Germán Sánchez called "the illusion of development and the impotence of underdevelopment" (Sánchez, 1985:
184).

The relative development reached by some branches of the nonexporting domestic industry from 1934 to 1957 was reflected in their
earnings. Since income declared by this part of the bourgeois class
is given together with that of commercial enterprises from 1937 to
1958, the earnings of the industrial bourgeoisie cannot be dis-
cerned in the statistics, but to the extent that these figures reflect
the capacity of the domestic market to absorb national and foreign

products, the rising or falling curve of industrial earnings can be deduced in general terms.

Thus, from 1934 to 1952 there was a slight sustained increase in the earnings of the commercial and industrial class as a result of the slow recovery of the economy. Of course, in the five years from 1948 to 1952, compared to 1953 to 1957, average annual income in the industrial and commercial sector declined from $75.5 million to $66.4 million (Martínez Sáenz, 1959: 214–215, table 5.1.1e). The contraction of the domestic market, caused by the sugar crop restriction in the 1950s, brought about a notable reduction in the production of footwear, textiles, alcoholic beverages, and so on by the industrial bourgeoisie. The growth of the nonexporting industrial bourgeoisie was maintained within the narrow limits of the structural dependence of the Cuban market on U.S. production. Industrial development was inconceivable under these conditions, which left room only for limited expansion within the margins conceded to domestic industry by U.S. financial capital.

At the Conference for the Advancement of the National Economy, organized in 1947 by the industrial bourgeoisie, the above-mentioned reduction-plus-stagnation tendencies were already in evidence. The participants advocated stimulating foreign investments and their harmonization with national interests. This program would be applied, in its general terms, in the following decade, with the merger of foreign and national capital in many joint ventures. Dependence on foreign capital became acute since these industries required technology and raw materials from the U.S. market. From that time on, the Cuban industrialists called openly for more intensive forms of worker exploitation and compensated dismissal.

Oscar Pino Santos, who held executive responsibilities in the Institute of Agrarian Reform (INRA), pointed out with reference to the non-sugar-producing industrial bourgeoisie that when the agrarian reform of 1959 began to be applied, "some of its most economically powerful members had made considerable investments in the acquisition of land, that is to say, they were large landowners" (Pino Santos, 1964: 276). This historian also found that no sharp separation existed between the interests of the industrial bourgeoisie and those of U.S. financial capital, "nor were these interests always absolutely contradictory," since not only were capitals merged with those from the United States, but they had grown under their wing or depended on them to supply equipment and raw materials, the use of patents, and so on. The same could be said of the financial and importing bourgeoisie, which, according to Pino Santos, was also closely linked to foreign capital.

Because the non-sugar-producing industrial bourgeoisie could not compete with U.S. products that entered the country protected by the reciprocal trade treaty of 1934, it opposed industrial development based on new national investments in the branches of production it aspired to control. Decree Law 2144 dictated by the Grau government in 1948, which granted important fiscal and tariff benefits to national production destined for the domestic market, was impugned not only by the large importing sector but also, paradoxically, by the Association of Industrialists (*Cuba Económica y Financiera*, 1948, no. 273: 19–20). Opposed to the stimulating effects of the decree in providing bases for the creation of future industries, the executive committee of the association called for its suppression and its replacement by a project that would expressly deny the category of "new industry" to those manufacturing centers whose products on the date of publication of the decree law were "substitutes for others manufactured in the country in sufficient quantity to supply it." Thus the already established industries reserved for themselves a monopoly of the country's domestic market, inhibiting the creation of new industries for which fiscal and tariff exemptions had been granted and whose duly protected production would be able to compete favorably with foreign products.

In reality, what was involved was a sharing of the domestic market among the already established national industries, the large U.S. exporters, and the Cuban importers, in detriment to the prospect of national industrial development. The tariff exemptions that they demanded for themselves did not by any means imply the displacement of U.S. competition but only a readjustment that would permit them to survive without entering into contradictions with the U.S. monopolies. Nevertheless, Cuban industrialists at the Conference for the Advancement of the National Economy held in 1947 favored a moderate tariff revision so that foreign products would not be able to compete with the country's established industrial production. Such a posture stimulated a heated controversy with the Cuban owners of sugar mills in the 1940s and 1950s, since the hacendados favored sacrificing domestic industrial production in order to gain a better position in the U.S. sugar market (*Boletín ANIC*, no. 11, July 1955; no. 10, May 1955).

The tendency of capital to withdraw from economic activities in the 1930s and 1940s became accentuated in the years prior to the economic recession unleashed by the sugar restriction of 1953. The domestic capital accumulated during the prosperous postwar years was diverted abroad, hoarded in banks, or invested in speculative activities or real estate. Between 1946 and 1952, the total of fixed capital investment in the country constituted 9.3% of national income; in comparison, it reached 18.6% in Argentina, 18.7% in Brazil, 18.6% in Colombia, 13.4% in Mexico, and 13.1% in Chile (United Nations, 1955: 52). During the 1940s the investment capacity of the nations of Eastern Europe reached 15% of their national income. Cuba, with its 9.3% of gross investment of the national income, was on a level with the most backward group of Asian countries, whose investment capacity, according to estimates of Harry Oshima, was below 10% of national income (Oshima, 1961). The investment capacity of Malaysia was 10% in 1947, as was that of Ceylon in 1951. In 1948 the Philippines had 9%, Thailand 6%, and India 5%. What caused Cuba's backwardness, therefore, was not a scarcity of capital but the withdrawal of capital from all types of reproductive economic activities. The indices of the United Nations and Oshima show clearly the extent to which the Cuban economy was prostrated prior to the short-term crisis of 1953–1957.

In Paul Baran's view, the main obstacle to development was the way in which the economic surplus was used. The surplus was absorbed by financial capital, by the maintenance of enormous bureaucracies and their armies, by the extravagant spending of the oligarchies, and by the uninterrupted increase of money hoarding in domestic and foreign banks (Baran, 1971: 257).

At the time some ideologists of development and an independent economist, Raúl Cepero Bonilla, repeatedly exhorted the Association of Industrialists to work out a program of national recovery, but the association obstinately refused to second their proposals. The attitude assumed by the industrialists made it clear that this class was organically linked to the bourgeois-landowning power bloc and could not conceive of development independently of the interests of U.S. industrial financial capital, whose production impeded it from advancing its own interests beyond certain limits. Its perspective concerning the need for economic development was thus individual or at most corporative, not national. This does not mean that no conflicts of a secondary nature, which the parties and organizations opposed to U.S. neocolonial domination could exploit, existed between this sector of the bourgeoisie and the bourgeois-landowning power bloc, as we have just seen. The insistence of Marxist and democratic-revolutionary discourse on the need for industrialization made clear which classes opposed its development and the role of U.S. financial capital in the economic backwardness of the country. Of course, as we have seen, the domestic industrial bourgeoisie was not the historical agent capable of bringing about that industrialization.

Bourgeois Agrarians and Precapitalist Landowners:
The Vicissitudes of the "Junker" Path

Around 1890 the key positions in the tobacco and sugar industries were held by the Spanish sector of the island's bourgeoisie, which aspired, despite its conflicts with the interests of the bourgeoisie in Spain, to maintain colonial domination in Cuba as a means of preserving its predominance over the Cuban sector of the bourgeoisie, represented politically by the Autonomist Party. It should be kept in mind, however, that although the Spanish maintained a greater degree of economic power, the Cubans were numerically superior and exercised greater cultural, political, and social influence over the other social classes of the island. In 1899 in the provinces of Matanzas and Santa Clara, where 91% of the country's sugar was produced, the majority of sugar mills were Cuban owned. According to U.S. general James H. Wilson, during the U.S. military occupation (1899–1902) fifty of these mills were Cuban, twenty-one Spanish, eleven U.S. owned, one English, two German, and one French (Wilson, 1899). With few exceptions, however, the Cuban owners of sugar mills belonged to the Autonomist Party until the end of the war of independence in 1898 and closed ranks with Spanish colonial power. The end of the war brought ruin to the Cuban owners of large and medium-sized mills, many of whom were obliged to sell their properties to the financial capital of their powerful northern neighbor or cede them to their Spanish creditors. Nevertheless, in the first two decades of the twentieth century, a nucleus of Cuban owners of sugar mills and large cane plantations was slowly and arduously reconstituted. In this process of reconstruction, the Cuban bourgeoisie followed what might be called an abnormal path, adopting four fundamental strategies in the first decades of the republic:

1. Considerable investment of Spanish commercial capital in sugar mills and large plantations (*colonias*) that, over the course of the first three decades of republican life, passed into the hands of their Cuban descendants.
2. The transformation of Cuban cattle-raising landowners into owners of cane plantations and sugar mills. Landowners responded to the sustained rise in the price of sugar by converting their surplus land to sugarcane plantations or investing in the construction of new sugar mills.
3. The conversion of high officers of the liberation army and politicians into large plantation owners (*grandes colonos*). U.S.

planters as well as many Cuban and Spanish landowners also followed the policy of turning over cultivation of cane plantations to outstanding Cuban politicians in the region.

4. The transformation of bureaucratic capital into a part of the sugar bourgeoisie, which brought wealth to politicians, bourgeois contractors, entrepreneurs, and others associated in illicit state activities who acquired large plantations or sugar mills.

The process by which the Cuban bourgeoisie was reconstituted economically seemed evident to José Sixto de Solá around 1913. Luis Marino Pérez also affirmed, in 1916, that important Cuban capital was being accumulated, "and the number of wealthy natives is steadily growing" (Pérez, L.M., 1915–1916: 521; Solá, 1915–1916: 52).

We can trace the general decline of Spanish landownership by looking at data provided by the *Boletín de la Secretaría de Hacienda*. According to this data, in 1915 forty-two sugar mills belonged to Spaniards; by 1922 the number was twenty-seven. In 1925 the Secretariat of Agriculture listed only thirteen Spanish sugar mills. In contrast, in 1915 sixty-seven mills belonged to Cubans; in 1921, 103; and in 1925, ninety-three. The figure dropped to fifty in 1930. The reasons for the progressive reduction of Spanish properties are, first of all, their transformation into Cuban properties and, second, their sale to U.S. enterprises. The rise in the number of Cuban mills up to 1921 is explained by the influx of bureaucratic and commercial capital into the sugar industry and the subsequent passing of Spanish property to Cuban heirs.

The dip in the number of Cuban-owned mills around 1930 resulted from the incapacity of small mills to survive the conditions of the sugar crop restriction. Moreover, many of the Cuban investments made at the end of the second decade had a speculative character— that is, the mills were built with the purpose of selling them at a moment when the market was favorable. According to the records, only ten Cuban-owned mills disappeared between 1921 and 1925, despite the well-known fact that in 1921 some twenty such mills passed into the hands of U.S. banks based on the island.

As Pino Santos has correctly pointed out, beginning in 1912 the U.S. financial oligarchy launched an assault on Cuba with the intent of monopolizing the country's sugar industry. The rise in the number of U.S. properties is evident in the sugar statistics of the epoch. According to the *Boletín de la Secretaría de Hacienda*, U.S. proprietors held forty-three sugar mills in 1915, fifty-five in 1922, sixty in 1925, and ninety in 1930.

Following the revolution of 1930, as a result of the subsequent economic crisis and a powerful social movement, many U.S. owners returned to their country, selling their smaller and less profitable mills to Cuban buyers. The increase in the number of Cuban-owned mills at the start of the 1930s evidences the existence of a considerable accumulation of domestic capital, which was again invested in the sugar industry.

Bank vaults on the island held deposits of national capital in current and savings accounts amounting to $100 million annually in the 1930s and $370 million in the 1940s, evincing the solvency of the national bourgeoisie and its capacity to manage the sugar industry (*Cuba Económica y Financiera*, 1950, no. 289). The Cubans who had sold their mills in the 1920s were in positions to repurchase them in the following decade and the early 1940s.

In my view, the retreat of U.S. investments from the sugar industry between 1932 and 1959 did not come about because of the simple fact that the Cuban sugar bourgeoisie was progressively displacing them. The so-called Cubanization of the sugar business, as López Segrera has pointed out, occurred because U.S. capital emigrated toward other sectors of the economy in its own country in search of higher dividends after selling out its older and smaller mills to Cubans and retaining the most modern and profitable. In 1939, U.S. citizens were the proprietors of sixty-six mills that produced roughly 55% of Cuban sugar; Cubans owned thirty-six mills that produced 22.4% of the total; Spaniards owned thirty-three that manufactured 14.3%. The remaining mills—ten Canadian, four English, three Dutch, and two French—produced 7.7%.

By 1956, U.S. citizens owned thirty-nine sugar mills that produced approximately 40.1% of Cuban sugar. In turn, Cubans owned 118 with a production equivalent to 58.7%. Spanish-owned mills turned out 0.89% and a single French mill 0.27% of the total sugar. U.S.-owned sugar companies held 127,500 *caballerías* of land and controlled, by means of contracts or leasing, another 56,500 *caballerías* in 1958. This total of 184,000 *caballerías* represented 27% of the national farmland.

After the blow dealt to the domestic bourgeoisie by the acquisition of its sugar by U.S. refineries in 1920, the most active Cuban producers, especially the nonexporting industrial bourgeoisie, regrouped around the government of Machado, constituting an effective pressure group with the aim of obtaining the abrogation of the tariffs that gave U.S. producers absolute control of the internal Cuban market.

The criollo representatives of the most powerful sector of the sugar-mill-owning class (the hacendados), among whom were Julio

Lobo, José Gómez Mena, and Vinato Gutiérrez, favored a plan presented by a sector of U.S. banking capital that financed Cuban sugar
crops and the sugar enterprises not linked to the refineries. The plan
would restrict the sugar harvest by segregating 1.5 million tons of
sugar that would be acquired by the government through the
issuance of government bonds (Freyre de Andrade, 1931). The
Chadbourne Plan, as it was known, would make the Cuban state the
guarantor of sales operations for a period of five years to provide an
outlet for the sugar accumulated in warehouses, committing the state
to assume losses caused by depreciation or prices lower than those
the state had paid for the sugar, without the Cuban treasury's receiving any benefit from optimum sales prices. The actual intent of the
plan was to protect the interests of the U.S. financial corporations
and the large Cuban and Spanish sugar mill owners who, after acquiring the bonds issued by the government, presented them to the banks
as guarantee of the payment of debts and obligations acquired in the
preceding harvest. In this way the U.S. financial corporations became
creditors of the Cuban state. The only ones who remained outside the
guarantees implied by this gigantic operation were the smaller sugar
mill owners, who lacked sufficient capital to face a reduction in their
yearly production of sugar. With the reduced harvest, the large plantations retained a quota large enough to allow them to mill, but that
of the small producers was so diminished that their profits could not
cover the costs of the harvest.

The agricultural sector of the sugar bourgeoisie developed parallel to the industrial sector. The large plantation owners became the
most prosperous sector of the large and middle agricultural bourgeoisie. When a large plantation was ceded as a donation by the sugar
mill to the lawyer who represented the mill, to the most prominent
politician of the region, or to small neighboring landowners, its
development did not at first have the capitalist, entrepreneurial character of enterprises in which money is invested to earn more money.
Nevertheless, over the years and given the considerable income
obtained by the large plantation owners, such development that had
arisen from certain political relations inevitably acquired the nature
of a capitalist enterprise.

Of course, the dependent situation of these *colonos,* who entered
economic life by virtue of an agreement that implied loyalty to the
sugar mill vis-à-vis the other social classes that participated in sugar
production, was much greater than that of those who leased land
from a sugar mill with a view to investing money to earn more money.
The latter, obviously, were capitalists who were keenly aware that
sugar production is a business. Despite the dynamic character of this

activity, it formed a part of the presuppositions of neocolonial domination in the first years of the republic, and the *colonos* benefited from the reciprocal treaty together with the owners of sugar mills.

The figures offered by the *Times of Cuba* of February 1926 on the participation of large *colonos* in the harvest are highly indicative of the development of this agrarian bourgeoisie. According to this newspaper, in the 1924–1925 harvest, more than 500,000 *arrobas* (1 *arroba* = 25 lbs.) of cane had been cut at more than ninety-six sugar mills. The same source reported some 1,200 *colonos* with annual earnings of at least $15,000 each; 395 *colonos* had cut as much as 1 million *arrobas*; 148 of these 2 million or more; and fifty-nine approximately 3 million, for which they had received yearly gross earnings amounting to at least $100,000.

The great majority of these *colonos* were situated in what were then the provinces of Camagüey and Oriente, where the U.S. companies organized sugar production on the basis of large plantations. Meanwhile, in the provinces of Matanzas, Havana, and Santa Clara, small planters predominated. From 1898 to 1920, as a consequence of the sustained rise in sugar prices and the increase in sugar production, the foundations were laid for what would later be the large Cuban sugarcane plantations with monthly incomes above $1,000.

According to the *Times of Cuba*, in 1926 more than 1,200 plantations had incomes above $12,000 per year, and Ramiro Guerra estimated that 1,176 plantations earned approximately $12,187 annually in 1939. These figures show that the agrarian bourgeoisie was definitively formed as a part of the sugar industry as a result of considerable U.S. financial capital investments in new sugar mills in the 1910s and 1920s and the subsequent transformation of many cattle-raising landowners into cane growers, stimulated by the continued rise in the price of sugar. In those decades multiple investments were also made in sugar plantations by bureaucratic capital acquired from politics. The most significant fact of this process is that in 1899 the island had only 269 plantations of more than 10 *caballerías* of cane each, capable of obtaining earnings above $15,000 yearly; by 1926 more than 1,200 plantations of this size had earnings above $12,000. It is thus clear that the formation of this important sector of the agrarian bourgeoisie as a compact and numerous group took place in the first two decades of the republic. This sector of the dependent bourgeoisie was originally shaped as the social base for foreign domination in Cuban agriculture.

The decline in the earnings of cane planters from 1945 to 1957 was not as severe as that of the workers at the end of this period. Table 2.1 illustrates their situation.

Table 2.1   Earnings of Cane Growers, 1945–1957 (in millions of pesos)

1945	1946	1947	1948	1949	1950	1951	1952	1953	1954	1955	1956	1957
84.6	81.2	166.4	146.0	134.8	130.0	173.9	144.0	125.4	131.3	127.8	129.1	174.9

Source: Martínez Sáenz, 1959: 214–215, table 5.1.1e.

Compared to the five years between 1953 and 1957, in the years between 1948 and 1952 the earnings of the *colonos* decreased by $40.2 million, from $728.7 to $628.5 million. A close examination of the earnings for these periods shows, however, that this drop is in fact due to the giant harvest of 1952, that is, the high earnings obtained by the *colonos* that year in comparison to other years.

The development of cattle raising in the first thirty years of republican life was linked in part to the incorporation of a sector of these landowners into the agrarian bourgeoisie. From 1930 on, as we will see, the development of this sector also depended on investments made in cattle raising by a considerable nucleus of capitalist-type lessees.

The censuses of 1907 and 1919 register an important growth in the number of cattle-raising properties. Between 1894 and 1899, the number of cattle ranches in Cuba declined to 489 as a consequence of the war of independence. By 1907 they had increased to some 1,536 and in 1919 to 3,059. The statistics for those years also show a rise in heads of cattle, parallel to the number of ranches, from 872,381 animals in 1899 to 970,216 in 1902, 3.2 million in 1912, and some 4.1 million in 1919 (Arredondo, 1945). As the cattle census of 1919 indicates, 92% of these ranches were the property of Cubans.

The 1931 census shows an increase in the total number of cattle ranches to 27,423; that is, cattle-raising property grew ninefold in just ten years. This fact, together with the rise in the number of large Cuban-owned cane plantations, provides evidence of the existence around 1930 of a strong Cuban landowning class and agrarian bourgeoisie.

A comparative analysis of the data given by the agricultural census of 1946 and the livestock census of 1953 reveals the concentration of cattle raising in the hands of a relatively small number of large ranch owners. At the same time, it shows that between 1946 and 1953 the number of ranches with more than 100 head of cattle increased by 249, whereas those with fewer than 100 animals decreased by 30,075.

This process of concentration of cattle-raising wealth may have arisen from the intention of the large landowners to introduce large-scale livestock exploitation at the expense of small ranchers. For this purpose, they may have rescinded the profit-sharing and lease contracts of thousands of small cattle ranchers on the large haciendas of their property. Simultaneously, between 1946 and 1953 the large landowners and the bourgeois lessees who owned more than 100 head of cattle undertook the extensive and intensive breeding of more than 80,000 animals. The increase in the number of cattle of the large ranchers may have been based on the cancellation of profit-sharing contracts by the large landowners and on purchases of cattle from small ranchers inside the country and abroad. The sources I have consulted, however, do not explain this process. The disappearance of more than 30,000 cattle ranches should have left traces in the periodicals of the time or publications that specialized in cattle raising, in the records of the Association of Cattle Ranchers, or in the diverse property registers of the country. Of course, the fact that in only seven years 30,000 ranchers seem to have abandoned their activities might be explained by an overcount in the census of 1946 and an undercount in the livestock census of 1953.

In any event, when the revolution occurred in 1959, a group of forty families and cattle-raising enterprises owned more than 1,000 *caballerías* each, covering a total of 73,931 *caballerías*. The Cuban process of concentration of landownership continued to swallow up small owners. According to the estimates of Antonio Riccardi, in 1949 the *terratenientes* (landowners) devoted to sugar, cattle, and coffee production held some 56% of the land in Cuba (see Table 2.2).

As we have seen, the number of cattle increased fourfold between 1899 and 1919 but remained stationary between 1920 and 1952. In 1919 the number of heads of cattle was 4.1 million, but in 1953 the

Table 2.2   Land Distribution, 1949

	Caballerías	%
Large sugarcane plantations	219,526	26.34
Coffee and cattle raising	248,498	29.82
Small cultivated areas	119,279	14.31
Uncultivated land	140,094	16.81
Cities, roads, mountains, etc.	105,899	12.70
Total	833,296	

Source: Riccardi, 1955.

number registered decreased to below 4.0 million. Although the population grew by a factor of 2.01 from 1919 to 1953, the country's cattle herd decreased by a factor of 1.01. But cattle raising was not the only branch of agricultural commercial production that remained stagnant or declined proportionally in relation to population growth. The period from 1927 to 1958 was in general one of stagnation.

The development of capitalism in Cuban agriculture was closely linked to the process of proletarianization of the rural population, to be analyzed later in this study. Of course, these transformations did not take place by the mere fact of the growth in population or the increase in immigration: Their appearance was intimately related to the existence of a class of bourgeois entrepreneurs in the countryside. Unlike the landowners, who submitted the peasantry to severe links of dependency, this class preferred to employ salaried workers. In this way thousands of peasants' sons who reached working age each year joined the ranks of the rural proletariat contracted to work on the farms of the new class of capitalist leaseholders. As Lenin pointed out in describing another process similar to that which took place in Cuba, "a complete interdependence is observed between the formation of the class of rural employers and the increase in the inferior group of 'peasants,' that is, the increase in the number of rural proletarians. Among other rural employers, an outstanding role is played by the rural bourgeoisie" (Lenin, 1954, vol. 3: 242).

The quantitative leap in the size of the rural proletariat between 1927 and 1957 was the result in great part of the development of that agrarian bourgeoisie. The agricultural census of 1946 reveals this relation in its enumeration of the high percentage of rural workers employed on large and medium-sized farms of entrepreneurial leaseholders: 41.7% of the temporary laborers (176,653) and 36.4% of permanent salaried workers (19,555) in 1946 were employed by leaseholders (*Memoria del Censo Agrícola Nacional, 1946:* 473). The proportion of salaried workers employed on farms of leaseholders must in fact have been higher, since 46.7% of them worked on farms operated by administrators, a considerable part of which were held by lessees. (For the purposes of this study, I have classified as capitalist-type lessees those who appear in the census enumerations as having usufruct of farms of 100 hectares or more and receiving annual incomes above $1,500. Lessees of farms with lower income or less area I consider as peasants.)

The large and medium-sized leaseholders not only contributed to the expansion of capitalist relations of production but also introduced the most advanced agricultural machinery and technology from the world capitalist market. The lands of large, medium-sized, and small lessees accounted for 38.2% of the area under irrigation and 42.37% of areas using fertilizers (*Memoria del Censo Agrícola Nacional, 1946:* 434). The large and medium-sized leaseholders—that is, the capitalist lessees—were much more economically powerful than the small ones—that is, the peasants—so probably as much as 90% of the fertilized and irrigated land belonged to the former. Because the census of 1946 combines in a single category all types of leaseholders, we must make estimates based on the different tables presented in that census. The proportion of areas using irrigation and fertilizers on farms of capitalist lessees must have been much greater, since 19.9% of the area under irrigation was cultivated by administrators, who, as pointed out earlier, were usually employees of large, capitalist-oriented entrepreneurial leaseholders, whereas 16% of the total area of fertilized land also belonged to farms operated by administrators.

The farms of the leaseholders, in contrast to those of proprietors, devoted 28.2% of the total of their areas to diverse crops; the large, precapitalist landowners employed only 7.7% in a variety of crops, as they were cattlemen who owned great expanses of idle land (*Memoria del Censo Agrícola Nacional, 1946:* 434). As in the preceding cases, the area cultivated by leaseholders must have been greater, since 17.5% of the land was operated by administrators, of which a high percentage must have been lands held by leaseholders.

Of the total area of farms worked by their proprietors, large and small landowners, 50.1% was devoted to pasture, whereas in the area of farms worked by leaseholders only 39% were destined for this purpose. Evidently, cattle raising was carried out fundamentally by the owners of large-scale, semi-idle lands and, secondarily, by large lease-holders, that is, members of the agrarian bourgeoisie who devoted 28.2% of their lands to crops and only 30% to pasture.

As to the use of tractors and other types of agricultural machinery, 32% of these were situated on farms held by the large capitalist entrepreneurial leaseholders, which made up only 26% of all the farms registered by the census of 1946.

No statistics exist on the expansion of fertilized and irrigated land or the number of tractors and other agricultural machinery of the new proprietors who acquired farms from 1931 to 1946; that is, the owners of capital invested in a capitalist sense in this era for the purchase of expanses of land greater than 100 hectares. But their enumeration would certainly have indicated the predominance of the developmental path promoted by the agrarian bourgeoisie, made up of large and medium-sized leaseholders and the new proprietors who bought land through what we might call the "Junker" path, which turned precapitalist *terratenientes* into agrarian entrepreneurs. As we will see, the number of new proprietors grew considerably between 1931 and 1946.

The introduction of fertilizers and agricultural machinery by the large and medium-sized leaseholders, the new capitalist proprietors, and the large landowners-turned-agrarian bourgeois—a decisive step in the extension and deepening of capitalism in agriculture—represented serious difficulties for the proletarianized rural population, which was displaced by the mechanization of agricultural work. Throughout this period, numerous protests were heard from the organized labor movement against the dismissal of agricultural workers owing to the introduction of new and modern cultivation equipment. As in all contradictory processes, the capitalist development of agriculture opened new work opportunities for the rural population at the same time that it displaced contingents of agricultural workers already employed on the entrepreneurial farms. The large sugar mills were inclined to adopt precapitalist forms of social organization of agricultural work: Despite their close link to the world market, their technology (relatively advanced for the time), and the capitalist conception that determined all their economic activity, the U.S. and Cuban cane plantations and sugar mills feared the struggles of the rural proletariat and so opted to "feudalize" the small cane growers on their lands, forcing them into indebtedness by demanding a high price for land leases.

With respect to the oft-debated question of capitalist development in Cuban agriculture, I am not inclined to assent to the thesis of predominance of the Junker path beginning in 1930. The growing preponderance of leaseholders of capitalist orientation in the cultivation of sugarcane, who accounted for 49% of the value of production, and in other branches of agriculture, such as henequen and rice, in which they again accounted for 49% of the harvest, gives a clear idea of their increasing importance. The process of conversion of old *terratenientes* into agrarian capitalists in this century—that is, the Junker path—does not constitute the decisive feature in the capitalist development of agriculture.

In some crops, such as coffee, the preeminence of the small peasant owner can be recognized alongside that of the large landowning class, which destined a part of its lands to the cultivation of this branch of the Cuban economy. Thus, large landowners and small peasant proprietors produced 49% of the total value of coffee. The capitalist-type leaseholders did not constitute the decisive sector in this crop. Of course, in general terms the capitalist development of agriculture tended to depend on the entrepreneurial activities of the capitalist leaseholders. Table 2.3 illustrates this tendency.

Table 2.3   Production Value of Leased Farms Versus Owned Farms

Type of Landholding	Farms with a Production Value Below $1,500 Yearly		Farms with a Production Value Above $1,500 Yearly	
	Number	%	Number	%
Leaseholders	71,687	48	15,829	59
Owners	78,319	52	11,113	41

Source: *Memoria del Censo Agrícola Nacional, 1946:* 1013.

As seen in Table 2.3, the capitalist leaseholder, rather than the large and medium-sized landowners, played the leading role in Cuban agriculture. The great majority of leaseholders invested in the most profitable sectors of commercial agriculture. They rented the lands; acquired agricultural machinery, implements, seeds, and fertilizers; and exploited the business from a capitalist viewpoint. Even the small leaseholders of tobacco plantations with yearly incomes between $1,500 and $2,000 had a capitalist orientation in their economic activity. Leaseholders in branches of commercial agriculture, both large and small, bought in order to produce for the capitalist market, obtain profits, and, in general, employ salaried workers. The decades between 1931 and 1958 were decisive in the advances of the capitalist sector in agriculture as it gradually displaced the large landowners, since they did not undertake bourgeois-type business activities. In my view, capitalism followed a double path of development in Cuban agriculture: on the one hand, a direction followed by the capitalist leaseholders; on the other, a slower, Junker-type transformation of *terratenientes* into agrarian bourgeois.

Progress along both paths, however, was slow owing to the massive penetration of products from the United States and the stagnant character of the cattle-raising sector, which held the greater part of the land. Then, too, the most significant investments of the new agrarian bourgeoisie were made in cane plantations as the large U.S. and Cuban sugar mills leased their lands. The only new crops of particular economic importance for the capitalist leaseholding class were rice, henequen, and cereals. In 1952, 47.5% of the area devoted to rice cultivation was held by capitalist leaseholders, 35.3% by the owners of farms, and 8.5% by small farmers (squatters, *partidarios* [renters], sharecroppers, and subtenants).

The slight growth in agricultural production in crops other than sugarcane in the 1950s was due primarily to increases in tobacco and rice production. This small growth, however, provided employment for only 5% to 10% of rural workers, condemned in general to unemployment as a result of the sugar crop restriction. Potato production also rose in those years, but this did not bring about a reduction in import. As a whole, the value of noncane agricultural production was 1.91 million pesos in 1946–1951 and 1.94 million pesos in 1952–1957.

The importation of food products from the United States contributed to the relative stagnation of agricultural production. In the 1950s Cuba surpassed by ample margin the leading Latin American countries as a large importer of foodstuffs, as shown in Table 2.4. From 1952 to 1958, the value of the island's average imports of foodstuffs rose to more than $140 million annually.

Although the large leaseholders tended to adopt capitalist relations of production, contracting salaried workers, the large landowners resorted to precapitalist means of appropriation of surpluses, such as land ceded for sharecropping, a system that goes back to the slave societies of antiquity and still survived in the late 1940s in highly developed European capitalist countries such as France and Italy, in which from 10.8% to 33.3% of the land, respectively, was worked by sharecropping (Byres and Stolcke, 1983: 21). The dimensions and importance of medium-sized farms and large areas leased by the class of bourgeois entrepreneurs are suggested in Table 2.5.

Table 2.4   Value of Imported Foodstuffs by Country, 1956 and 1957 (in millions of pesos)

	1956	1957
Cuba	124	147
Mexico	69	104
Venezuela	72	82
Brazil	29	39
Chile	20	25
British Caribbean islands	13	20
Peru	9	12
Panama	9	9
Guatemala	9	9
Bolivia	20	9
Argentina	24	2
Others	67	60
Total	465	518

Source: Cuba Económica y Financiera, August 1958.

Table 2.5 Types of Landholding, by Size of Land

Type of Landholding	100 to 499.9 ha	500 to 999.9 ha	1,000 to 4,999.9 ha	5,000 or more ha
Proprietors	3,831	452	235	35
Leaseholders	3,592	465	190	26
Administrators	2,027	432	303	49

Source: *Memoria del Censo Agrícola Nacional, 1946:* 401.

As I have pointed out, farms operated by administrators were in many cases farms leased by a capitalist entrepreneur. Only some of these were the property of large landowners. The singularity of the Cuban social process seems to be explained, therefore, by the double path capitalism followed in agriculture and the process of formal *descampesinización,* or reduction in the number of peasants, that occurred with the proletarianization of the rural population and the simultaneous increase in the number of *minifundios,* or small landholdings. (I return to this subject in Chapter 6.)

We should note, finally, some facts that explain the process of formation and consolidation of the class of large and medium-sized capitalist leaseholders and the new capitalist proprietors in the last three decades of the neocolonial republic. The law of sugar coordination of 1953 sought to guarantee the permanence of the small *colono* on the land. In the 1930s and 1940s, a series of other measures tended to prevent the eviction of peasants and limit the rents charged by landowners. This combination of legal regulations should have induced the landowners to employ salaried workers rather than cede land for sharecropping or leasing to the peasant class. Contrary to what might have been expected, however, the desired effects were not achieved. Apparently, the pressure exerted by the communist unions in defense of the rights of agricultural workers led many of the landowners to cede the land preferentially for sharecropping. At the same time, campaigns carried on by the reformist national press through such widely read publications as *Bohemia, Prensa Latina,* and *Luz,* insisting on both the need to enforce the precept of the constitution of 1940 that proclaimed the social function of property by obliging large landowners to cultivate large expanses of idle land as well as the need to raise rents to maintain the living standard of the capitalist class, persuaded a considerable sector of the *terrateniente* class to increase the number of peasants settled on their idle lands as sharecroppers or tenants. The number of sharecroppers rose considerably in relation to the number of proprietors of all types from 1931 to 1946. Nevertheless, throughout these decades one sector of the large landowning class that felt more pressured by the measures that limited their rents and tended to guarantee the permanence of the small *colonos* and peasants on the land decided to become a part of the agrarian bourgeoisie, modernizing its methods of land exploitation and hiring salaried workers. The 1946 rural census stated that of 423,690 permanent rural workers, 41.7% labored on farms operated by tenants, that is, mainly by their capitalist leaseholders, whereas only 18.1% were employed most of the time by large landowners (owners of latifundia). Thus capitalist lessees were the landholders that employed the greatest number of workers on their lands. The set of governmental rulings issued in this period determined the slow progress along the Junker path compared to the capitalist path based on the new investments of leaseholders and new capitalist proprietors.

The slow advance of Junker evolution was also attributable to another factor: A considerable part of the farmers who used salaried workers on their lands were new proprietors who between 1931 and 1946 acquired farms for the purpose of working them under intensive capitalist-type exploitation. In this way the new proprietors of large and medium-sized farms, together with the large and medium-sized leaseholders, became the principal driving force toward capitalist development in agriculture. It is not possible to determine precisely the number of new nonpeasant proprietors (that is, bourgeois entrepreneurs who acquired lands during that period), but the agricultural census of 1946 gives an idea of their growing importance. From 1931 to 1946, a total of 21,204 proprietors who had worked their farms fewer than fifteen years of permanence were established, 43% of the total number of proprietors registered in that census. If we add to this new agrarian bourgeoisie the capitalist leaseholders of farms larger than 100 hectares, it is clear that they were a majority compared to the *terratenientes* who owned farms of that size, among which are included both those who hired salaried workers and those who exploited peasants by submitting them to links of dependency such as sharecropping. I have already noted that 59% of the farms with a production value above $1,500 annually were in the hands of capitalist leaseholders. It can be calculated that with the addition of an important part of the new proprietors established between 1931 and 1946 (21,204), the new agrarian bourgeoisie made up an indisputable majority over the *terratenientes*. If we add to this that the group of *terratenientes* who had become agrarian bourgeois constituted only a fraction of the class of large landowners, it is evident that the Junker transformation fell far short of being the leading force in agriculture and that the dominant form was that promoted by the capitalist lease-holders and new capitalist proprietors.

Although the predominance of capitalist relations in agriculture seems to be an incontrovertible fact, it hardly appears that a modern mentality prevailed among the agrarian bourgeoisie. Of 159,958 farms registered in the census of 1946, only 1,364 had tractors; 1,053 reported the possession of trucks, 1,186 automobiles, 9,764 power mills, and 6,410 windmills. According to Minneman, 80% of the land was plowed by oxen and 95% of the sugarcane was transported by these animals in 1947. Thus the agricultural attaché of the U.S. embassy in Havana did not hesitate to affirm: "On the majority of Cuban farms, the work methods continue to be more or less the same as those of one hundred years ago. Until recently, they have used very few tractors. . . . It can be safely stated that at least three-fourths, and perhaps more, of the work in the countryside in Cuba is still being performed almost exactly as it was in colonial times" (Minneman, 1947: 1–4).

The difficulties of mechanizing agricultural production was not simply a matter of backward perspectives, however; the agrarian bour-geoisie would have liked to follow the example of U.S. farmers. But the shortage of credits constituted an unsurpassable obstacle for many agricultural entrepreneurs, who were obliged to resign them-selves to low-yield harvests and low productivity. The Truslow Report complained about the high customs duties and taxes that the Cuban government imposed upon imported machinery: Altogether those taxes amounted to 18% of the U.S. free on board prices. The report also lamented the way U.S. distributors of farm equipment raised prices on tractors and implements, averaging 35% above U.S. prices, with repair parts 40% higher (Truslow, 1951: 99). At the same time, the halting progress along the Junker path kept great expanses of land idle, preventing capitalist-minded leaseholders from using them. And finally, competition from U.S. farm products ensured a relative stagnation in Cuban agricultural production.

In 1950 the U.S. industrial consortium International Harvester, a manufacturer of agricultural equipment, conducted a survey of 100 mechanized sugarcane plantations. As Table 2.6 shows, Cuban agri-culture had made some progress. Although these farms had tractors, fertilizers, or irrigation equipment, the majority could not com-pletely mechanize irrigation, fertilization, soil preparation, and

Table 2.6   Percentage of Mechanization of Work on 100 Plantations, ca. 1950

	All	Part	None
Fertilization	39	48	13
Irrigation	27	29	44
Soil preparation	50	47	3
Cultivation	24	67	9

Source: U.S. Department of Commerce, *Investments in Cuba*, 1956: 34.

cultivation. Apparently, however, in rice cultivation 60% of these tasks were completely mechanized and 30% partially.

The number of tractors used in agriculture increased by a factor of 3.8 from 1946 to 1950, but only 4.4% of farms had these machines in 1950 compared to 1.1% in 1946. Table 2.7 shows these changes. With the slow pace at which mechanization was introduced in agriculture, capitalist development in this sector would have to wait several decades.

The large *colonos* and the sugar mill owners of large tracts that were worked under the system of "administration cane" generally used oxen to plow and to transport cane and at the same time collected abusive rents from the small *colonos* and paid them in company store chits. A historian once described these as "feudal forms of exploitation." Certainly the backward character of dependent capitalism on Cuban plantations is beyond dispute, although the appropriation of surplus value by the agrarian bourgeoisie in the republican period was a system of survival employed by slaveholding, not feudal, landowners. Thus despite their modern conception of development and the high technology employed, the large sugar mills and

Table 2.7   Use of Tractors, by Type, 1946 and 1950

	Caterpillar Types	Wheeled Tractors	Total Tractors	Available Horsepower
1946	1,416	472	1,888	57,075
1950	2,020	5,130	7,150	185,900

Source: Gutiérrez, G., 1952: 209.

plantations backed by U.S. financial capital adopted antiquated forms of agricultural exploitation, affirming the assertion that any means of earning capital is good.

The Absentee Bourgeoisie

A conceptual problem confronts us with respect to given strata of the dependent bourgeoisie whose capital was not invested in reproductive economic activities or the circulation of goods. Some researchers, following the example of André Gunder Frank, have defined this idle sector of the bourgeoisie as the absentee bourgeoisie or as the lumpen bourgeoisie. Others have observed that the main features of these strata are common to the generality of the dependent bourgeoisie, thus tending to confuse them with other strata of the same class.

In fact, it was because financial capital appropriated the national economic surplus that national capital, accumulated historically, tended to withdraw from the commercial and reproductive economic cycle. The prolonged domination exerted by neocolonial mechanisms in this period led to the gradual formation of a rentier and hoarding sector of disproportionate dimensions. In the existing conditions, capital transferred from generation to generation tended to be employed in relatively stable and profitable activities unrelated to the process of production. At the same time, the precariousness of the Cuban economy, subject to the vicissitudes of sugar prices, the system of sugar quotas, and periodic crises, inhibited owners of capital from undertaking agricultural and industrial activities as entrepreneurs. The most eloquent statistical evidence of the process of accumulation of absentee capital in bank vaults from 1920 to 1959 is found in the relation between deposits and loans. The recessive economic cycle began in 1928, but not until 1935 was there a marked discrepancy between deposits and loans. In 1928 loans began to diminish progressively until 1949, whereas deposits increased constantly until 1957. Bank vaults thus remained crammed with immobilized money at the same time that requests for loans declined or were rejected by bank managers, fearful of the risks implied by investments in a time of economic recession. In the 1950s, nevertheless, the Batista regime's free-handed spending policy encouraged commercial banks, under pressure from the National Bank, to finance the building boom and other investments in nonreproductive economic activities. Under these circumstances deposits rose steadily, a sign that the tendencies to inertia or withdrawal dominating absentee capital

Table 2.8   Total Bank Deposits and Loans, 1920–1957 (in millions of pesos)

	Deposits	Loans	%
1920	441	282	64
1926	168	227	135
1929	229	183	79
1933	108	94	87
1935	106	77	72
1937	138	69	50
1939	128	69	43
1941	139	60	29
1943	261	77	25
1945	432	110	29
1947	586	174	29
1949	554	191	34
1951	727	382	52
1953	704	388	55
1955	716	422	51
1957	1,106	552	50

Sources: Cuba Económica y Financiera, April 1950; Revista del Banco Nacional de Cuba, February and September 1958.

conserved their vigor. Table 2.8 indicates the reciprocal relation of bank activities with respect to deposits and loans from 1920 to 1957.

Absentee capital was made up as well by a sector of bureaucratic capital that came from the enormous fortunes amassed by embezzlement, contraband activities, and illicit contracts for government works, which sought greater security in the vaults of U.S. and European banks.

Absentee capital must be distinguished according to the functions it performed in the economy. In industrialized capitalist countries, the capital of the real-estate-owning bourgeoisie does not have the relative importance that it holds in agrarian and dependent nations. One of the most revealing indices of the magnitude of capital invested in the construction of apartment buildings in Cuba is the constantly growing income of this nonreproductive sector compared to other sectors of the dependent bourgeoisie (see Table 2.9).

Between 1946 and 1951, only the earnings from industry and commerce surpassed those of the owners of real estate. Between 1952 and 1958, however, the rents received by the real-estate-owning bourgeoisie were greater than the earnings derived from industrial and commercial activities. The earnings of this sector in this period were also higher than those of the professional sector, which indicates its

Table 2.9   Income of the Real-Estate-Owning Bourgeoisie, 1946–1951 and
1952–1957 (in millions of pesos)

	1946–1951	1952–1957	Total
Rents from real estate	444.7	540.5	985.2
Earnings from industry and commerce	539.2	416.8	956
Earnings of professionals	98.7	115.4	214.1

Source: Martínez Sáenz, 1959: 214–215, table 5.1.1e.

growing importance in the overall Cuban economy. With respect to
gross capital outlay, the value of the buildings erected from 1945 to
1949 accounted for a considerable portion of the total investments
made by the domestic bourgeoisie in those years: In 1945 it was 45%;
in 1946, 51%; in 1947, 22%; and in 1949, 29% (Truslow, 1951: 513).

It is not possible to determine how representative these investments in real estate are in the gross Cuban capital outlay from 1942
on, as the importations of fixed capital by U.S. enterprises operating
on the island are not separated from those domestic enterprises in
estimates of national income. Nevertheless, the estimates of capital
formation in the private sector made by the U.S. Department of
Commerce in Cuba reveal that the distribution of investments in the
building sector rose from 16.8% in 1952 to 47.2% in 1953 and to
32.8% in 1954 (U.S. Department of Commerce, *Investments in Cuba,*
1956). The proportion of fixed capital importations in building compared to other sectors of the economy must have risen considerably
between 1954 and 1958, given the building boom that took place in
the 1950s and the recession in the majority of economic activities.

The real-estate-owning bourgeoisie was made up essentially of
persons of high and middle income. As a whole, this sector of the
dependent bourgeoisie shared a fear of losing its capital in investments in branches of the economy exposed to the competition of
products imported from the United States or in those areas monopolized by U.S. enterprises operating in Cuba. The hoarding of large
sums of money in Cuban or foreign banks, together with investments
made in the United States, characterized the parasitic sector of the
marginal bourgeoisie. A large part of the savings of this stratum took
the form of inactive deposits in Cuban and U.S. banks. Another considerable part emigrated to the New York and Florida exchanges,
where it was invested in real estate. The distinguishing feature of this
capital was its liquidity.

Investments of Cuban capital in U.S. securities, amounting to $30 million at the beginning of the 1930s, reached $42 million in 1941. Some $79 million in Cuban capital was deposited in U.S. banks in 1942 (Torras, 1984, vol. 1: 631). Independent deposits of Cuban capital reached $39 million in 1939 and $260 million in 1950; the flight of private capital climbed to $150 million in 1955. Other calculations for the period 1954–1958 place the flight of private capital to U.S. banks closer to $129 million (U.S. Department of Commerce, *Investments in Cuba*, 1956; Collazo, 1989: 46).

By 1950 Cuban investments in real estate in the state of Florida amounted to $100 million; income in passive accounts in U.S. banks reached $58 million; investments equivalent to $70 million were made in building, for a total of $228 million. If we compare this figure with the $140 million invested in fixed capital equipment, repairs, and maintenance in agricultural, commercial, and industrial activities, we see that the investments of the absentee bourgeoisie reached 62% of total investments that year, surpassing those of the bourgeoisie involved in productive or commercial activities (Truslow, 1951: 519–520; Banco Nacional de Cuba, 1953: 106). (Investments in gambling and vice are not included in these estimates for lack of statistics.)

The stratum of the marginal bourgeoisie devoted to illicit activities such as gambling and vice, the so-called lumpen bourgeoisie, was closely linked to diverse sectors of the dependent bourgeoisie. An investigation carried out by the Central Economic Board in 1958 found that some 26,710 people were proprietors of illegal games or involved in the administration of other organized gambling activities. According to historian Louis Pérez Jr., Havana was transformed into a center of commercialized vice of all sorts, underwritten by organized crime in the United States. American-owned gambling casinos emerged as a major industry, receipts reaching $500,000 a month in 1957. Batista's notorious chief of police, Rafael Salas Cañizares, received in his office daily the sum of $25,000 in proceeds from the capital's brothels and gambling houses. The lumpen bourgeoisie played an intermediate role in relation to the U.S. mafia in the exploitation of the luxury hotels and gambling dens built in Havana in the 1950s. Money was in constant movement, but no new Cuban jobs were created nor were salaries raised.

3

The Urban and Rural
Middle Classes Dislocated

The distinct sectors of the urban middle class continued to be fundamentally Cuban in both composition and ideology, in contrast to the working class, whose ranks were swollen by tens of thousands of workers of Antillean and Spanish origin, and in contrast as well to the bourgeoisie, in which a national consciousness had not yet jelled at the beginning of the twentieth century. The urban middle class bore the brunt of the contradiction of living "outside" the nation until the 1920s, when the changes that took place in their composition and in the structure of society awakened them to new awareness of the country's neocolonial situation. The data appearing in the 1907 and 1919 censuses allow us to reach certain conclusions concerning the nationality of the intellectual and professional sectors of the middle class. In 1907, 91% were Cuban, and this continued to be true in 1919. Among these intellectuals and professionals, only the clergy was, for the most part, Spanish. The national educational system was also in Cuban hands, so that the presence of foreigners in this sphere was insignificant.

The sector of the middle class made up of small proprietors and merchants, who were predominantly Spanish, diminished as a result of the emigration of Spanish subjects at the end of the war of 1895 and following the liberal insurrection of 1906. Thus, of a total of 42,430 merchants registered in the country in 1899, 24,588 were Spanish and 17,842 were Cuban. In 1907, of a total of 46,348 merchants, 23,973 were Spanish and 22,375 were Cuban. With respect to small grocers, the composition varied: Of a total of 13,817 in 1899, 10,169 were Spanish and 3,648 Cuban; in 1907, of 30,758 small grocers in Cuba, 20,787 were Spanish and 9,971 were Cuban.

By 1919 the trend had reversed: Of a total of 60,735 Cubans and Spaniards engaged in larger-scale commercial activities, 31,730 were

Cuban and 29,005 were Spanish. The proportion of small grocers had also evened up notably, with 7,962 Spanish and 6,270 Cuban out of the total of 14,232. According to figures for 1931 published by the National Commission of Statistics and Economic Reform, 1,427 of the country's small grocers were Cuban and 1,289 were foreign. Cuban capital invested in wholesale commerce amounted to $1.5 million, whereas foreign capital reached $4.3 million. In 1919, of the 1,389 pharmacists registered in Cuba, 1,262 were Cuban and only 127 Spanish. By 1930 the gradual passing of these commercial activities into Cuban hands played an important role in the new nationalist attitude of the middle classes. These sectors had become hostile toward the political corruption rampant in the country, since they were the most direct victims of the extortion practiced by venal administration and treasury department functionaries. Between 1898 and 1914, the middle-class sectors devoted to commercial activities had constituted an impregnable wall defended by Spaniards, impenetrable by any national sentiment. The island's small Spanish merchants and producers had faithfully adhered to policy of abstention vis-à-vis all national problems laid down at the beginning of the republic by Nicolás Rivero (Rivero, 1929: 235). But by the sheer weight of their numbers and their preponderant role in the economy by the 1920s, the Cubans devoted to commercial activities were a powerful force opposed to political corruption and to the country's neocolonial status, and they joined with the working class to protest against the Machado regime.

The census of 1907 reports 25,599 public employees, indicating that public employees were not numerous in the early years of the republic and that the struggle for political posts was no more than grasping at straws, resulting from the critical economic situation of the bourgeoisie and petty bourgeoisie. Nevertheless, jobs for teachers, soldiers, policemen, day laborers, and other government workers were the object of bitter political disputes.

According to 1931 data of the National Commission of Statistics and Economic Reform, the state paid more than $30 million to 41,817 employees in 1924. In 1914 the amount paid in salaries was $24 million, which translates into 25,000 to 35,000 government jobs. The growth of this sector dependent on government salaries meant greater political influence of governing groups over the urban middle class. Public employees were thus the portion of the middle class most closely linked to national political groups.

At the same time, these employees constituted the largest sector of the Cuban middle class. Their function as political clients of the government did not signify loyalty to a given party, since each change in power implied changes in the loyalty of the enormous mass of public employees who wished to retain their posts. The vicissitudes of government employees in their struggle to earn their daily bread resulted in the depoliticization of this portion of the middle class. Attitudes of bitterness, disbelief, and skepticism ended by corroding the foundations of patriotism in the early period. Nonetheless, this apparently made up only one of the tendencies existing in this sector. Around 1920 rebelliousness and disagreement with the existing state of affairs were palpable among the mass of second-class employees. Although the existing bureaucratic instability tended to make them dependent on the ruling political groups, it also generated a current toward rupture not only with the politicians in power but with neocolonial society in general.

The evolution of the urban middle classes from 1931 to 1953 was conditioned to a great extent by the growth of the tertiary sectors—employees of commercial establishments, services, and the government—more than by the increases that occurred in the number of self-employed persons, small proprietors, and merchants employing salaried workers. Thus, the number of government employees more than doubled from 1939 to 1953, going from 58,731 jobs to 133,862, which represented an increase in salaries paid from $40.2 million to $177.8 million (*Cuba Económica y Financiera*, March 1953: 7). The total number of workers in service jobs (including employees, professionals, and technicians) expanded by a factor of 3.8, from 48,011 in 1943 to 184,362 in 1953. In these same years, the number of employees in commerce also increased, 3.47 times, from 38,368 to 133,438. In absolute numbers, this meant that the sum of employees in the tertiary sector rose from 170,584 to 490,988, for a total increase of 320,404. These were government, commercial, and service employees, that is, the salaried middle stratum, which constituted 50% of the Cuban middle class.

The quantitative estimates I have made of the number of self-employed persons and small proprietors employing salaried workers are based on the supposition that the latter composed some 95% of all those classified in the censuses as "proprietors" or "owners," who presumably employed salaried workers. Because the number of large and medium-sized proprietors was insignificant, I decided to make my estimates for the 1943 census in relation to the petty bourgeoisie by adding the total of self-employed workers and "owners," since it was not possible to separate these categories from the others in the census.

In 1910, 31,000 public employees were working in government administration. By 1915 this number had grown to some 40,000.

From 1924 to 1937, government payrolls expanded considerably. Between 1924 and 1930, the Machado dictatorship increased the number of public employees by 9,096, from 42,294 to 51,390. The first Batista dictatorship further inflated these numbers. From 1933–1934 to 1936–1937 alone, the Caffery-Batista-Mendieta government raised the number of public posts by 18,385 (Abad, 1937: 9). This was an easy way to broaden its political base at a moment when the majority of the population repudiated the counterrevolutionary coup d'état carried out by Batista and the U.S. embassy against the revolutionary process of 1933. The number of employees added to the public payroll in the 1930s and 1940s provoked frequent criticisms from the daily *Diario de la Marina* and *Cuba Económica y Financiera.*

The hypertrophied character of the Cuban bureaucracy becomes obvious by comparing it to figures on government employment in other Latin American countries. For example, Colombia, with a total population double that of Cuba in 1940, had only slightly more than half the number of public employees: It had a population of 8.7 million and a public payroll of 38,893, whereas Cuba, with 4.2 million inhabitants, had 60,760 public employees. Equally significant was the proportion of the public payroll with respect to the national budget. In the case of Colombia, the payroll accounted for 27% of the budget; in Cuba it amounted to 57%. In other words, whereas a substantial part of the Colombian state budget was devoted to public works and activities promoting agriculture, which had a positive effect on the economy, in Cuba the budget was destined largely to creating bureaucratic posts that had no major influence on the economic development of the country (Abad, 1942: 36).

The urban middle strata, which perform services and carry out commercial or productive activities, are made up of the small manufacturers and merchants who employ salaried workers and those who are self-employed, with no employees. In the cities, according to the 1943 census, this sector was made up of those who carried out activities "for their own account" in construction, manufacturing and industry, transport, communications, commerce, services, electricity, banks, for the state, and in nonspecified activities. For the purpose of obtaining these estimates, I considered as urban those areas in which agricultural, forestal, or mining activities were not carried on. Between 1943 and 1953, the number of self-employed and owners decreased by 102,723.

An example of the decline in entrepreneurial activities in urban zones is seen in the category of managers, high-level employees, and owners who carried on activities "for their own account" or as owners in the census of 1943 and in the homologous category of managers, administrators, and owners who carried on the same activities as self-employed persons or as owners in the census of 1953. Thus, in the 1943 census the category of owners, managers, and high-level employees included 108,089 self-employed persons and owners, whereas in the 1953 census the number of managers, administrators, and owners had been reduced to some 73,459. Similarly, the census of 1943 reported 143,404 workers in all occupations who undertook activities as owners or "for their own account," whereas the 1953 census counted 110,809 self-employed workers or owners.

Nevertheless, these reductions in the number of self-employed persons and owners seem to have taken place only in manufacturing, industrial, and other highly specific activities. In construction, transport, and state and commercial services, stimulated by the giant harvest of 1952, the economic activities of self-employed persons increased. The rise in the total number of self-employed persons was also a result of growing unemployment. The presence of self-employed persons (and, apparently, owners) in reproductive economic activities, manufacturing, and craft industries is thus reduced because of imported U.S. merchandise, yet activities linked to commercial traffic grew, stimulated by the large post–Korean War crops.

The disappearance of some 102,723 persons from the rolls of the self-employed or owners reveals the proletarianization of the property-owning middle classes in the cities. A part of the owners and self-employed in the census of 1943 not registered as such in the 1953 count passed into the sector of the middle urban stratum of government employees in services and commerce; others were effectively proletarianized by becoming a part of the working class in industry, transportation, or construction. Still others must have joined the ranks of the large army of unemployed.

Parallel to this process of proletarianization of small manufacturers, the number of employees grew in the sectors of commerce, services, and the state, that is, the salaried middle strata. Government employees totaled 60,763 in 1943; and employees in commerce and industry numbered some 139,730, of which "the great majority," according to the census, were employees of commercial enterprises, in addition to 41,966 employees in commerce and services classified under the heading of "not known," making a total of some 242,459 commercial, service, and government employees. The increase in commercial and service employees resulted from demographic pressures as well as from modernization, driven by the consumption patterns of the wealthy classes (Zanetti, 1993: 152).

Nevertheless, the proletarianization of the middle classes was much more drastic than these estimates may indicate. Some non-Cuban authors have suggested that the middle class in Cuba in the 1950s continued to be a numerically decisive class, a notion that can scarcely be maintained. These observers based their conclusions on certain tables in the two above-mentioned censuses, ignoring the phenomenon of growing proletarianization reflected in other tables of the last census count. According to Hugh Thomas, the Cuban middle class included 680,000 persons (Thomas, 1967). The scholar C. M. Raggi stated in 1950 that the middle class made up 35% of the total active population (Raggi, 1950: 79). These authors did not bear in mind that the different census enumerations included many persons who declared only their usual or last occupation and were registered by the census takers as engaged in those occupations, whether or not they were actually employed. As a matter of fact, a high proportion of those who described themselves as having middle-class occupations were not working. At the time of the census, they held working-class jobs or were in fact unemployed. For that reason, scholars often overestimated the size of the middle class. There is, then, a need to elaborate middle-class estimates that take into consideration the existence of one stable sector and another that is in the process of disintegration—that is, of becoming proletarianized.

    López Segrera (1972: 443), who was the first to call attention to this historiographical error, quantified the ascendance of the middle classes using as an apparent base certain data from the 1953 census. His estimates, then, are hardly more accurate than those of the authors he criticized. However, the census of 1943, taken at a time when the process of proletarianization had not yet reached its zenith, reports that of some 445,912 persons classified as professionals, managers, proprietors, office workers, salespeople, shop clerks, and providers of personal services, 297,433 offered sufficient information to be able to classify them as employed and 62,952 as unemployed, whereas 85,537 could not be classified as either, for lack of sufficient information. The ratio between those who could be effectively classified as employed and those who were unemployed was approximately 5:1; the unemployed in the "unknown" group thus reached some 14,541. If we add these 14,541 to the 62,942 that appear registered as the total of unemployed in the categories of employees, small proprietors, or providers of services, the number of unemployed in these categories reaches 77,483. The stable urban middle class therefore did not exceed 370,000 persons.

    The census of 1953, in contrast, does not allow us to establish the proportion of employed persons with respect to small proprietors and providers of services, nor the relation between the middle class as a whole and the total population of working age, since the tables of employment and underemployment do not include the different occupations. The data show only that of a population of 3,828,464 persons fourteen years old or above, 1,779,236 were working for or without payment the week preceding the census count, so it is impossible to determine the number of employed or unemployed members of the middle class.

We can only calculate in general terms that unemployment and underemployment had increased considerably in this part of society in 1953 compared to 1943. As we have seen, during these years the number of people who made up the middle class of owners was notably reduced, with fewer persons reporting their habitual occupational status to the census. This does not mean, however, that at the time of the census they were employed, so we can simply speculate as to the possible number of individuals from the middle strata who were not working. If we consider that 41.3% of the total labor force worked fewer than thirty-nine weeks in the year, we can estimate that from 20% to 40% of the owning classes and employees were in the same situation. That is, 120,000 to 180,000 middle-class people were employed and underemployed. These calculations reduce the size of the middle classes with stable, permanent employment from 604,531 included in the census in the categories of employed and self-employed to 424,600 to 484,000 persons in urban zones.

The portion of the middle class made up of service, commerce, and government employees, which grew by more than 248,500 persons, suffered a decline in its standard of living between 1941 and 1947 as a result of the increase in the food cost index from 99.9 to 248.8. No significant increase of salaries over prices sufficient to raise the standard of living took place between 1947 and 1957. Government salaries, which had been raised by a law of the senate on November 14, 1951, were cut by 16% to 10% as a result of a budget readjustment carried out by the Batista dictatorship following a drop in fiscal income caused by the sugar restriction. This last measure held salaries at this level until 1958. The monthly salaries of teachers and public employees that had been raised from $102 to $126 in 1951 were reduced in 1953 to $119. In other words, the cost of food rose 31% from 1944 to 1957, whereas the salaries of public employees and teachers increased only 14.4%. The difficult situation these intermediate strata of employees faced is suggested in the summary in Table 3.1.

The events that brought about a global diminution in the earnings of commercial and service employees from 1944 to 1958 are difficult to quantify. With the complicity of the Auténtico and Batista

Table 3.1   Income of Commerce, Service, and Government Workers, 1943

Salary	Commerce		Services		Government	
	Number	%	Number	%	Number	%
$30	24,639	20.5	39,567	49.3	10,361	20.9
$30–59	62,238	51.8	24,996	31.5	22,788	36.6
$60–99	21,357	17.8	7,558	9.4	16,521	38.3
$100–199	9,549	7.1	5,173	6.4	3,332	6.7
$200–299	1,206	1.5	1,398	2.9	565	1.1
$300 or more	1,359	1.1	1,107	1.3	443	0.9

Source: Census of 1943.

governments, relying on the connivance of the head of the Confederation of Cuban Workers (CTC), Eusebio Mujal, and aided by the lack of militancy among employees, the owners in the commercial and service sectors drew up a list of urban underemployed persons, who were given work for fewer than five days, rotated, and paid lower wages for the same work as that performed by permanent employees. The group that received less than $30 per month in the commercial and service sectors thus increased considerably through the incorporation of apprentices and substitute workers who, by law, were paid less than permanent workers. This was one of the main mechanisms used to depress the salaries of employees in these sectors.

The argument that growth in the number of workers in distribution and service sectors corresponds to the degree of economic development reached by a society has been widely disseminated in the social sciences. According to this point of view, an increase in the number of employees in government and commercial activities constitutes an indication of a high standard of living and industrial prosperity. A rise in employment in the tertiary sector has also been taken erroneously by some Marxist authors as an index of numerical growth of the working class in underdeveloped countries and thus of the development of capitalism. These concepts have repeatedly run up against the contrary sociological and historical reality of underdeveloped countries.

The decrease in the number of small proprietors, manufacturers, and artisans and the increase in employees and professionals do not indicate a growth of the working class but rather a transfer from one category to another within the sector of the middle classes. In urban shops and small retail establishments, the workers are frequently the majority of the members of a family, who are classified by census takers as commercial employees or workers. This growth of employment in the tertiary sector constitutes an index of the pauperization of small producers. The result of this phenomenon is that worker productivity tends to fall. As Witold Kula has correctly pointed out, one of the regressive phenomena observed in periods of crisis and of depression is an increase in the number of commercial and manufacturing employees. To this could be added the fact of an increase in government employment in such periods. Populist or oligarchic governments frequently resort to agreements for foreign loans with the aim of offering new job possibilities to their numerous political clientele (Kula, 1973: 460). Finding themselves incapable of promoting economic development during the cyclic crises of the world capitalist system and facing mounting popular discontent, these governments use the resources of public power to absorb, albeit in a very small measure, the large contingent of unemployed generated by the lack of jobs. Referring to the growth of the tertiary sector in underdeveloped countries, Paul Baran has pointed out that employment rates are like obesity: At times they indicate opulence and at other times want (Baran, 1971: 247).

In periods of crisis, Cuba also experienced an increase in the number of small retail establishments in the cigar and shoe industries, which does not in general terms contradict the drastic reduction in the number of small manufacturers that occurred between 1943 and 1953. Since the basic tools of cigar and shoe production (sewing machines, lasts, knives, benches) were easily acquired, many people who were left without jobs became artisans, that is, self-employed workers. This process took place in the shoe industry during the 1930s and later, beginning in 1953, in the tobacco industry (Lugo, 1963). The following comments give an idea of the modus operandi of the industry:

> The crisis of 1930 accelerated this process. Improvised shops using the labor of all members of the family appeared everywhere; manufacturers became monopolizers by supplying lasts, leather, etc., to the family producers and "buying" their production at cutthroat prices. The manufacturers found it more profitable to close the factory—where they were obliged to pay rent, electricity, taxes, and salaries corresponding more or less to the general standard of living and to comply with social laws—and contract the labor of these small producers, who worked themselves to death 16 hours a day, making the shoes in their homes, paying no taxes, using the labor of all the family and of apprentices and, finally, turning over the shoes to the monopolizer for a pittance. (Roca, 1960: 56)

The rise in the number of artisans in these sectors in the 1930s and 1950s was thus a result of the crisis that threw into the streets thousands of workers, some of whom began to work for themselves or in small, hole-in-the-wall shops, using the labor of all family members. All this helped accentuate the low level of earnings of the small manufacturing bourgeoisie, which, together with its employees, suffered a considerable decline in its standard of living in the critical decades of the 1930s and 1950s.

The hypertrophy of the Cuban tertiary sector, shaped by the mechanisms of neocolonial domination, went beyond that which occurred on the Latin American continent. As Bairoch has justly emphasized, a disproportionate growth in this sector, in the context of an economy whose industrial productivity is still weak, contributes to the continuing stagnation of the economy. In these cases the disproportion of the tertiary sector proves to be a negative factor for an economic takeoff because of the living standards it tends to reproduce, inasmuch as it is not the result of industrial development, and above all because of the high prices caused by distribution costs. The pressure of the tertiary sector on mercantile circulation also reduces the possibilities of profits, limiting the rate of profitable investments. Table 3.2 shows Cuba leading fifteen underdeveloped countries when it reached the highest percentage of population employed in the tertiary sector in the 1950s.

Of course, copper in Chile and oil in Venezuela have enabled these countries to advance since the 1950s at a rate similar to that of Cuba because of sugar, but the monoproductive nature of these economies, as well as their hypertrophied tertiary sector, impeded their development and determined the dependent character of their economic structure.

A study carried out by the National Bank of Cuba to determine the dimensions of the Cuban tertiary sector within the Latin American context yielded the results shown in Table 3.3. The average percentage of the Latin American population employed in the tertiary sector reached 29.1%; in Japan and Europe it did not exceed 10–12% prior to their economic takeoff and approached 15% during the first decades of their development. In England it reached 10%, in France 12%, in Japan 10%, in Sweden 11%, in Italy 15%, and in Finland 19%. In the course of their industrial takeoff, then, the European countries benefited from a low percentage of population employed in the tertiary sector. In contrast, the underdeveloped countries faced the obstacle of a tertiary sector reaching 29%, whose participation in the national product was equivalent to 40%. In the case of Cuba, the tertiary participation in the national product

Table 3.2   Percentage of the Population Employed in the Tertiary Sector, by Country

		Percentage
Cuba	1953	37
Chile	1952	36
Venezuela	1950	35
Ceylon	1953	28
Brazil	1950	25
Egypt	1947	25
Philippines	1959	24
Malaysia	1957	23
Mexico	1958	21
Morocco	1952	21
Pakistan	1954	21
Iran	1956	20
India	1951	19
Ecuador	1961	20
China (Taiwan)	1956	24

Note: The tertiary sector includes electricity, gas, water, sanitation services, commerce, banks, insurance, transportation, communications, services, and storage.
Source: Bairoch, 1969: 176.

Table 3.3   Percentage Distribution of the Population by Occupational Sector, Latin America and Cuba

	Latin America		Cuba	
Sectors	1940	1954	1943	1954
Primary	62.0	51.6	41.5	40.9
Secondary	14.5	19.3	20.0	28.5
Tertiary	23.5	29.1	38.5	30.6
Totals	100.0	100.0	100.0	100.0

Sources: Alienes, 1950: 34; *Revista del Banco Nacional,* 1955, 1, 2: 479.

had a larger dimension (31%) and represented an additional hindrance to economic development.

Before formulating any conclusions about the historical evolution of the middle class, we must refer to the strata that composed it, inasmuch as these diverse strata (commercial and government employees, professionals, small manufacturers, and merchants) had differing

structural characteristics on the economic plane but behaved similarly on the political and ideological planes. Both their position in the
economic structure and their political-ideological behavior distinguished them, however, from the bourgeoisie and the working class,
classes situated at the extreme poles of the economic structure. The
explanation for this singular phenomenon lies in the fact that the
diverse middle-class strata occupied a common place in the country's
relations of production, different from the places occupied by the
working class and the bourgeoisie. In other words, although the different middle-class strata held diverse positions in the economic
structure, they held a common place with reference to the other classes of society, the bourgeoisie and the working class. Nevertheless, the
different political and ideological effects that might have derived
from the different economic positions existing among the strata of
the middle class underwent leveling changes as a result of the impact
of the other classes and institutions of society and of objective movements of the economy (processes of proletarianization, the decline of
real salaries) in the historical conditions of neocolonial domination.
All these factors tended to further differentiate the middle classes
from the bourgeoisie, pushing them nearer to the working class,
which—as a result of the struggles of the 1930s and 1940s—had a
more stable position and greater job security than did government
and commercial employees, easy victims of dismissals and cuts in real
salaries.

At the same time, small manufacturers and merchants and self-
employed individuals also suffered the consequences of the
depressed economic cycle of 1928–1958. This traditional sector of the
petty bourgeoisie identified itself with workers in their strikes in the
country's large industries and sugar mills. In general, this sector provided for workers' families during prolonged worker resistance and
favored better salaries for the working class, which constituted the
basic clientele of its establishments. Small merchants and manufacturers, furthermore, were the victims of venal exactions by tax collectors, sanitary inspectors, and the police. Thus, the most imperceptible
movements of the economy and of public administration exerted similar destabilizing effects on government and commercial employees
on the one hand and small manufacturers and merchants on the
other, determining attitudes of repudiation of politics. Nevertheless,
to the extent that these strata of the middle class sustained similar
relations of dependence on the state, attitudes of idolatry toward the
state and fetishism of political activity arose among them. Their position with respect to the state was therefore much more subordinate
and vulnerable than that of the workers, even when the latter began

to become dependent on increasing government intervention in labor conflicts.

The cultural levels of the middle class in general tended to be higher than those of laborers, who worked with their hands. Historically, many members of the middle class had come from the middle bourgeoisie and had access to middle-level or higher education, and this better education tended to create in them a disdain for physical labor. The most cultured sectors of the middle class were in general descendants of criollo families of the nineteenth century, whereas the workers were in general Spanish immigrants, poor peasants, or racially mixed descendants of slaves.

The middle class repudiated easy enrichment, squandering and ostentation, rapacious exploitation, and anticapitalism of the status quo because this class had a property-owning as well as a salaried sector that feared proletarianization. They despised as well the financial capital and the great commercial capital that pushed up the prices of the products of small shopkeepers. This repudiation extended to exploiters such as the large real estate owner Sarrá and the despoiler of the public treasury José Manuel Alemán. What they hated was not "the class," the bourgeoisie, but its more ostentatious representatives. The middle class did not identify itself with the powerful, hence its rejection of U.S. economic penetration—above all that part that exploited it most directly, such as the so-called Cuban Electric Company and the Cuban Telephone Company. They were also aware that the high prices of products were due to the massive penetration of merchandise from the United States. The majority of the middle class, of course, lived a tranquil existence without excessive aspirations to wealth or social position, but the more ambitious sector of the class tried to imitate the dependent bourgeoisie in every way, for they believed the future belonged to the most capable, to the best. These attitudes, especially those that united the middle class around certain fears and aspirations, fed its most intimate myths and isolated it in relation to the other classes.

The rejection of administrative corruption and proletarianization was a basic part of the ideology of the middle classes throughout the first half of the century. Their principal crises and moments of rupture were linked to this attitude. In this sense, it should be remembered that the wars of liberation at the end of the nineteenth century, with their terrible destruction of property and wealth, ruined the urban and rural middle class. It was thus that the republican state was obliged to become a shelter, where tens of thousands of helpless persons found employment. Very soon the competition for government jobs and electoral posts became the keynote of government adminis-

tration. Massive displacement of employees with the advent of each
new administration, electoral deals designed to ensure the triumph of
candidates of the party in power, the physical misappropriation of
government funds by ministers and high functionaries, scandalous
business transactions carried out under contracts conceded by the
government or by the introduction of contraband goods through the
country's customs office provided not only a partial solution to the
employment problems of the middle class but also the enrichment of
politicians seeking to become part of the bureaucratic bourgeoisie.
Thus, security in public posts was not guaranteed, and robbery was
encouraged with the aim of reconstituting the bourgeois class ruined
by war. The result was that the state as shelter or catalyzer of development became a bilgewater state. In these circumstances the life of the
urban middle class was extremely insecure and unfruitful; during the
first fifteen years of the republic small-scale commercial and industrial activities had only the slightest development. Only the expansion
of the sugar industry in the first two decades of the century contributed indirectly to the beginning in the following decades of an
increase in the number of small urban businesses and industries. But
that development was not sufficient to free the urban middle class
from dependence on state largesse.

The repudiation of political and administrative corruption by
given sectors of the middle classes manifested itself in the first half of
the twentieth century through the protests of the most representative
and incorruptible institutions of Cuban national sentiment. In 1914
the Association of Veterans, whose leaders were outside of politics,
began a moralizing campaign against the illicit handling of public
funds; the Association of Veterans and Patriots, composed of the most
prestigious figures among the high officers of the liberation army and
of Cuban intellectuals, was created in 1923 in protest against administrative immorality; and the Grupo Minorista made itself known that
same year through its "protest of the thirteen," as leading members of
the young Cuban intelligentsia demonstrated against the administrative excesses of the Machado government. The denunciations and
moralizing campaigns of these institutions responded to middle-class
sentiment that opposed corruption.

The failure of the Auténticos, the national-popular party of the
masses headed by Ramón Grau San Martín, to live up to the principles of administrative honesty it had expounded led one of its most
respected leaders, Eduardo Chibás, to break away from the party and
found the Cuban People's Party, which took up the slogan "decency
versus money." A large part of the nonproletarian masses and a
reformist sector of the working class soon abandoned the Auténtico

Party to join Chibás. The populist Ortodoxo program appealed particularly to the masses of small merchants and industrialists, self-employed persons, and government and commercial employees, as well as the intelligentsia. The program denounced the venal functionaries who practiced extortion against small merchants and manufacturers and favored a law of administrative nondismissal to protect the jobs of government employees. At the same time, it called for the nationalization of public utilities (electricity, telephones, and transport) and a reduction in the rates of these public services and rents. Chibás also opposed the arrangement of foreign loans, whose liquidation implied new burdens on taxpayers. He further challenged indirect taxes on the population, at the same time favoring direct taxation of the prosperous dependent bourgeoisie. Another important facet of Ortodoxo policy was the denunciation of speculation and the black market, which pushed up the prices of consumer products, and the penetration of U.S. merchandise, which had the same effect through its monopolizing character. The Cuban People's Party criticized U.S. political interference in the internal affairs of the country, which appealed to the national sentiment of the middle classes. Chibás was also one of the most ardent proponents of admitting the public to the beaches controlled by private clubs of the bourgeoisie. But the main fire of his moralizing campaigns was aimed at the scandalous embezzlements of the leading Auténtico personages. His ethical crusade was directed against the credibility of the party then in power, but it was based on middle-class opposition to administrative corruption that had prevailed since the beginning of the twentieth century.

One of the most important aspects of the middle class between 1910 and 1930 was the relatively stable and consolidated character it reached as a result of the development of small-scale commercial and industrial activities. Its ideological representatives, the intellectual sector of this class, with a greater awareness of its interests, posed its participation in the popular movement in terms of the class, the middle class, rather than as a part of the people. In this sense, it coincided with the working class, which formulated its demands strictly in class terms and not as a part of the people. It should be pointed out, however, that from 1920 to 1930 its decision to confront the neocolonial relation had a more radical character than from 1940 to 1950, as evident in the political and ideological discourse of the earlier period compared to that of the following decades.

The confrontation with U.S. economic penetration was stimulated in the 1930s by the elements of the middle class most conscious of their interests as a fairly stable and cohesive class. In the 1940s and

1950s, in contrast, the increasing deterioration of the middle class resulting from the recessive economic cycle induced many of its members to aspire to solvency through politics, allowing them to join the ranks of bureaucratic capital, a true bourgeoisie that had its origin in the enrichment of venal politicians. Thus the access to power of these money-seeking elements of the middle class signified, paradoxically, a weakening of their class positions, a tendency that would begin to manifest itself in the government of Grau San Martín and become consolidated in the administration of Prío Socarrás. As had occurred between 1902 and 1923, once the political representatives of the middle class had obtained power—and become corrupt—the middle classes lost their nationalist sentiments: Political corruption and weakening of nationalism were mutually inclusive. With the reorganization of the Auténtico Party in the 1930s, Conchita Casteñedo first observed and Ruben de León subsequently admitted that in the electoral activities of this political group, the revolutionary candidates were replaced by upstarts hungry for power and money. Years later Chibás would summarize this process in an article entitled "Vendepatrias y ladrones" (Traitors and thieves), in which he equated those who had abandoned the national ideal and the nouveau riche of the Auténtico Party. In this way the process of depauperization and proletarianization of the middle class stimulated its most insecure elements, avid for wealth, to take over the most relevant positions among the Auténticos and led its most consequent nationalist elements to break away from this group and join the Ortodoxo Party. Thus the growing instability and impoverishment of the middle class appears to have resulted in a double process of embourgeoisement and denationalization among the corrupt political sectors and of intensified patriotism among the most politically aware sectors of the opposition.

The Ortodoxos offered a continuation of the program of the revolution of the 1930s, buried by the intervening Auténtico governments, with a series of measures in favor of the country's popular sectors, especially the middle class. Although its program was merely redistributive, inasmuch as it did not propose basic structural transformations that would imply displacing the dependent bourgeoisie from power, Chibás kept alive faith in the possibility of changes at a moment when the traditional political parties were in full crisis.

4

Disintegration of the Independent Peasantry

The *campesinado* (peasantry), properly speaking, included the small proprietors, subtenants, sharecroppers, and others who owned or had usufruct of farms smaller than 50 hectares. The majority of such owners and tenants can be classified as campesinos, or peasants. This conventional classification, however, is subject to variation, depending on the region of the country and the type of crop. A tobacco grower with fewer than 5 hectares of land can be considered a small landowner or rich campesino, not an ordinary campesino. In certain very fertile regions, some crops yield profits four, five, or ten times greater than in others, and in these cases the factor differentiating the peasant from the landowner is not the amount of land but its yield. In fertile regions a farm of only 1 *caballería* can yield more than a farm of 8 or 10 *caballerías* of exhausted land. For the purposes of this book, I used census figures, ignoring the particularities of the soil, its fertility, and the demand for a given type of crop and basing my classification solely on farm size.

The definition of tenants of farms of less than 50 hectares as capitalist tenants is also controversial. In reality, despite their small landholdings, the aim of the small tenants is to produce in order to sell—that is, their economic activity would appear to be governed by a capitalist conception. If we take these circumstances into account, we might consider the small tenant no more than an agrarian bourgeois, not a peasant. But the investment in equipment made by tenants of farms smaller than 50 hectares is usually so insignificant that it can scarcely be considered a capitalist type of investment. Moreover, it is difficult to specify the motives of these small tenants in settling on their parcels of land. We cannot ascertain precisely whether their purpose is simply to sustain their families economically, that is, to produce for family consumption and avoid the need to sell their physical labor to a rural employer, or whether it is to earn money and become an agrarian bourgeois who produces for the market. In my view the majority of these small tenants are peasants who cannot find any other way to have access to land than by renting a parcel.

Another controversial question concerns the classification of the squatters, sharecroppers, and others who have usufruct of tracts of land greater than 50 hectares. According to the 1946 census, 55,776 campesinos had this type of link to land. For my purposes, I count the subtenants, sharecroppers, and other types of landholders not classified in the census but with usufruct of farms of more than 100 hectares not as peasants in the strict sense of the term but as rich peasants who can be classified as agrarian bourgeois. The subtenants, sharecroppers, and squatters I define as peasants occupied 97% of farms of fewer than 100 hectares and numbered 55,776, whereas the remaining, agrarian bourgeois, on farms of more than 100 hectares, occupied 5.2% of the farms and numbered only 2,903.

A comparison of farms by size and type of tenancy in the censuses of 1899, 1931, and 1946 presents difficulties as well: (1) In classifying farms by type of tenancy, both the 1931 and 1946 censuses include those that have an administrator, farms with a proprietor or those held in usufruct by a tenant who employed a person to administrate them. This classification makes it impossible to clarify precisely the number of farms that had a proprietor and the number that had a tenant. The census of 1899 does not include administrators. (2) The census of 1931 does not show, among the types of land tenancy, farms worked by sharecroppers and subtenants, although it is possible that the latter are included among those classified as farms worked by a tenant. (3) The 1899 census also fails to take into account sharecroppers, who are classified as tenants, and therefore their evolution can be traced only from 1931 on.

Despite these problems, it is possible to make a relative comparison and estimate of the number of proprietors, tenants, administrators, and sharecroppers in the three census enumerations. The number of proprietors grew from 16,990 in 1899 to 32,314 in 1931, an increase of 15,324, and from 32,314 in 1931 to 48,792 in 1946, an increase of 16,478. The same occurred with tenants and subtenants, whose numbers rose from 35,340 in 1931 to 46,138 in 1946, that is, by 10,798. The number of farms operated by administrators, however, decreased from 10,798 in 1931 to 9,341 in 1946. The number of sharecroppers, in turn, expanded considerably during those fifteen years. Between 1931 and 1946, it went from 8,944 to 33,064, an increase of 24,120. In absolute numbers, and proportionately, sharecropping (*aparcería*) was the type of land tenancy that experienced the greatest growth during this period.

According to my estimates, the number of agrarian proletarians in the year 1946 (265,538) was 3.8 times greater than the total of landless campesinos who worked as sharecroppers (33,064) and those who were subject to precapitalist links of dependency on farms of fewer than 50 hectares as subtenants or tenants (35,210). These calculations indicate the parallel development in agriculture of capitalist forms of contracting, corresponding to bourgeois tenants, and precapitalist types of links, imposed by landowners on the campesinos.

The development of capitalism in agriculture by way of large tenants and new capitalist proprietors brought about a considerable increase in the number of wageworkers—that is, of the rural proletariat in relation to the sharecroppers and other subordinate roles to which the campesinos were subjected. These figures thus stand as testimony to the existing tendency toward this type of capitalist development beginning in 1930. Nevertheless, the number of landless campesinos linked to precapitalist types of relations of dependency rose notably from 1930 to 1957 as a result of the need of landowners to augment their income and their aspiration to enjoy a high living standard in accordance with the prevailing levels of consumption of the bourgeoisie in general.

The sustained growth in the number of sharecroppers contrasted sharply with the slow increase in the number of small proprietors. Despite what some apologists of the capitalist system in Cuba postulated, in the sense that the basic path of mercantile development in agriculture was determined by the growing access of campesinos to land as proprietors, the fact is that this development followed other paths. The fundamental path was determined by the growing proletarianization of the campesinos, who found themselves obliged to sell their labor to capitalist agricultural tenants and to the landowners who became a part of the agrarian bourgeoisie. The general development of capitalism impelled landowners who did not modernize to submit the campesinos to ever more severe links of dependency of the precapitalist type, such as sharecropping, in order to increase their rents. This process was derived from the general commercialization of all economic relations.

The former Cuban provinces where squatting most proliferated were Oriente, Camagüey, and Las Villas. According to the census of 1946, the squatters numbered 636 in Las Villas (4.6% of the total), 924 in Camagüey (6.7% of the total), and 11,447 in Oriente (83.4% of the total). The average area of farms occupied by squatters was

12.9 hectares in Oriente and 17.8 hectares nationally. Only the farms of sharecroppers, with an average of 16.7 hectares, had a smaller area than those of the squatters. On a national scale, the remaining farms covered much larger average areas: The farms of proprietors averaged 60.6 hectares, those of tenants 58.9, those of subtenants 30.8, and those of other, nonclassified types of tenancy 35.9 hectares. The area of the farms of the squatters and sharecroppers in the former province of Oriente, each less than 13.42 hectares, suggests that these farms corresponded in dimension to the parcels of land occupied by rural workers during the "dead season" after they had sold their labor during the year in the diverse harvests of the region. These parcels had the function of providing subsistence to the families of unemployed agricultural workers.

The farms occupied by squatters on a national scale also had the lowest average value of production, reaching only $475.32. These were followed by other, nonclassified types of tenancy with an average value of $1,325.78, the sharecroppers with $1,379.98, the subtenants with $1,888.18, the proprietors with $1,759.37, and the tenants with $2,749. The higher value of production registered for the farms of tenants shows the bourgeois entrepreneurial character of exploitation on the greater part of the farms in this category. The low average value of production on the farms of squatters indicates that the greater part of this production was not marketed but destined for family consumption. It also reveals that the squatters did not devote sufficient workdays to commercial crops because they were employed in the harvests of other farms or in the sugar harvest.

The small coffee growers, tobacco growers, and cane growers constituted the most dynamic sector of the campesinos. According to the National Commission of Statistics and Economic Reform, the average small-scale coffee-growing farm had 12 hectares in 1925; the average such farm in 1930 had an area of 15.4 hectares. The product of the harvest left the coffee farmers with a monthly income of just over $56 in 1925 and $21 in 1933, without taking into account costs of production or payment in kind or money for sharecropping rights or tenancy. In 1946, coffee-growing farms with an income of less than $1,000 per year averaged earnings of $494 for the sale of their crops—that is, $46 a month.

According to the agricultural census of 1946, 7,527 farms (53.1% of the total) had fewer than 25 hectares, a smaller area than what the National Association of Coffee Growers considered profitable. The average earnings of 3,057 farms of squatters devoted to coffee growing in Oriente Province reached only about $270 per year, whereas farms operated by administrators had annual average gross earnings of $1,086. All this made for a situation of extreme poverty and backwardness among the campesinos and rural population of the mountainous regions. In the end, the very poor campesinos with earnings of less than $40 monthly and the poor, with less than $100 monthly, were usually obliged to sell their labor on nearby farms.

The landlords of the mountainous regions resorted to the most rapacious exploitation, following the methods of appropriation of peasant labor of precapitalist agrarian societies. Landholders granted campesinos parcels of land to develop coffee plantations. After three years of work, campesinos had the right to the product of the first harvest, and each received another parcel in another place to continue developing coffee plantations, which then passed to the owner to be exploited directly as soon as they reached full production (Roca, 1960: 38). Also common were sharecropping contracts that stipulated payment to the landlord of 40% of the coffee produced annually. The contract was canceled if the sharecroppers promoted "political or any other kind of discussion on the farms" or did anything that the landlord considered prejudicial "in any way" to the farm (Vilar, 1949: 1021, 1022). Sociologist Lowry Nelson of the U.S. Department of State quoted some informants as saying, "After the landowner turns over a piece of land for a period of 8 years, the only benefit derived by the *colono* consists of 3 harvest gatherings. . . . Inasmuch as the coffee trees require from 4 to 5 years to come to bearing, the *colono* meanwhile leads a miserable life" (Nelson, 1950: 129).

According to the Truslow Report, the usual interest rate that coffee hullers, wholesalers, and local retailers charged coffee farmers was in the neighborhood of 25% per annum (Truslow, 1951: 593). The majority of coffee growers found themselves, like the tobacco growers and cane growers, forced to join agricultural associations dominated by the landlords; far from raising their class consciousness and promoting their demands, this distanced them from practical action in favor of their rights. The regulations of the associations of cane growers, coffee growers, and tobacco growers recognized the right of all campesino members to elect their officers, but these were in fact controlled by the large and medium-sized landlords. Because the majority of these members had legal representatives or were lawyers themselves, the campesinos trusted them to handle everything related to the sale of the harvest. In general, these associations held one or two meetings each year, in full harvest season and without prior notice, in one of the urban centers. Consequently, few growers could attend these assemblies, with the result that elections were held and decisions were made behind the backs of the rank and file. Compliance with the agreements reached at these meetings was, in general, obligatory (Regalado, 1973; Martínez Allier, 1977: 1065).

Coffee harvests grew in the 1950s in comparison to the 1920s, 1930s, and 1940s, but the precarious situation of the poor coffee growers scarcely improved. Table 4.1 illustrates the large coffee sales of those years. The bearish speculations stimulated by this increase in production enriched wholesalers and functionaries of the government agencies who were charged with stabilizing coffee prices. The former obtained profits ranging from $10 to $20 per quintal, acquiring the greater part of the harvest from the state. The minimum prices of $44.50 per quintal were not sufficiently backed up. In 1955, for example, the decision to segregate 35% of the total of the harvest for export left the producers defenseless, since no minimum price was fixed, and the government financial agencies, as was customary, delayed in order to allow wholesalers to buy in advance. The Bank of Agricultural and Industrial Development of Cuba (BANFAIC), which had to finance and mortgage the harvest, did not fulfill its duties properly during those years (Cepero Bonilla, 1983: 215, 361, 365, 405).

Table 4.1   Growth of Coffee Sales, 1937–1956

	Pounds
1937–1938	71,164,479
1938–1939	50,333,501
1939–1940	53,405,283
1940–1941	59,935,170
1941–1942	59,256,348
1942–1943	78,798,871
1943–1944	75,773,847
1944–1945	57,140,539
1945–1946	49,822,852
1946–1947	76,908,291
1947–1948	71,877,665
1948–1949	71,877,665
1949–1950	86,444,489
1950–1951	71,374,683
1951–1952	62,516,896
1952–1953	58,721,173
1953–1954	77,589,000
1954–1955	83,770,345
1955–1956	118,169,573

Source: Boletín Informativo, 7, 2, February 1957: 89.

The links of dependency that prevailed in the lives of the coffee-growing sharecroppers in the mountainous regions of Oriente Province were extended in great measure to the small cane growers and tobacco growers. By 1899 Cuba had 15,881 cane growers, of whom 8,735 were tenants and 7,146 proprietors. It must be kept in mind, however, that, according to the authors of that census, "given the disturbed state of the industry—just after the war—the occupant of the farms was frequently unknown." According to the New York–based Foreign Policy Association, the number of cane growers in 1914 had grown to nearly 20,000. The same source gives 28,660 in 1934, an estimate based on the number of quotas assigned to cane growers in the census of 1931. By 1935 the numbers had grown to 40,000 (Foreign Policy Association, 1935). Nevertheless, in the 1915 report *Portafolio de la industria azucarera*, based on information provided by the plantation owners to the Secretariat of Agriculture, Industry, and Commerce, the number of *colonos* in 1914 totaled 37,353, of which 33,100 were Cuban and 4,253 foreigners, predominantly campesinos from the Canary Islands (Secretariat of Agriculture, 1915).

According to these data, the number of *colonos* seems not to have decreased. By 1935 their number was estimated to have grown to 40,000. The reduction in 1931 probably meant simply that in that year only the *colonos* who had received quotas were registered. In any event, the figure of 40,000 cane growers in 1935 testifies to an increase over the number offered by the Foreign Policy Association in 1914 (20,000) and that of the Secretariat of Agriculture (37,353), which refutes the supposed proletarianization of the *colonos* in the first thirty years of the republic.

For the landowners and the sugar companies, the *colono* system represented the safest way to keep a considerable nucleus of workers tied to the land by means of the legal fiction represented by the milling contract and by the proprietorship or lease of the small cane farm. At the same time, the cost of producing cane by the system of administration was higher than by the system of *colonos*. The Tariff Commission of the United States determined a cost of $2.19 per ton for administration-produced cane and $1.70 for that produced by *colonos*. The data of the Foreign Policy Association are significant in this respect. In 1904, sugar mills ground 30.3% of administration cane; in 1930 20%, and in 1933 15.5%. The controlled *colonos* produced 35.2% of the cane ground by the mills in 1904, 63.5% in 1930, and 64% in 1933. Independent *colonos*, owners of their land, who had produced 36.5% of the cane ground in 1904, dropped to 16.3% in 1930 and to 10.3% in 1933. The tendency in the first decades of the republic was toward an increase in the number of *colonos* controlled by the sugar mill and a reduction in the cane produced by administration and independent growers. Thus, the number of *colonos* tied to the sugar mill grew at the expense of the independent *colonos* and the sugar-mill-owned plantations of administration cane cut by paid cane cutters. From all this data, one cannot reach the conclusion that the *colonos* were proletarianized in the first decades of the twentieth century but rather that more and more of them were submitted to extraordinarily harsh links of dependency by the sugar mills. The sugar mills found it convenient to keep them as enslaved *colonos* rather than ruin them in order to convert them to proletarians.

The effect on the *colono* system, as we have seen, was not one of proletarianization but of conversion of the independent cane grower into one controlled by the sugar mill. As the *colonos* became tied to the land, raising families and becoming indebted to the mills, they found themselves tightly bound to the landowners or the sugar companies. The controlled *colonos* gradually became the dominant figures of cane plantations at the same time that the independent *colonos,* owners of their land, tended to disappear.

As to the standard of living of the small *colono,* the rural proletariat had little to envy. In the first place, we should recall the calculations of the Foreign Policy Association: Drawing on the cane census of 1931, it estimated the average amount of cane cut by each cane grower at 14.2 hectares. If we take into account that these averages also include the total amount of land owned by the large and medium-sized cane growers, we get a better idea of the poverty of the small cane grower, who represented the overwhelming majority in the *colono* system.

The cane growers' absolute dependency in relation to a typical sugar company, the Cuban Sugar Cane Company, is described by the Foreign Policy Association: In September 1925 the company reported that growers owed $12.2 million. By September 1933 the company had on its books cane growers' debts of $13.4 million.

The sugar coordination law of May 3, 1937, was intended to help the small *colonos* survive. To this effect, it created a protection fund based on contributions of 6% of their quotas to be made by *colonos* who produced more than 500,000 *arrobas,* 12% by sugar mill lands managed by administration, and 2.5% by the sugar mills. The contributions stipulated by the law were to permit the small *colonos* to grind up to 30,000 *arrobas* of cane, a right they could not cede or encumber. Small *colonos* were also obliged to devote a limited area to minor cultivation to tide them over during the "dead season." The *colonos'* participation in the production of sugar ranged between 46% and 48%, depending upon the yields of the sugar mill. Small *colonos* had to devote a minimum of 5% of their cane to the payment of land rent to the sugar mill or the landowner.

The legislation of 1937 reversed the decline in the numbers of cane growers who worked their own land or leased or sharecropped land outside the mill owners' jurisdiction in order to sell their cane freely to any sugar mill. The proportion of cane ground by independent *colonos* had diminished threefold between 1904 and 1933, whereas the controlled *colonos* had increased their production twofold in the same period. In contrast, between 1938 and 1945 the number of small *colonos* increased in a proportion similar to that of the controlled *colonos*. In these same years, cane plantations managed by administrators diminished progressively. Data do not show the ratio between independent *colonos* and controlled *colonos* beginning in 1946, since the two categories appear as a single item. We should keep in mind, however, that the number of free *colonos* without a quota increased as a consequence of the sustained growth in production brought about by World War II. These were *colonos* who were not established prior to promulgation of the sugar coordination law and who did not have the right to sell up to 30,000 *arrobas* to a sugar mill. Since participation of the small *colono* in the harvest was not guaranteed by a quota, the conditions of poverty and helplessness that had characterized the first decades of republican life reappeared. Thus, the number of free and independent *colonos* with and without quotas must have increased since 1946 in relation to the controlled *colonos*. The sugar crop restriction of the 1950s prevented thousands of small independent *colonos* without quotas from selling the cane they grew on their leased or sharecropped land. In this way, they found themselves virtually driven from the land and obliged to join the reserve labor force as proletarians.

The growth in the number of small independent *colonos* without a quota prior to the sugar crop restriction of 1953 is apparent in the production statistics of the *colono* system for the years 1939–1951. The distribution of cane production in those years reveals considerable differences. The number of small *colonos* who harvested fewer than 30,000 *arrobas* grew from 18,639 in 1939 (62% of the total) to 27,134 in 1951 (68%).

Ramiro Guerra's data concerning the situation of small planters in 1939 allow us to evaluate the standard of living of this sector. Of the 30,020 planters in existence in 1939, 15,865 (52.8%) received earnings ranging from 243.75 to 478.50 pesos annually (Guerra, 1940). This averaged approximately 20 to 40 pesos per month, equivalent to the wages of a field hand during the harvest. Planters with quotas of between 30,000 and 50,000 *arrobas* numbered 3,249, or

10.8%, calculated on the basis of their earnings of between 731.25 and 1,218.75 pesos. This means that 72.9% of the country's cane planters earned less than $100 per month (Guerra, 1940: 121–122). Planters with a quota under 50,000 *arrobas* must therefore be considered poor farmers. This group was hard hit by the policy of crop restriction of the Batista government. Overall earnings of cane planters increased slightly from 1947 to 1952 and then fell again. Only in 1957 did signs of recovery appear. Earnings of the sector for 1947–1951 reached $751 million then dropped to $658 million for 1952–1957. Its earnings thus decreased by $93.5 million during the Batista dictatorship (Martínez Sáenz, 1959: 214–215).

A considerable reduction in the number of tobacco plantations is shown for the intervening years by the statistics of the 1899 census and the census of tobacco farms of 1929. In effect, 15,831 tobacco plantations were registered in 1899; their number reached only 7,690 in 1929. The area devoted to tobacco growing covered 523 *caballerías* in 1899 and 4,578 in 1929. The decrease in the number of tobacco plantations together with the increase in the number of *caballerías* devoted to this crop by 1929 show a 50 percent reduction in the number of tobacco growers at the same time that the area planted expanded eightfold.

It is possible, however, that the 1899 census recorded as tobacco growers in possession of land (owned or rented) campesinos who in reality had been ruined in the wars of independence and were in fact unable to resume agricultural activities. I believe the census included as tobacco growers all those who in one way or another, as proprietors or sharecroppers, had at one time a piece of land devoted to growing this crop. Statistics on the number of tobacco plantations given in the 1899 civil report of the U.S. military government of the island are more precise than the 1899 census—which does not mean that they are more reliable. According to this report, the country had 9,259 tobacco plantations, of which 3,859 had been destroyed, 1,583 had been rehabilitated, 2,081 were in production, and 2,006 awaited reconstruction.

During the first decades of the republic, scarcely 200 bales of 120 pounds per *caballería* were produced by the majority of tobacco plantations, and these were sold at prices that fluctuated between 37 and 65 pesos—which was necessary to cover the costs of production in Pinar del Río (Magoon, 1907: 437; Lindsay, 1919: 194 and 195; Porter, 1899: 310 and 311). Tobacco growers were able to survive only by employing the labor of their families. The estimated production costs for a tobacco grower who was a proprietor or the lessee of 1 *caballería* who employed from two to four workers were invariably much higher than sales prices. These figures as a whole are evidence of a precarious economy, subject to the tyranny of usurious tobacco merchants and to the slightest imbalance in world market prices. Tobacco growers lived a feudal existence on the land under an inflexible system that barely permitted them to survive.

From 1914 to 1917, the restriction on tobacco purchases by Britain, the United States, and other countries seriously affected Cuba's tobacco zones. Leading newspapers of the time described widespread hunger in those regions. Yet the tobacco growers, in contrast to the sugar workers, did not participate in the social agitation and strikes that convulsed the country from 1914 to 1920. The extreme cultural backwardness of the province of Pinar del Río impeded this type of feudalized campesino, tobacco growers as well as tobacco sorters, from finding organized forms of protest. Spanish anarchists who had carried out intense activity among the sugar proletariat were unable to enlist the tobacco workers for combative action.

Tobacco farms worked by *partidarios* (sharecroppers) had real incomes of some 450 pesos per year (37 pesos monthly) in 1933 and 1934 (Foreign Policy Association, 1935). From this, they had to deduct the payment of rents and usurious loans. The incomes of these farmers were close to those of agricultural field hands.

According to the labor press of the era, sharecropping reached 33% on the lands devoted to tobacco cultivation. In Pinar del Río the majority of tobacco growers were sharecroppers and lessees of large farms. Few growers were owners of land, and some of these acquired it by leasing, that is, by paying as a minimum 10% per year of the value of the land. Sharecropping contracts stipulated that campesinos could not set a price for tobacco. Around 1945 a quintal (100 lbs.) of tobacco of inferior quality from Semi-Vueltas brought a price of 25.75 pesos, that from Santa Clara 26.09 pesos, and that from Oriente 26.08 pesos, leaving reduced margins for subsistence (*Memoria del Censo Agrícola Nacional, 1946*).

Figures presented in the census of 1931 differ slightly from the results of the land registry of 1929 and are much more congruent with those of the agricultural census of 1946, the best conceived and executed in the republican era. Of the 22,750 farms that reported tobacco as their chief source of income, 48.2% had gross earnings of less than 80 pesos per month. Annual incomes of 1,000 to 2,000 pesos were reported by 38.5%, and 13.3% received incomes of 3,000 pesos or more. That is, the gross earnings of approximately 49% of the country's tobacco planters amounted to 80 pesos per month, from which they were obliged to deduct the payment of rent and loans that absorbed 50% to 60% of their gross earnings.

Average annual production of tobacco from 1952 to 1956 increased considerably in relation to the preceding five-year periods. This growth enabled the province of Pinar del Río to escape the effects of the restriction, and the total volume of salaries of tobacco sorters was increased. Table 4.2 shows clearly the increases that took place. During these last years, the purchase of harvests by tobacco industrialists led to speculation, with the complicity of governmental financing agencies, through which the most needy tobacco growers were paid 20 pesos per quintal, although the minimum official price was 25 pesos. Thus, the fortunes of the majority of tobacco planters must have improved little despite the increase in production (Cepero Bonilla, 1983: 290).

The 1953–1954 restriction on tobacco growing seriously hurt the economic situation of tobacco planters. A decree of the Ministry of Agriculture ordered a reduction of 30% in the total national quota of 900,000 quintals the ministry had set in its decree of July 27, 1954. In the words of one campesino leader of the time, "That crisis, officially and publicly recognized, was once again shifted onto the long-suffering and exploited tobacco growers by the government of landowners and reactionaries, while the magnates continued to enjoy substantial profits" (Regalado, 1973: 138).

From 1955 on, the strong demand for tobacco on the world market spared tobacco planters the erratic fluctuations in demand experienced by cane planters and coffee growers. Lowry Nelson declared that the *partidario* system in Cuba was harsher than the sharecropping system in the Cotton Belt states of the U.S. South, since "the Cuban *partidario* has to meet all the expenses of making the crop in addition to providing his own farm implements and paying a full interest rate

Table 4.2   Average Annual Tobacco Production, 1931–1956

	Average in Quintals
1931–1940	495,672
1941–1945	530,456
1946–1950	730,464
1952–1956	923,950

Source: Cepero Bonilla, 1983.

of 8 percent per annum. He is also supposed to do the hand labor" (Nelson, 1950: 130–133).

According to the Truslow Report, the tobacco *partidarios* paid as much in interest rates as the coffee sharecroppers. Thus in Remedios, 90% of all the tobacco planters paid an interest rate of 20%. As collateral, many gave their creditors title to their land, cattle, and buildings. In some regions in Pinar del Río, 8% per annum was charged on credit to sharecroppers (Truslow, 1951: 593–594).

At Consolación del Norte in Pinar del Río, *partidarios* paid from $600 to $800 per *caballería* per annum. On a large latifundio owned by an American, *partidarios* had to work 140 days a year on his best lands in order to pay their rent (de la Osa, 1960: 249). Their position of absolute dependence on the large landowners is corroborated by the testimony of Blas Roca: "In tobacco the sharecroppers had the character of real serfs. The lord of the land was also the owner of the local store, the provider of water, the supplier of fertilizer and seeds, for all of which he collected an extraordinary overcharge. And for years and years, these same lords of the land were the political bosses of the campesinos, who told them how and for whom they should vote when elections came around" (Roca, 1960: 38–39).

As we have seen, the situation of the small cane planters, tobacco growers, and coffee growers approached that of the rural proletariat and at times was even worse. In these conditions the poor farmers were obliged to sell their labor during one or another season. The distinctions between poor farmers and the rural proletariat in Cuban neocolonial society are difficult to establish.

Sharecroppers and *colonos* constituted the backbone of the Cuban peasantry. Although they produced the principal commercial crops, the severe precapitalist bonds to which they were subjected determined their dependent status. The rents and interests they were obliged to pay to landlords, sugar mill owners, and commercial intermediaries provided them no escape and no possibility of rising above the condition of peasants. This situation of subordination did not permit them to play a vanguard role in rural affairs, but it did not prevent them from taking part in social struggles. Thus, in the first two decades of the twentieth century, the sharecroppers and *colonos* were subordinated to the political caciques of the agrarian bourgeoisie, for whom they were invariably forced to vote in electoral processes (Ibarra, 1992; James, 1976). Only as the rural links of dependency became more severe and poverty was intensified in the 1920s and 1930s did the coffee sharecroppers and small *colonos* take part in the struggles of the rural proletariat. With the increasing deterioration of caciquism in the 1930s, considerable numbers of sharecroppers and *colonos* spontaneously joined the Auténtico and Ortodoxo populist parties, becoming their primary political base in the rural areas, although relations of caciquism were maintained in tobacco and other zones, where the peasants continued to vote for regional bosses. Beginning in 1933, the electoral machinery that bought peasant votes became the dominant conservative force in the countryside, replacing the traditional relations of caciquism.

The attitudes of these peasants tended to become identified with those of the rural proletariat. In reality, the small *colonos*, sharecroppers, and rural workers made up a single social fabric. They had approximately the same incomes and, in the majority of cases, came from the same families and coexisted in the same rural milieu. Thus these rural masses, undifferentiated in living standard and cultural condition, tended to take part in similar ways in the social protests of the 1930s. Although lacking a labor union such as that of the rural sugar workers, the small *colonos* and sharecroppers responded in critical situations to their mobilizations. The small coffee sharecroppers, somewhat more conservative than the small *colonos,* also joined the social struggles initiated by the rebel army in the 1950s. The squatters in the mountains of Oriente Province had taken refuge in the Sierra Maestra after having been driven off their land, settling on properties without the landowners' authorization. A large part of them sold their labor in the sugar and coffee harvests and frequently took part in strikes of the rural proletariat. These peasants were rural rebels who did not hesitate to enlist in the rebel army in the 1950s (Mayo, 1979). In contrast, tobacco squatters, because of their cultural background and traditions of dependency as well as their peculiarly conservative social psychology, remained aloof from the rural protest movements of the 1930s and 1950s.

5

The Industrial Proletariat
and the Urban Working Class

In order to study the urban proletariat, we must separate it from artisan industry, just as we distinguish the rural proletariat from the farmer. We must also disregard any type of quantitative evaluation of income in defining the different social categories. Marxist definitions of classes and social strata have a qualitative rather than quantitative character, based on the position classes and strata occupy in the totality of relations of production and type of rent. Nevertheless, there is no consensus among Marxist social scientists as to the application of these categories in history. They frequently disagree on the extension of these concepts and their applicability to the different social groupings found in the societies they study. In the view of the outstanding Spanish historian Tuñón de Lara, both craftspeople and tenant farmers belong to the working class because they receive their income from work. The social class, however, as he points out, is defined as well by the position that it holds in the social organization of labor. It would thus be necessary to depart from this essential criterion to distinguish the urban proletariat from artisans. There is no doubt that a considerable part of the working class originally came from artisan industry and that the son of the artisan is, as a general rule, already a worker (Tuñón de Lara, 1984: 63).

We need to distinguish between two types of artisan: the artisan merchant and the artisan worker. Artisan merchants believe that the value of their merchandise is the result not only of their labor but also of their negotiating skills as merchants, by means of which they obtain higher prices for their merchandise. In this way artisan merchants confuse value and price. Given the conditions in which they realize their work, individually and isolated from others, without employers who appropriate part of the value of their labor, artisan merchants cannot be considered workers. From the moment that they buy in order to sell, nothing differentiates them from capitalists. Artisan workers, in contrast, come closest to salaried workers. The French historian Labrousse has even defined their work as a "disguised form of salaried work" (Labrousse, 1967: 176–181). Obviously, it is necessary to establish the differences between such artisans who primarily sell their personal and manual work, incorporated into raw material supplied by merchants or manufacturers, and salaried industrial workers. Artisans work at home and, in principle, independently, although under certain control of their employers, who can always reject the products of their work or the price of its manufacture. But so long as artisans do not work in factories, have not joined the ranks of the working class, and have not identified themselves with the exploitation suffered by workers, they have not lost their relative independence in production. The main fact that differentiates them from salaried workers is that they do not communicate with, are not identified with, and do not share the situation of those who are exploited in a factory by an employer. The artisan worker is one of the diverse types of workers "for their own account" that appear in Cuban censuses, differentiated from the census category of "employee," that is, from the salaried employee of an employer. Artisans, then, offer difficulties only in relation to their conceptual classification, since in Cuban censuses they appear unequivocally differentiated from salaried employees.

The other question to be clarified is related to the category of salaried employee: Are all salaried employees workers? There were, first of all, office employees. Many of them were in positions of trust and provided the capitalist enterprises that employed them with all the data required for production and the productivity of workers—in other words, everything that helps the enterprise to control the work of the industrial proletariat. At the same time, they frequently do not identify their interests with those of other industrial workers or participate in their organized struggles.

Commercial, service, and government employees as well have no clearly defined place in the working class. In societies in which industrial capitalism has not been definitively established, the relations of dependency of these employees on the bourgeois employer or government authorities would seem to determine their class placement. The main function of trade, or commercial, employees is to represent or personify the employers in relations with the consuming public, to endorse the value of the articles sold by the commercial establishments that employ them. Their work does not consist in creating new value but in attributing this to the articles they offer in representation of their employers with the aim of increasing the employers' profits.

As the social scientist Victor Semionov has pointed out, this type of salaried employee does not create added value (Semionov, 1965: 95).

Another difference is that these employees in general do not perform physical labor, though this is not an essential distinction. Nowadays workers in automated factories do not lose their proletarian character because they do not do physical labor. The primary criterion is that workers are linked in a direct way to the process of producing added value.

In his study of the process of production of added value, Marx defined the situation of employees when he pointed out that "only two points of departure exist: the capitalist and the worker. The third persons of all the categories must receive the money of these two classes in exchange for some service or, if they receive money without providing any service, then they are coproprietors of the added value in the form of rent, interest, etc." (Marx, 1946, vol. 2: 298).

From this point of view, it is evident that the mass of employees does not pay itself, unlike the workers, who in transforming the products they manufacture create new value. The employees instead receive a salary from the proprietors of the profit or exchange their work for part of the wages of the workers. Marx highlighted this idea with his observation, "From an economic point of view, only the salaried worker who produces and gives value to 'capital' can call himself a 'proletarian,' and he is thrown into the street as soon as he is no longer of use to Monsieur Capital, which is the name that M. Pecqueur gives to this personage" (Marx, 1946, vol. 1: 518, n.).

In the beginnings of European capitalism and even in the early twentieth century, the salaries of employees were approximately twice as high as the wages of skilled industrial workers. At present they tend to be the same or lower. The increase in working-class wages is a result of the historic struggles of workers to raise their standard of living, and the rhythm of this tendency has been accelerated by the scientific-technological revolution as engineers, technicians, and skilled workers have become more directly linked to the process of producing added value. The majority of employees, meanwhile, have not participated in the historic struggles of the proletariat, are not directly implicated in the productive process, and are less well remunerated than industrial workers. The 1943 census gives evidence of this process in Cuban society of the 1940s.

With respect to employees, employers appropriate a part of the value of their labor just as they do in the case of industrial workers, but the former have some administrative power in representing the enterprise for which they work that the latter lack, leaving these employees obliged simply to execute the tasks assigned to them. The position of employees in the organization of work becomes even more clear when we understand their limited participation in the struggles of the working class. According to the German historian Jürgen Kuczynski, employees belong to the urban petty bourgeoisie (Kuczynski et al., 1973). During the first sixty years of the Cuban republic, the majority of employees came from these middle sectors. In general, they were elements who found themselves obliged to sell their labor because of reduced financial circumstances of their families. Despite this origin, commercial employees in Cuba have had greater participation in the historic struggles of the working class to raise their standard of living than have employees in advanced capitalist countries. Some historians and Marxist social scientists consider them an underdeveloped sector of the working class. I believe, on the contrary, that they do not constitute a part of the proletariat.

To classify government employees as members of the working class is still more difficult. As a rule, in Cuba they belonged to the traditional clientele of political groups. They did not participate in struggles to raise living standards nor did they belong to labor unions. Nevertheless, within these government employees, teachers were clearly differentiated, since they were organized in associations and on occasion presented their demands and complaints to the higher educational authorities. In general, they had a very clear perception of the problems that affected the nation as a whole. The nucleus of the urban working class, therefore, was the industrial proletariat, around which the transport, building, mining, and electric power proletariat was grouped.

One peculiarity of the situation of commercial, service, and government employees is that in general they were victims of the country's economic crises in a more acute way than the urban proletariat, because their salaries were fixed and since they were not organized in unions or were not sufficiently combative, they did not have adequate channels to protest against labor conditions. It was for this reason that during critical points in the 1930s and 1950s these sectors formed groups independent of the working class within the democratic-revolutionary organizations that struggled against the prevailing situation. Thus, in urban zones artisans, teachers, government employees, and employees of private enterprises together with small merchants and manufacturers, professionals, and intellectuals constituted the "nonproletarian masses" Lenin described as capable of organizing themselves independently of the proletariat, in opposition to the domination of the landowning bourgeoisie.

The professional and intellectual sectors are generally considered an inherent part of the petty bourgeoisie. It is often affirmed that they belong in part to the bourgeoisie by virtue of their relations, opinions, and so on and in part to the sector of salaried employees because capitalism subordinates them and transforms them into salaried dependents, depriving them of their autonomous position.

Antonio Gramsci's definitions are based on the *function* of the intellectual in the social organization of work. According to this outstanding Italian Marxist theoretician, it is necessary to know who intellectuals serve and what conception of the world they embrace. Thus, the bourgeoisie will have its organic intellectual sphere, the proletariat another, and the middle class another (Gramsci, 1975: 107, 108). This definition seems the most convincing, but for the purposes of my census-based, quantitative study of the social structure, it is inapplicable, since it is impossible to know how the persons who responded to the census actually thought. Still, distinct socioprofessional categories can be defined, based on the data provided by the census. In this sense, managers and administrators are intellectuals who serve and represent the interest of the bourgeoisie, although certain engineers and skilled technicians who sell their labor can be classified as workers. Obviously, on the basis of the designations of the censuses, the whole of the intellectual sector cannot be sorted into the different classes and strata that make up the social structure.

Determination of the dimensions of the urban proletariat in relation to the petty bourgeois, artisan, and semiproletarian whole of the population should give us an idea of the specific importance and the real influence of that sector in those first years of republican life. A quantitatively preponderant or qualitatively decisive industrial proletariat did not arise ipso facto with the abolition of the slave system on plantations and the constitution of the capitalist plantation system in the 1880s. The population was made up principally of the nonproletarian mass, according to the Leninist definition of this type of formation, as I have pointed out earlier. The numerical, organizational, and ideological weakness of the proletariat in the first twenty years of the republic prevented it from constituting the fundamental social base of the nation.

If we look at the size of the nonsugar, principally urban industries based on the number of their workers, we see a considerable increase in the number of factories employing fewer than ten workers between 1925 and 1954, according to broad statistical reports that did not include all factories. Thus, in a 1923 sample, factories with fewer than ten workers made up only 24.7% of the total, whereas in 1954 a similar but more extensive sample showed that these made up 63.2% of the total. A slighter increase was registered in factories with more than 100 workers, from 1.7% in 1925 to 5.8% in 1954. Nevertheless, in the same period a decrease, from 73.5% in 1925 to 30.9% in 1954, was registered in medium-sized factories employing between ten and 100 workers. These statistics suggest a notable rise in the number of workers laboring in hole-in-the-wall shops and in craft industries belonging to small owners and self-employed persons who used the help of family members or ill-paid workers, in violation of labor legislation. According to other sources, this increase took place in urban zones in the interior of the country. The growth in the number of factories with more than 100 workers, meanwhile, suggests the presence of large U.S. investments and a modern industrial proletariat, with high salaries, job security, and protective labor laws. The reduction in the number of medium-sized factories evidenced the difficulties of surviving the competition of U.S. production and the weakening and diminution of the worker sector that could have been most combative. In general, the increase in craft enterprises and the reduction in medium-sized industries revealed a debilitation of the capacity for struggle of the working class.

More than bourgeois industrial development, this would seem to have been a manufacturing development of small artisan producers. In every sense, this sector had a preindustrial, manufacturing character dominated by an artisan consciousness. The predominant feature of this sector was its nonintegration and dispersion resulting from its inability to organize itself into unions and demand its rights. The majority of the workers were underemployed part of the year and protested only when their standard of living fell below what was physically tolerable. Their ideological militancy between 1930 and 1950 was for the most part in the ranks of the democratic-revolutionary movements, especially in the rural zones of the country.

Workers of the tobacco industry had a long tradition of struggle dating from the nineteenth century that included the contribution of immigrant workers to the country's fight for independence. As a result of the shutdown of many cigar factories belonging to the tobacco trust based in Cuba and their transfer to the United States with a view to manufacturing the cigars there with Cuban leaf tobacco, the number of cigar workers declined considerably. Whereas some 29,500 cigar workers were employed in Cuba between 1901 and 1907, this number had declined to some 12,000 by 1929. The census of 1899 and that of 1907 counted 27,169 and 27,503. According to Álvarez de Acevedo, there were 11,586 cigar workers in 1927. The National Commission of Statistics and Economic Reform reported 8,450 workers in the cigar industry in the first semester of 1926.

The attempt to determine the size of the urban working class within the economically active population according to the data provided by the different censuses carried out between 1907 and 1953 presents serious difficulties. I concluded that the only way to approach the real growth of the urban working class was to identify it with the concept of the general group of professions, classified as "manufactures and mechanical industries" in the censuses of 1907, 1919, 1931, and 1953. This determination is based on the following characteristics of the information offered by these censuses: (1) The censuses of 1907 and 1919 do not permit an evaluation of the number of workers in the transport sector, since these are merged with workers in commerce. Construction and electric power workers are classified with workers in mechanical industries and manufactures. (2) The 1931 census breaks down manufacturing, construction, and electric power workers so that they can be classified in a group by themselves. (3) The census of 1953 includes all workers of the sugar industry among artisans and factory operators, but these are broken down, which makes it possible to group industrial workers with those in construction and electric power.

Using this information, I was able to calculate the number of workers in industry, construction, and electric power in 1907, 1919, 1931, and 1953. These sectors of the urban working class made up 6.15% of the economically active population in 1907, 6.57% in 1919, 8.94% in 1931, and 19.47% in 1953. Since the censuses classify industrial, electric power, and construction workers together with every kind of artisan, self-employed worker, and employer among the persons occupied in the diverse economic activities mentioned above, these calculations are not based on the actual specific importance of the working class in the society as a whole.

The results of the censuses of 1943 and 1953 do not allow the possibility of making a term-by-term comparison to measure the quantitative changes that took place in the working class, the bourgeoisie (small and large) that employed workers, and the intermediate strata of artisans, sharecroppers, tenants, *partidarios*, merchants, and producers "who work for their own account" and do not employ workers. A large part of the information these censuses offer is so heterogeneous as to make them radically incompatible with one another. A host of factors mitigates against the possibility of reaching definitive conclusions about the growth of these classes and groups and their relative magnitude in the whole society: For one, the census of 1943 was taken in the dead season, whereas that of 1953 was carried out during the cane harvest, preventing any comparison between the rural proletariat of those years. The census of 1943 consequently must have undercalculated the agricultural proletariat and that of 1953 overcalculated it. The same can be said with respect to the proprietors, sharecroppers, tenants, and others who appear classified as "self-employed workers" in agriculture. Inversely, the number of these must have been larger in 1943 and smaller in 1953.

To this practically insurmountable difficulty we can add others. The census of 1943 did not classify some 156,158 persons of the economically active population in agriculture, fishing, and forestry as belonging to the categories of "owner," "self-employed," or "employee"—that is, 26% of the total economically active labor force was not classified because the census takers obtained insufficient information with respect to the labor status of these individuals. In contrast, the census of 1953 sorted all the economically active population into the categories of "employee" (of both private enterprises and the government), "self-employed," or "working for a relative." This classification makes it impossible to differentiate between proprietors who employ salaried workers and those who do not. The censuses also prevent a quantitative differentiation between the petty and the upper bourgeoisie.

With respect to the classification of workers employed in industries and manufacturing, it must be supposed that both censuses include the industrial workers of sugar mills in this category. Inasmuch as the first census was taken during the dead season and the second during the harvest season, the first did not classify thousands of workers from the industrial sector of sugar production as workers in manufacturing and mechanical industries. It is thus impossible to compare the numbers of workers in manufacturing and mechanical industries appearing in the two censuses, since logically the number increased extraordinarily in the second of these counts.

The only category of workers unaffected by the fact that 20% of the workers in all categories were not classified by the census of 1943 was that of employees and workers of the government. The situation in this case is absolutely clear in that among them there were no "employers," "self-employed persons," or workers who could be classified as such.

In the 1943 census, the category "nonclassified industries and commercial establishments" included 314,297 persons but did not specify how many worked in industry and how many in commercial establishments, although according to the census authors the majority of this group was made up of commercial employees. This fact hinders any comparison between the industrial worker sectors in 1943 and 1953.

If we make a global comparison of the qualitative evolution of the industrial proletariat together with that of artisans, with which it is united in a single category, we may be able to obtain a general though vague idea of its real evolution between 1907 and 1953. Industrial workers constituted a very small sector in 1953 with respect to the rest of the classes making up the population. In the forty-six years from 1907 to 1953, the number of workers and artisans employed in manufacturing and mechanical industries grew only from 6% to 19.47% of the whole economically active population.

Given the small percentage of workers whose labor status was listed as "unknown" in the 1943 census, the category of workers in mining, construction, transport, and communications offers the possibility of studying their evolution quantitatively. The number of construction workers in 1943 oscillated between a minimum of 10,342 and a maximum of 16,942. In 1953, this number reached some 51,525, an increase of between 34,583 and 41,183, that is, of between 67.1% and 79.9%. In mining the number ranged from 3,669 to 4,374 in 1943, and in 1953 had reached 8,447, growing from 4,103 to 4,808, or from 48.4% to 56.7%. In transport and communications, the number was between 24,721 and 29,097 in 1943 and grew to 76,786 in 1953, an increase of 47,689 to 52,065, or from 62.1% to 67.8%.

Beginning in 1925, the struggles of the working class, led in large measure by the Communists, led to higher salaries. This rise in income of the proletariat is reflected in the tables per salary group where the greater proportion of industrial, construction, and transport workers and service and commercial employees was concentrated. In the groups with monthly salaries of 30 to 59 pesos and 60 to 99 pesos, the proportion of the proletariat tended to equal or surpass that of the employees.

Thus, the tendency of salaries of the proletariat to exceed those of employees, as a result of working-class struggles, was confirmed. Table 5.1, based on the tables of the 1943 census, allows us to compare the salaries of the proletariat with those of employees.

Table 5.1   Salaries of the Working Class, 1943

Salary (in pesos)	Working Class (industry, construction, transport)	
	Number	%
Less than 30	47,457	25.6
30–59	84,635	45.7
60–99	38,486	20.8
100–199	11,401	6.2
200–299	1,592	.8
300 or more	1,626	.8

Source: Census of 1943.

Although it is true that the industrial proletariat represented a higher proportion (27%) than commercial employees (20.5%) among the groups that earned less than 30 pesos, this was primarily because of the dispersion of a considerable part of the workers in a variety of small manufacturing and hole-in-the-wall shops, where all labor laws were violated and the lowest salaries were paid. The workers who found employment in these small shops were in general unskilled workers who were underemployed a large part of the year and found themselves obliged to accept this type of salary. Despite the relatively high proportion of industrial workers (27%) in the group of those who received less than 30 pesos, it was much lower than that of service employees (49.3%), who were the worst paid in this group.

In the group that earned 30 to 59 pesos the percentage of workers in industry, transport, and construction (48.5%) was higher than that of service employees (31.46%) and close to that of commercial employees (51.8%). In the group with salaries of 60 to 99 pesos the proportion of industrial workers (22.01%) surpassed that of commercial employees (17.8%) and that of service employees (9.4%). These salaries were usually paid in large industries that required skilled workers and where labor struggles had successfully imposed their demands. In the group that received 100 to 199 pesos, which was the remuneration generally paid to employees in confidential posts, that is, the small group of first-class employees, the proportion of industrial workers (6.5%) was less than that of commercial employees (7.1%) and only slightly higher than that of service employees (6.4%). The majority of workers in this salary group were considered members of the labor aristocracy. Those with salaries above 200 pesos were the privileged: confidential employees, managers, administrators, heads of work crews, and so on.

The salary increases of 1944 corroborated the tendency toward a greater representation of the industrial proletariat than of employees in the 60–99-peso salary group. In labor sectors and centers such as ports, electricity, railroads, telephones, and textiles, workers obtained salaries higher than those of other sectors of the working class and, of course, higher than those of commercial and service employees in the 60–99-peso salary group (*Cuba Económica y Financiera*, 1944, January 15–16; February 19–20; May 19; August 19). In the 1940s and 1950s, the struggles of industrial workers to raise their standard of living had boosted their salaries to the highest levels in Latin America.

Martínez Sáenz and J. Domínguez argue that the economic situation in Cuba in 1953–1957 was not so difficult for the working population (Martínez Sáenz, 1959: 163–165; Domínguez, 1978: 72–75).

But the salary tables, by province, I have compiled reveal the mislead-
ing character of the global per capita salary and earning indices these
authors used to demonstrate their hypothesis. The indices of the total
amount of salary paid for industrial and commercial activities per
province show that after having reached very low salary levels for
urban zones during the 1930s, salaries gradually rose until World War
II, remained stable during the conflict in Korea, and again declined
as a result of the economic recession of 1953. The most notable
aspect of this curve is the slow rise in the global amount of salaries
paid in the provinces of Matanzas, Las Villas, Camagüey, and Oriente
throughout this period and its sudden drop in the brief period
between 1953 and 1957.

The nonagricultural, commercial, and industrial salary series by
province from 1937 to 1953, reproduced in the *Memorias del Banco
Nacional*, gives a clear picture of the depth of the crisis that depressed
the country from 1953 to 1956 and the ineffectiveness of the policy of
compensatory spending to offset the effects of the recession outside
the province of Havana. In fact, the slight increase in the volume of
salary paid in Pinar del Río Province from 1953 to 1957 was a consequence of the growth in demand for tobacco on the world market in
those years. Thus, in 1957, 62.6% of the bank loans were destined for
public services in the province of Havana, such as the tunnel under
Havana Bay and the Vía Blanca highway; 28.9% to industry, with more
than 90% for the capital and its surroundings; and 6.1% to agriculture, especially in the western provinces. Credits were also extended
to the oil refineries of Santiago de Cuba, the mines of Charco
Redondo, and the rice plantations of Aguilera and other capitalist
leaseholders of Camagüey, but such loans could not compensate for
the drop in salary volume, the result of the sharp economic contradiction existing in the rural zones of the country.

The fundamental monographs of Cuban revolutionary historiography for this period, written by Carlos Rafael Rodríguez and
Francisco López Segrera, touch on the situation in the hinterland but
accentuate the nonreproductive character of the investments made
by the Bank of Economic and Social Development (BANDES). Basing
his assessment on the situation in the capital, López Segrera (*Cuba,*
1979: 325) mistakenly generalizes for the whole island when he states
that "workers and employees outside of the sugar industry were not
affected by the sudden economic contraction."

The most conclusive evidence of the drop in the global amount
of commercial and industrial salaries can be found in the central and
eastern regions of the country. In Oriente Province, real nonagricultural, commercial, and industrial salaries, which had risen by 1.5 from

1941–1944 to 1949–1952, declined 1.3 times from this last four-year period to 1953–1956. In Camagüey, where the volume of salaries had grown by a factor of 1.9 from 1941–1944 to 1949–1952, it diminished 1.22 times from that date to 1953–1956. In Las Villas Province, the salary volume of 1941–1944 rose 1.5 times compared to that of 1949–1952, and in the following four-year period of 1953–1956 it dropped by a factor of 1.1. Matanzas Province increased its salary volume by 1.7 from 1941–1944 to 1949–1952, then remained more or less stagnant with a growth of a factor of only 1.1 times in 1953–1956. In contrast to these provinces, Havana Province raised its real salaries 1.5 times from 1941–1944 to 1949–1952 and 1.2 times in 1953–1956.

Finally, in Pinar del Río Province, the real salary grew 1.3 times in the first periods and 1.5 times in 1953–1956. In absolute numbers, this situation was expressed as follows for 1953–1956: In contrast to the four-year period 1949–1952, in 1953–1956 real nonagricultural, commercial, and industrial salaries declined by $36.2 million in the provinces of Las Villas, Camagüey, and Oriente. In the last province, not even large U.S. investments in nickel and in the Santiago oil refinery (Texaco) and Cuban investments in flour mills and cement factories in Santiago de Cuba were able to counteract the economic recession. The foreign investments responded to other stimuli than those of Cubans.

The reduction in earnings of the sugar industry provoked a contraction in the rest of the country's industry, which—like commercial activities—produced for internal consumption. Hundreds of work centers closed their doors under the impact of the economic crisis, and tens of thousands of workers were left without jobs in the cities and towns of these provinces. According to the census of 1953, during the years between 1953 and 1956 more than 344,000 young people between the ages of fifteen and nineteen entered the labor market in the provinces of Oriente, Camagüey, and Las Villas. According to my estimates, more than 90% of this young workforce did not find employment in these provinces from 1953 to 1956. These estimates take into account the number of deceased persons of working age as well as provincial migrations during the period.

In Havana, on the contrary, the economic contraction produced by the recession was in part controlled, although the economy could not maintain the same pace of development during 1953–1956 as in the preceding periods. Thus, the volume of salaries for Havana Province increased in absolute numbers by only 114.3 million pesos from 1953 to 1956, whereas it had increased by 134.1 million pesos over the preceding period. This means that of the 125,789 young people in Havana who reached working age between 1953 and 1956, plus some 40,000 immigrants (both foreigners and Cubans from the rural zones of the country who arrived in the capital), 10% to 15% remained without employment.

In Pinar del Río Province, the total of salaries in 1953–1956 increased by 5.1 million pesos over the preceding four-year period. Of the 44,691 young people who reached working age during this period, 20% to 30% did not find employment. In Matanzas, where the salary situation remained practically stagnant, increasing only by 1.03 in 1953–1956, 38,226 young people between the ages of fifteen and nineteen reached working age, according to the census of 1953. My calculations indicate that 34% to 44% of these did not find employment. Salary volumes in the provinces of Oriente, Camagüey, and Las Villas allow us to estimate the number of workers in these regions who entered the army of permanently unemployed in the four-year period of 1953–1956. Using the reduction of 36.2 million pesos in real commercial and industrial salaries, we can calculate that some 30,000 to 40,000 men and women who had held jobs between 1949 and 1952 lost their employment. If we add to this figure the approximately 349,259 young people who reached working age between 1953 and 1956 in these provinces, it becomes obvious that unemployment increased considerably.

As significant as the reduction in the total salaries paid from 1953 to 1956 in the provinces of Las Villas, Camagüey, and Oriente is that this total remained at a stationary level from 1947 to 1951, indicating that commercial and industrial activities stagnated from then on, with commercial salaries being stimulated by the giant harvests brought in during the Korean War (1951–1952) only to fall abruptly as a result of the aforementioned policy of sugar restriction. In other words, the growth in economic activities between 1947 and 1956 in the provinces of Matanzas, Las Villas, Camagüey, and Oriente was insufficient to provide employment for tens of thousands of Cubans who reached working age during this crucial ten-year period. The stagnation of 1947–1951 and the economic recession of 1953–1956 exercised their most deleterious effects on the thousands of urban workers who could not find employment after 1947 and on those who began to lose their jobs starting in 1953, primarily in the rural areas of the country.

Unlike what happened in the years 1929–1933, the individual nominal salary of the urban proletariat did not drop precipitously between 1953 and 1956. Rather, it descended progressively from 1941 to 1947 and then remained relatively stable until 1958. The nominal salaries frozen from 1944, the year of the last increase, until 1958 in urban commerce and industry barely permitted urban workers to maintain the living standards they had in 1941. Moreover, the individual real wage of the urban proletariat suffered a sharp decline between 1944 and 1947 as a consequence of the rise in prices that caused the purchasing power of the peso to fall.

By raising prices, the capitalists unleashed an inflationary process that tended to offset the salary increases of 1942–1944, restoring salaries in great measure to the levels of 1941. Efforts of the Confederation of Cuban Workers (CTC), under the leadership of Lázaro Peña, to reestablish equilibrium between prices and salaries at the 1944 level were unsuccessful. The Auténtico governments, after making Mujal head of the CTC, were not interested in raising salaries more than prices. Denunciations by Cuban Communists of the scandalous profits being obtained by capitalist enterprises, especially foreign firms, and their campaigns for a rise in the living standard of workers were ignored by Grau San Martín and Prío Socarrás. Beginning in 1947, Peña argued that the 250 million pesos paid to workers in 1946 in relation to wages of 1941 "did not represent a significant increase, inasmuch as the purchasing power of the peso had declined by 56%" (Peña, 1947: 17, 18). A year later, Jacinto Torras, in his column in the newspaper *Hoy,* wrote that Cubans had to spend three times more money than in 1940 for the purchase of food, with the result that families whose income had remained static after the salary increase of 1944 found themselves in a precarious situation. He added that even those who had received nominal increases of some importance as a result of agreements between unions and owners after 1944 had seen their living standard fall to a level lower than that of 1941 (Torras, 1947: 1).

Real salaries did not deteriorate in all industries, however. In large companies with more than 100 workers, the active struggle of the communists obliged the followers of Mujal to demand higher salaries from the bourgeois employers in order to maintain their leadership. In work centers where the unions were led by Communists or by workers who defended the rights of their class, no transactions prejudicial to proletarian interests took place. Salaries and working conditions of the proletariat in the most important industries thus reached a higher level than those in small and medium-sized industries in urban areas.

The list of salaries for some categories of skilled and unskilled industrial workers reproduced by the Bohan Report of the U.S. Department of Commerce shows that these were much better remunerated than the majority of industrial workers, who according to the census of 1943 received salaries lower than 60 pesos per month. The Bohan investigation covered nine of the leading industries of the country and included refineries and public utilities. Table 5.2 gives an idea of the salary differences.

Table 5.2   Salaries of Skilled Versus Unskilled Industrial Workers, 1955

	Pesos per Hour		
	Minimum	Maximum	Average
Unskilled: heavy manual work	0.71	1.07	0.92
Loader and unloader of cargo	0.87	1.36	1.08
Mechanic's assistant	0.72	1.23	1.05
3rd-class mechanic	0.99	1.46	1.20
2nd-class mechanic	1.08	1.61	1.30
1st-class mechanic	1.25	1.83	1.45

Source: U.S. Department of Commerce, Investments in Cuba, 1956: 186.

In large urban industries, the united labor movement, taking advantage of the situation created by World War II, managed to wrest from employers salaries that were relatively high compared to those earned by the general population of workers. Included in this group were those employed in electricity; telephone communications; the beverage industry; cigarette manufacturing; some branches of graphic arts; the docks of Havana, Nuevitas, and other ports; hotels and nightclubs (where workers augmented their wretched basic salaries with high earnings in tips); banks; and transport. The salaries in these fields contrasted with the low pay of workers in small enterprises, especially those in shoe manufacturing, cigar making, retail stores, mechanics, the textile industry, tobacco stripping, part of the railroad sector, the graphic industry, domestic service, dry cleaning, laundries, and diverse types of day labor. But differences existed even within a single industry, as occurred in the sugar industry, where workers in the mills earned much more acceptable salaries than did field-workers. Other notable inequalities in salary were found among workers in a single industry in the capital and in the provinces. Referring to the differences between large and small industries, García Galló and Mier Febles (n.d.: 86, 87) pointed out that "workers in beer factories received an average salary of $1.40 per hour; those in cigarette factories, $1.50 or more; those in soap and perfume factories, $1.00; metalworkers, $0.75, and sugar producers, lumping together both agricultural and industrial workers, $0.50. But those in the last group worked only four or five months of the year, while those in the other sectors as a general rule worked longer." According to their findings, 62% of workers earned less than 75 pesos per month.

The high salaries paid by large industries and public services tended to create a labor aristocracy in those branches of the economy in which the labor leaders and Communists obtained advantages over the rest of the proletariat, lending a purely economic character to their activities. Coinciding with this process, by 1947 many of the industries created during the war were either partially paralyzed or shut down. The number of workers in the tobacco industry fell from 6,206 to 1,853. The textile industry was reported to have nearly 11,000 unemployed. In the province of Havana, only ten of some thirty-six lumberyards and sawmills continued to function. The metal and machinery industry confronted the closure of a considerable number of diamond workshops, can manufacturers, and machinery industries. The foundry of San José de las Lajas and the Continental Can Company halted their operations. Factories that produced crackers, sweets, and preserves reduced work schedules to a few days a week and dismissed 2,000 workers. Other thousands of workers were thrown into the streets by the shoe, glass, and paper industries. The end of World War II meant the return to Cuba of merchandise massproduced in the United States that had been temporarily diverted to the war fronts and now saturated the Cuban market, forcing the closure of many industries that had sprung up during the war (Luzardo, 1946: 986, 987).

The recession in industrial activities was not reflected in the salary statistics of the era thanks to the 6-million-ton harvest and the 300-million-peso budget approved by the Grau government in 1947. Nevertheless, from that moment on the slow growth sponsored by the industrial sector of the dependent bourgeoisie came to a stop. As U.S. goods again flooded the internal market, the recession in industrial activities grew more acute. The process was particularly dramatic in the provinces, where commercial and industrial activities languished. The total amount of wages paid that year in Cuba remained at the same level until 1957, rising only during the Korean War. The sudden drop in salaries resulting from the sugar restriction of 1953, in relation to the harvests of 1951–1952, triggered the definitive crisis of the system.

The total of real wages paid by province in nonagricultural activities, commercial and industrial, plus those paid in the sugar industry allow us to evaluate the situation of the working class as a whole in the diverse regions of the country. The total amount of real wages increased only in the provinces of Havana and Pinar del Río. In Havana this amount grew by 98.7 million pesos in 1953–1957 in relation to 1948–1952, from a total of more than 817 million pesos to almost 916 million pesos. In Pinar del Río, the sum of real wages rose only slightly from one five-year period to the other, from 64.8 million pesos to 68.7 million pesos. Meanwhile, total wages in

THE INDUSTRIAL PROLETARIAT

Matanzas, Las Villas, Camagüey, and Oriente diminished considerably from 1953 to 1957. The wage situation in those provinces is summarized in Table 5.3. In short, real wages in these four provinces diminished by nearly 142 million pesos in 1953–1957 in relation to the preceding period.

Nominal wages decreased by more than 477 million pesos in 1953–1957. Nominal wages constitute a more reliable index for measuring the dimensions of the overall economic crisis and the existing situation of unemployment than do real wages, which serve best to measure the individual living standards of workers employed in the diverse branches of the economy. Table 5.4 illustrates the situation of nominal wages in the provinces and the exact dimensions of the slowdown provoked by the sugar restriction of 1953.

The drop in total wages paid from one five-year period to the next in nonagricultural commercial and industrial activities, as well as in the sugar industry, is seen in absolute numbers in the following reductions: in Matanzas 42,189,948 pesos; in Las Villas 106,860,471 pesos; in Camagüey 203,624,564 pesos; and in Oriente 124,707,150 pesos.

This severe reduction in wages meant that tens of thousands of workers lost their jobs in the cities and in the sugar industry. Although individual real wages of the urban proletariat employed in diverse economic branches were not significantly lowered in those last two five-year periods, unemployment in urban commercial and industrial activities increased drastically. At the same time that thousands of workers lost their jobs, young people reaching working age

Table 5.3   Total Wages of the Nonagricultural Working Class by Province, 1948–1957 (in pesos)

	Matanzas	Las Villas	Camagüey	Oriente
1948–1952	122,396,962	222,110,041	277,035,933	304,778,001
1953–1957	109,886,943	185,189,961	201,865,188	253,241,402

Table 5.4   Nominal Wages by Province, 1948–1957 (in pesos)

	Matanzas	Las Villas	Camagüey	Oriente
1948–1952	371,425,748	668,243,471	821,154,451	910,435,470
1953–1957	329,235,800	561,383,000	617,529,887	785,728,310

(seventeen to twenty-one years) found it almost impossible to obtain employment.

A better idea of the scope of the reduction in nonagricultural and sugar industry wages is provided by various surveys carried out in the 1950s. One of the most significant was without doubt that made by the British government (Zeitlin, 1967:51). Of 252 industrial workers interviewed, 41% had worked fewer than nine months between 1953 and 1958. The highest percentage of part-time workers, with fewer than nine months worked during the year, was in the sugar industry (70%), followed by workers in the paper industry (66%), textile workers (44%), cigar makers (40%), workers in the shoe and leather industry (40%), and those of oil refineries (35%). A census of cigar makers in 1951, carried out two years before the decree on sugar restriction, showed the extent to which the recession had converted thousands of workers into unemployed and underemployed. Of 10,161 cigar makers, 5,124 (or 56%) were unemployed.

A series of surveys made by the National Economic Council in 1956, 1957, and 1958 clearly revealed the dimensions of unemployment among industrial workers. The unemployment of artisans and factory operators did not diminish substantially despite the magnitude of compensatory spending. Second only to those in agriculture, the largest number of unemployed were industrial workers. In January 1957, industrial workers made up 27.1% of all unemployed. In December 1957 they constituted 20.1%, and in July 1958 the figure had again risen to 24.1%. The next highest percentages of unemployment were among the transport workers, who made up 12.6% of all unemployed in January 1957 and 11.1% in December of the same year. The slowdown affected workers and artisans more than any other sector of society. Industries and transport companies, unable to confront the economic recession, laid off workers in much larger numbers than did commercial and service enterprises. This phenomenon was still more dramatic in the cities and towns outside the capital. The National Economic Council in 1956 and 1957 published several tables showing the geographic distribution of unemployment; its findings coincided approximately with my own estimates: These statistics show that the provinces most convulsed by the economic contraction were those with the highest indices of unemployment. The province of Oriente had 29.9% of the total of unemployed in the republic, Santa Clara had 23%, and Camagüey 11.19%. Combined, these provinces had 64.8% of all unemployed in the country. In absolute numbers, unemployment in the eastern region of the country reached 234,000 persons, according to the National Economic Council.

The decline in real wages and the growing numbers of idle persons in urban zones during the 1950s was directly reflected in the indices of consumption per capita of basic food products. Table 5.5 takes into account the figures for production and importation of these products and the annual increase in population.

The indices of per capita consumption of beef and wheat flour were developed on the basis of figures of beef production at slaughterhouses and of the importation of wheat flour. These figures closely approximate consumer indices in urban zones, since meat from slaughterhouses and bread from bakeries were not consumed in general in rural zones. The indices of consumption of wheat flour in Cuba constructed by the U.S. Department of Commerce tend to coincide with mine in showing a declining tendency in 1952–1955 compared to 1946–1951.

The indices of national consumption of rice per capita were obtained by dividing the figure of its importation and production by that of the total population. Nevertheless, the indices developed by the U.S. Department of Commerce differ from mine in that they show a marked drop in the consumption of rice for years 1952–1955 (U.S. Department of Commerce, *Investments in Cuba,* 1956: 184–188).

The struggles of the working class to improve its standard of living were mediated by the Supreme Court of Justice and through government intervention to settle controversies over wages and other matters. Collective bargaining rarely resolved labor-management disputes. Workers preferred political intervention and arbitration by the executive branch, as Cuban presidents were more sensitive to immediate political pressures than the courts or congress. The Auténtico governments chose intervention as a means of handling labor disputes, and since the Auténtico reformists were also populists, they sought to co-opt working-class sectors by siding more frequently with labor than with capital in the conflicts. For this reason, the domestic bourgeoisie extolled the virtues of legislative and judicial processes.

Table 5.5   Per Capita Urban Consumption of Beef and Wheat Flour and National Consumption of Rice, 1945–1951 and 1952–1958

	Index of Beef Consumption (base year 1944: 100)	Index of Wheat Flour Consumption (base year 1925: 100)	Index of Rice Consumption (base year 1925: 100)
1945–1951	98.7	81.8	103.6
1952–1958	80	76.1	103.2

As we shall see, from 1950 on, with the beginning of the cold war, courts favored employers in their conflicts with workers. Two well-known representatives of Cuban industrialists, Francisco Fernández Pla and Enrique Guiral, speaking at a 1947 conference on economic development, called government intervention "the professional illness of our public officials" and blamed the governments for their failure to restore "peace and tranquility to relations between capital and labor after 1933" (Pérez-Stable, 1993: 45–46). The prestigious publication *Cuba Económica y Financiera,* representative of important commercial and industrial interests, similarly expressed its dissatisfaction with government intervention and promoted judicial mediation.

A list of cases cited by the president of the Supreme Court, Carlos M. Piedra, shows that workers won eighty-seven court decisions and employers forty-nine between 1939 and 1945. Another study of labor legislation shows that from 1938 to 1948 the Supreme Court ruled in favor of the workers on forty-two occasions and in favor of employers on thirty. In the 1950s, during the Prío government, the situation changed radically when the Supreme Court, in line with the overall policies of the administration, ruled against workers twice as often as against employers. This tendency increased during the dictatorship of Batista. In 1953, 1954, 1957, and 1958, the ratio of rulings against to rulings for workers was four to one; in 1952 and 1955 it was three to one. Only in 1956 did this ratio drop back to two to one, as had existed during the Prío government. As the crisis worsened between 1944 and 1952, the most reactionary political and social attitudes intensified. Every labor conflict invariably led to intervention by the Auténtico governments with the aim of settling to the advantage of the owner class or meeting only the purely economic demands of the labor leaders. The rate of official intervention grew progressively from 1937 to 1952. Under Batista (1937–1944) the government intervened eight times, under Grau (1944–1948) twenty-five times, and under Prío (1948–1952) sixty-five times.

Government intervention immediately followed union declarations of strikes. Labor union leaders no longer faced management directly; in order to achieve at least some of their demands, they had to deal with government officials. In mediation processes that tended to conciliate labor struggles, antagonistic class passions and heated demands gave way to cold discussions on legal points and matters such as profit margins. Expecting favorable government mediation, Auténtico union leaders did not agitate among workers. At the same time, they frequently sold out to management. Perhaps the most notorious action of the Auténtico top labor leaders was their stealing workers' retirement funds.

Communist-led unions as well were forced to make frequent concessions in order to push through some of their demands. Since they were only rarely favored by official arbitration, they accused the government of collusion with management against workers, although for tactical purposes they were obliged in the end to accept some of the conditions imposed. In the 1940s and 1950s, it was widely recognized that communist union leaders were honest representatives of the working class who could not be bribed by employers or government. In any event, government mediation led to employer concessions, which tended to appease the workers and satisfy certain economic demands raised by both the Auténtico and Communist-led unions, though the secretariat of the Popular Socialist Party criticized reformist tendencies.

Proletarianization also played a role in the reformist character of the working-class movement during these decades. That the demands of highly skilled workers had been successful in raising salaries and obtaining relative job security was due in part to the process of proletarianization. For every worker with relatively stable employment in a factory, there were five or six unemployed men in the streets waiting to take his place. Revolutionary strikes against the government or protracted, costly strikes against employers would have been seen as justification for the dismissal of hundreds of workers who could be replaced from among the thousands of jobless all over the country. Thus, the fact of proletarianization, whose expansion influenced diverse attitudes in the different social strata and classes, also affected working-class attitudes. As Georges Gurvitch pointed out, a social phenomenon does not limit itself to its original starting point but impinges on and transfuses the whole social structure. Despite the position of the stable working class in the 1940s and 1950s, in the long run it was a part of the oppressed strata of the national popular Cuban historical bloc and could not extricate itself from its political and social determinations. Thus, workers from large industries and public service enterprises finally emancipated themselves from the threat of dismissal and replacement by playing a decisive role in the 1958 general strike that helped to overthrow the Batista dictatorship.

6

The Rural Proletariat

One of the most difficult and controversial problems for the social historian studying this period of Cuban history is that of precisely differentiating the farmer from the rural proletariat. One obstacle lies in the population censuses and republican statistics that have used the empirical categories of positivist social science. Another emerges from the historical reality of rural life, in which the different social categories overlap in considerable numbers of individuals. The most notable example of this overlapping is found among the semiproletariat, made up of proprietors or holders-in-usufruct of small parcels of land who at the same time sell their labor. Still another difficulty lies in the fact that many rural proletarians are classified as farm holders (campesinos) for the simple reason that they were considered as such in the censuses carried out in the dead season, without taking into account that they sold their labor on neighboring farms the greater part of the year and that the products of their land were not destined for the market but entirely consumed.

The categories closest to a scientific conceptualization of the social structure are those of the 1943 census, which defines those who sell their labor (workers), those who own their means of production and employ salaried labor (proprietors), and those who do not employ salaried labor but are their own bosses. But the semiproletariat does not appear defined among the owners of means of production. Also undifferentiated are the large landholders of the agrarian bourgeoisie, that is, the fundamental owning class in rural areas. Under the category of self-employed who are owners of their tools and equipment but do not employ salaried labor we find not only farm holders but also muleteers, cane carters, and others who do not work the land.

Gramsci and Lenin differed concerning the category of semiproletarian. Whereas Gramsci accentuated the rural characteristics of semiproletarians, Lenin emphasized their proletarian characteristics and even affirmed that they are "already proletarian," without denying the rural elements of their situation in the social structure (Gramsci, 1975: 115; Lenin, 1954: 176–178).

Using the criteria of Kuczynski, Fe Iglesias insisted that the definition of the rural working class in Cuba must take into account the fact that this class is characterized not by its direct link to the means of production but rather by the lack of ownership of such means (Iglesias and S. Moro, n.d.: 12). I agree that the lack of ownership of means of production is in itself a characteristic of the rural proletariat, but I do not think that a direct link with the means of production refutes proletarian condition of the Cuban rural proletariat. Take, for example, rural proletarians with small, subsistence-level parcels of land whose production is not destined for the market. Even when they are directly linked to their means of production, their parcels of land merely fulfill the function of providing subsistence and do not connect them to the large landholders or to the capitalist market. The proletarian is, in general, a squatter, a small tenant, or the owner of a small parcel. Nevertheless, the point concerning the fact of nonownership allows us to classify as proletarianized many rural dwellers who are not considered as such by some social scientists and by the censuses, which define them simply as campesinos.

I refer to those who work as part of a rural household without receiving a salary. The typical farm family, according to our censuses, had from four to five children and owned less than 1 *caballería*. The descendants of owners, tenants, sharecroppers, and others who had usufruct of land were destined over time to become proletarians who sold their labor. But because they were sons of campesinos, they were classified as such by the censuses. In reality, they did not have access to the reduced family patrimonies, and the time they worked on their fathers' farms was only a brief interlude before they found themselves obliged to sell their labor. But even when they do not work physically in production, because they must sell their labor we may consider them proletarianized elements. Of course, the proletarianized farmer or farmer's son cannot yet be defined, sociologically speaking, as either a proletarian or a farmer. What is involved is a kind of transitory situation in which proletarian elements predominate and in which the predominant capitalist tendency in agriculture leads him to join the ranks of the rural proletariat. For this reason, for the purposes of my study of censuses, I accept the Leninist definition to the effect that he is *already* a proletarian.

Another important characteristic of the rural proletariat can be found in the fact that the Cuban censuses of the republican period, with the exception of that of 1953, were carried out in the dead season, in which the large number of workers employed by the sugar industry could not be registered. One-fifth of the population reported as economically active in the census of 1943 was classified as taking part in nonspecified activities. The majority undoubtedly made up the service sector, in which a number of occupations lent themselves to classification in other sectors, or belonged to the agricultural workforce that because of its itinerant character also did not easily fit into the categories employed by the Cuban censuses.

Nevertheless, by including agricultural workers among the existing occupations and, particularly in the census of 1899, by reporting the number of farms and the percentage of owners, tenants, and so on, the censuses of the first three decades of the republic offered useful information, despite their occasional contradictions. According to one page of the census of 1899, the number of farms and plantations in 1894 was 22,238; three pages later, it appears as 90,960, a figure that was reduced in 1899 to 60,711 as a result of the war of independence. Of the farms that continued in production, only 15,521 grew sugarcane and 15,831 were dedicated to tobacco. From that point on, Cuban historiography confuses the picture further. Ramiro Guerra gives the number of cane plantations in 1899 as 60,711 (Guerra, 1961). The error is noteworthy, but I do not point it out merely to show how the most prominent historians can blunder; the mistaken figure took on a life of its own and became a "historical fact" on the basis of which other historians began to argue about the decline or the rise of cane growers as an independent class. According to this erroneous estimate, the number of *colonos* would be reduced by half in the period 1920–1930.

Lionel Soto (1977, vol. 1: 254–258) and Francisco López Segrera (1979b, vol. 2: 165) take the figure of 60,711 farms of proprietors and tenants from the census of 1899 as if it represented only farms of proprietors. They compare it to the 38,105 farms that appear in the census of 1929, which are characterized as or presumed to be exclusively operated by proprietors, without taking into account that the later census takers were instructed to classify as a farm "a piece of land operated by its proprietor, tenant, or sharecropper." In my view the error of Soto and Segrera consisted in following Alberto Arredondo, who mistakenly deduced that the 38,105 farms were in the possession of and operated only by their proprietors. This error led Segrera to affirm that a process of massive proletarianization of small farm owners took place as a consequence of the ruin or dispossession of thousands of farmers in the first twenty years of the republic. In fact, the

1929 census suffers from a considerable underestimate. The number of farms of *colonos* in 1914 given by the Secretariat of Agriculture (37,574), the number offered by the Foreign Policy Association for 1927–1928 (43,000), and the number that appears in the *Memorias de la zafra azucarera de 1935* (43,821) reveal the existence of a larger number of farms of cane planters than the total of farmers of all types (proprietors, tenants, and sharecroppers) listed in the census of 1929.

At the same time, the enumeration of 1914 gives almost an identical number of farms of cane planters (37,574) as the total number of farms of proprietors, tenants, sharecroppers, and so on dedicated to diverse crops in 1929 (38,105). If we add to the total number of farms of cane planters in the 1927–1928 estimates of the Foreign Policy Association the different enumerations made independently during those years of farms devoted to coffee, cacao, cattle, and tobacco, we can appreciate more precisely how erroneous it is to suppose that only the proprietors of farms were included under the designation of farms. According to the land register carried out by the Commission for the Defense of Tobacco in 1929, 7,690 tobacco farms were in existence. According to the National Commission of Statistics, the number of coffee plantations reached 7,994 in 1926. This commission also gave the total of cacao farms for that same year as 1,346. And finally, the census of 1919 listed 3,334 cattle farms. Since the production of cattle increased and there is no record of a reduction in the number of cattle raisers, we can assume, conservatively, that this same number of cattle farms was in existence in 1929. Adding together these farms devoted to cattle, coffee, cacao, and tobacco, as well as cane plantations, gives a total of 62,964 farms operated by farmers, a sum surpassing the 60,711 farms in the census of 1899.

But we have not included the small properties devoted to the cultivation of other agricultural products that provided the basic food supply for the entire population and that always constitute a high percentage of the total of farm owners. It is therefore impossible to speak of a proletarianization of farm proprietors, tenants, and sharecroppers. Another important aspect to keep in mind is that according to the first census of 1899, the number of farms operated by cane planters was 15,521; the total in 1914 was 37,574; in 1927–1928 it was 43,000, and in 1935 it was 43,821. The total of cane-growing farms is calculated on the basis of the reports presented by plantation owners to the Secretariat of Agriculture. Thus, the expansion of the sugar industry in the first decades of the republic resulted in an increase, not a drop, in the number of farms operated by cane planters.

It seems, then, that the most reliable source for determining the dimensions of the different social classes in the rural areas in the first three decades of the twentieth century is the census of 1931, not that of 1929. The revaluation of these sources enabled me to reconstruct the process of real agrarian proletarianization that took place in the periods between 1899–1931 and 1932–1943. In doing so, I used the quantitative methods of Soviet historian Boris Koval.

Although dispossession, expropriation, and the ruin of hundreds of farmers was a normal, everyday phenomenon in the periods mentioned, the number of proprietors increased uninterruptedly. From 1898 to 1958, the proletarianization of the farmer did not occur fundamentally as a result of a decline in the number of proprietors and holders in usufruct but as a consequence of natural population growth and the immigration of tens of thousands of Spanish and Antillean workers.

In 1931 the average farm family was composed of 5.8 persons. Of the three or four descendants of the head of the household, only one normally had access to the reduced family patrimony; the others were obliged to sell their labor. It is thus clear that the process of proletarianization can take place in an era in which the absolute number of small proprietors increases. At the same time, many new holders of small plots had to find supplementary income beyond their farms by selling their labor.

From 1899 to 1931, the number of farm owners rose by 26,122; The total grew from 16,990 in 1899 to 43,112 in 1931, according to the census of that year. In the same period, the number of tenants and sharecroppers increased by 3,300, their number going from 40,984 in 1899 to 44,284 in 1931. Thus, the number of proprietors, tenants, and sharecroppers increased by 29,422, and at the same time the active rural population above fourteen years of age increased by 102,975 persons, from 262,123 in 1899 to 365,098 in 1931. This means that some 73,554 persons incorporated into agriculture over a period of thirty-two years did not acquire land of their own or join the number of rural tenants or sharecroppers classified by the censuses of the time. As Koval has correctly pointed out apropos of the process of proletarianization in Brazil, "The increase in the proletarian and semiproletarian elements is often hidden behind the screen of formal agrarianization" (Koval, 1974: 124). That is, the increase in the total number of small rural proprietors by no means indicates that a process of proletarianization is not going on.

The process of proletarianization during the first thirty years of the republic had neither the characteristics nor the dimensions of what occurred after 1931. As a consequence of the occupation and more intensive exploitation of land deriving from the development of capitalism in agriculture, offers of salaried employment on the farms of capitalist tenants and landowners who had become agrarian bourgeois increased notably. Relations of capitalist production thus tended to become constantly more prevalent in agriculture. The number of salaried agricultural workers greatly exceeded that of sharecroppers, subtenants, and all other links of precapitalist type existing in agriculture. Simultaneously, the process of proletarianization of the rural masses was strengthened by the accelerated growth of population in the countryside.

As I have mentioned, according to the census of 1931, the economically active population above fourteen years of age devoted to agriculture reached 365,098. The census of 1943 showed an economically active population above thirteen years of age in agriculture of 626,921 persons. Consequently, from 1931 to 1943, the economically active labor force in agriculture increased by 261,823 persons. In the fifteen years between 1931 and 1945, the rise in the number of farms seems to be the result of the proliferation of the number of small plots, whose main function was to guarantee subsistence to agricultural workers, not to produce for the market. In the agricultural census of 1946, some 62,500 farms of up to 10 hectares seem to belong to this category of land parcels whose produce was destined for family consumption and that were not owned or held in usufruct by farmers but by agricultural proletarians. The census of 1931 reports some 27,685 farms of fewer than 12 hectares. From 1931 to 1946, the number of farms in this category was about 35,000 or more, that is, of the increase of 72,562 farms between 1931 and 1946, some 20,000 were probably small parcels intended for the sustenance of agricultural workers (note that the 1946 census was made in 1945). If from the number of persons older than fourteen incorporated into the agricultural labor force between 1931 and 1943 (261,823) we subtract those who exploited farms as proprietors or usufructuaries (72,562), we are left with 189,261 persons who, having no land of their own and not belonging to the ranks of farmers, tenants, sharecroppers, and so on, were sooner or later obliged to become proletarians. This number of eventual proletarians contrasts notably with those for 1899–1931. Thus, in the first period (1899–1931) some 73,554 persons became proletarians, whereas in the second (1932–1943), 189,261 passed into that category.

This growing rural proletariat that made up the bulk of the permanent reserve army of unemployed in the dead season was essentially a new phenomenon of the last fifteen years of the bourgeois republic and the gravest structural flaw in Cuban neocolonial society. The great increase reflected in these estimates does not cover the exten-

sive process of proletarianization that took place in the rural population. Some elements notoriously escape all calculations. For example,
it has not been possible to quantify the number of rural workers who
emigrated to urban zones between 1899 and 1931 or between 1931
and 1943 or to determine the number of those who were classified as
farmers in the censuses because they were working small subsistence
plots or working on the farms of their parents at the time of the census. Further contributing to the underestimation of the size of the
rural proletariat is that many agricultural workers answered affirma-
tively when asked if they worked "for their own account," as the question was formulated by the census takers in 1943 and 1953. A considerable number of them assumed that they were being asked if they
worked with their own hands, not if they worked independently of an
employer.

The proletarianization process in the rural zones from 1943 to
1958 paradoxically implied a considerable increase of *minifundia.*
Thus, from the rural census of 1946, when 111,278 plots of land of
less than 25 hectares were registered, to 1959, when 140,000 families
were reported working on small pieces of land of the same size prior
to the agrarian reform law of 1959, the number of these parcels of
land increased by 28,722 (Rodríguez, 1963, vol. 2: 224–240). The
small plots allowed the rural workers, cane cutters, and coffee bean
collectors the elementary means of subsistence during the time they
were unemployed, that is, during the dead season. These proletarian
minifundia differed from the small plots on which peasants grew most
of the agricultural products they cultivated and consumed and from
the small farms whose produce was destined for the market. The
increase in the number of *minifundia,* therefore, did not mean a rise
in the number of farm owners or tenants between 1943 and 1958,
since those tracts were cultivated by rural workers, not by farmers or
peasants.

If the census of 1943 exaggerated the dimensions of the rural
proletariat, that of 1946, as British sociologist Brian Pollitt has pointed out, enumerated more the nature and the *opportunities* for work
that the agricultural labor force had at one time or another than the
number of workers who obtained employment in 1945. Given the
methodology of the census—the information was requested from
farm proprietors and administrators—there was no way to avoid
counting workers employed on more than one farm two, three, or
more times, depending on the number of different farms on which
they worked (Pollitt, 1977). This method of collecting information
resulted in an extraordinary discrepancy in the relative proportions
of "agricultural workers" and "agriculturists" in the censuses of 1943

and 1946. The first reported some 46,000 "agricultural workers" and 575,800 "farmers" and the second some 489,000 "salaried workers" and 221,900 "farmers and truck farmers." The 1943 census offered an explanation for these deficiencies: "If the census had been taken during the months of harvesting, the percentage of agricultural workers would probably have been considerably higher, and it is possible that each increase would have been compensated by a decrease in the group of farmers, since the group of agricultural workers is made up in great part of farmers' sons, who have been reported in the census in the group of farmers."

Pollitt's 1964 survey of rural men, which tended to define the occupational status during the 1940s and 1950s of the families of his interviewees, sought to clear up the confusion concerning the rural proletariat that the two censuses had created. To this end, Pollitt formulated a series of questions to distinguish proletarians from semi-proletarians and these from farmers—proprietors, tenants, sub-tenants, sharecroppers, and squatters. According to Pollitt's definitions, of the 1,002 men he interviewed, 204 (30.4%) were farmers, 125 (12.5%) were semiproletarians, 77 (7.7%) were nonsalaried agricultural workers, and 496 (49.4%) were salaried agricultural workers.

An unexpected result of the survey was the low number of agricultural workers who found employment in the cities during the dead season: Only three salaried workers of the total of 496 went to the cities in search of employment. In my opinion, this was a point that confused the interviewees. When they were asked, "Where did your father work during the dead season?" they did not remember clearly if he had worked in the city or in the country. All evidence seems to indicate, however, that a significant number of cane cutters worked in the cities as peons in public works, street vendors, artisans, or in other casual occupations. A collateral consequence of the survey was the determination of the proportion of salaried agricultural workers who had parcels of land. A total of 38% were in this category and allotted their produce fundamentally to the sustenance of their families. Thus, 61.9% of the rural individuals Pollitt interviewed were wage earners. This figure approaches the estimates of the 1946 rural census, according to which 57% of rural inhabitants were workers earning wages. The 1919 census reported that only 31.3% of the rural population earned wages. These figures back up evidence of the growing process of proletarianization among the rural masses that other census data indicate.

According to Marx, the first requisite for the formation of a class consciousness in Europe was the existence of great concentrations of workers in industries. In the large sugar mills in Cuba, however, this condition existed only three or four months of the year—the duration of the sugar harvest—for a technically unskilled and culturally marginalized rural proletariat. Consequently, the awakening of consciousness among this proletariat of the need to adopt organized forms of struggle to achieve its demands came about fundamentally as a result of the intense physical labor and subhuman standard of living to which it was submitted and of the example set by the urban working class. The early struggles of the rural proletariat were led by Spanish anarchists and socialists employed in urban centers of the island or in the industrial areas of sugar mills. The short period during the year available to the workers' vanguard for developing class consciousness among the mass of workers impeded their effective action. Since the majority of sugar workers were dispersed during eight or nine months of the year, selling their labor in various agricultural harvests or in the cities, the formation of links of solidarity resulting from coexistence in a single place over a long period of time proved to be impossible. Yet the intensity of their physical exploitation meant that this sector of the working class had the greatest potential for upheaval. Thus, whereas the urban working class, with better organization and a higher cultural level, maintained a more moderate attitude, cautious of embarking upon total revolution against the system, the rural proletariat threw itself impetuously behind the first possibility of changing the basis of its existence, following the political leadership of the rural middle classes in 1895 and supporting the same leadership in the internal struggles for power of 1906. This attitude led to violent and drastic forms of protest and in the 1930s the call to constitute soviets.

Because a considerable part of the sugar proletariat was composed of a semiproletariat of part-time workers, it differed notably from the modern industrial proletariat. The organic makeup of this proletariat determined its social and ideological fragmentation, accentuated by the relations of caciquism that predominated in the rural areas during the first thirty years of the republic.

The irruption of capitalist mercantile relations into Cuban agriculture contributed powerfully to the dislocation of farmers from their land and to the generalization of the phenomenon of labor migration among the different regions and cities of the country. This process, which gained strength at the beginning of the twentieth century, had a progressive historical character. Migration not only provided economic advantages to tillers of the soil by offering them the opportunity to move to other regions or cities where salaries were higher; it also tended to liquidate earlier forms of economic subjugation, such as lifetime tenancies and payments in labor. In Lenin's view, the tenant farmer's lack of attachment to the piece of land he had worked all his life in virtual vassalage to the landowner prevented him from being buried under the moss of history.

The itinerant character of the Cuban rural proletariat arose with the abolition of slavery. The nearness of the most remote regions to important population centers in the interior of the country facilitated the mobility of the rural workers; at the end of a harvest, they simply moved on to other harvests or to the cities or towns to look for work. In Cuba there are no regions far from urban centers and civilization such as exist in Brazil, Colombia, and Peru. As Carlos Rafael Rodríguez has pointed out, these geographical characteristics and the proliferation of part-time work in services and public works in cities gradually assimilated agricultural workers into the urban proletariat (Rodríguez, 1963, vol. 2: 242).

The short periods of time for which lands were leased or ceded for sharecropping guaranteed that not even people born and reared in the countryside had the mentalities of typical farmers. Nelson's survey, designed to determine the previous place of residence of 742 farm families by their type of land tenancy in 1942, revealed the extent of geographic mobility in rural Cuba. The most telling aspect of this survey is not only that more than 63% of the farmers and rural proprietors interviewed had changed farms but also that the mobility of the farmers, tenants, and sharecroppers was similar to that of the agricultural proletariat. Thus, 72.3% of agricultural workers, 70.1% of sharecroppers, and 64.7% of tenants had worked in and come from places other than their current place of residence. According to Nelson, his survey revealed in a way similar to the census of 1946 the great mobility of the rural proletariat that "emigrated from the sugar harvest to tobacco and coffee harvests, moving within a very well-defined pattern" (Nelson, 1950: 170–173).

The phenomenon of interprovincial migration increased notably in the last three decades of the republic. Table 6.1 shows the movement of the Cuban population. As Table 6.1 indicates, Pinar del Río, Matanzas, Las Villas, and Oriente were depopulated by at least 421,000 persons in 1953. And the numbers were probably even much larger, since the census gives net rates. According to other estimates, 600,700 persons did not reside in their provinces of origin, which confirms still further the existing process of rural proletarianization. Cuba was among the three Latin American countries with the highest population density, fifty-eight inhabitants per square kilometer. Thus, there was greater uniformity in the distribution of the population, higher density, and a landownership system based on latifundia,

Table 6.1   Net Interprovincial Migration of the Native Population, 1953

Province	Net Loss of Population (in thousands)
Pinar del Río	106.0
Havana	—a
Matanzas	96.4
Las Villas	161.9
Camagüey	—a
Oriente	56.7

a. Havana and Camagüey received more people than they sent to other provinces:
Havana 345,600 persons and Camagüey 75,400.
Source: Pino Santos, 1973.

which brought the country nearer to relative overpopulation. The closeness of relations and the mobility implied by such a concentration of population helped the rural masses to become highly politicized under the leadership of the populist parties and the revolutionary movements in the 1930s. The island also had the second highest index of newpapers per thousand inhabitants and one of the densest networks of radio and TV stations in Latin America, which further contributed to the socialization and cultural homogeneity of the rural masses (*Revista Interamericana de Ciencias Sociales,* 1964: 68, 168).

Carlos Rafael Rodríguez, member of the Agrarian Commission of the Popular Socialist Party and president of the National Institute of Agrarian Reform, defined the tendencies animating the rural proletariat at the moment of the triumph of the revolution: "The vast majority of agricultural workers in Cuba saw as the solution to their problems not an agrarian reform that would grant them land and transform them into small farmers but a revolutionary process that would assure them permanent work and raise their standard of living *as workers*" (Rodríguez, 1963, vol. 2: 243).

The answer given by 74.5% of the rural proletariat and farmers interviewed by the Catholic University Association (ACU) to the effect that what the rural population needed most urgently was above all work and not education, medical and social aid, or rural roads seems to provide indirect confirmation of the opinions Rodríguez cited (ACU, 1972). Of course, these farmers and rural workers were not asked whether they aspired to a job or to a piece of land. Nevertheless, their emphasis on the fundamental need for work implied that cultivation of the land and the part-time work they obtained was insufficient for subsistence and that they most required permanent work. What the rural Cuban proletariat and semiproletariat desired was a means of earning a living, although the vision of poor farmers all around them who had slaved all their lives on the land only to receive an income equivalent or inferior to theirs inclined the majority of rural workers to prefer a job rather than land (Mintz, 1967: 93, 94).

Spanish sociologist Juan Martínez Allier, who consulted more than 500 letters from farmers and rural workers requesting work or land in the archives of INRA—and who cannot be said to have shared the viewpoints of the revolutionary leadership with regard to the first steps of the agrarian reform—also tends to confirm the assertions of Rodríguez that the mass of rural workers did not have a farmer's mentality. According to Martínez Allier, "The workers who were unemployed part of the year wanted work or land; that is, when they asked for land, it was with the aim of obtaining assured work" (Martínez Allier, 1977: 138). At the same time, as Martínez Allier pointed out, in 1959 and 1960 the only way that the rural proletariat could survive the dead season was by possessing a plot of land. The possibilities of work on state farms and cane cooperatives were still insufficient to meet the existing demand for jobs in those early years in which the 500 letters asking for work or land were sent to the INRA. What is more, the revolutionary government rejected the demand of rural labor unions to create a fourth work shift at sugar mills to solve the problem of unemployment, saying it was excessively costly on the one hand and politically inconvenient on the other, since it could provoke the alignment of the sugar bourgeoisie with the landowners at an inopportune moment. Nevertheless, by May 1961 agricultural workers in cooperatives and on state farms totaled 149,700 permanent employees and 115,700 part-time, indicating that between mid-1960 and May 1961 tens of thousands of workers requested entrance into or were induced to enter into the new forms of agrarian production that were beginning to take shape all over the island.

The situation of unemployment during more than half the year led the agricultural workers of the sugar industry, under the leadership of their unions, to demand that each worker be granted 0.45 hectares of land for supplying his family with food. This demand, of course, did not tend to encourage a petty bourgeois spirit in the rural proletariat, since its purpose was to assure a minimum consumption level for the families of cane cutters and rural peons, not produce destined for the market. A study carried out by the Central Planning Board showed that workers permitted to hold parcels of land were reluctant to give them up, considering them necessary for their family's self-sufficiency and for obtaining modest additions to their earnings as workers.

Another important ideological characteristic of the Cuban rural proletariat and of the country population in general is that in contrast to the rural inhabitants of other Latin American countries, they had not been taught resignation and social conformity by the Catholic Church. Nelson's survey to construct the domestic budget of 746 farm families in nine different rural districts revealed that only "a few families" in two of those districts made expenditures on baptisms, burials, weddings, and church donations. And of these rural families Nelson wrote: "The Church has only occasional contacts with them. The priest appears only about once a year, when infants are baptized—usually at three dollars per head—and that is about the extent of his ministry" (Nelson, 1950). The survey carried out ten years later by the ACU showed that the rural workers and farmers hardly ever attended church or had relations with the parish priest of the municipality where they resided (see Tables 6.2 and 6.3).

Table 6.2   Attendance at Mass by Agricultural Workers and Farmers, 1956

Number of Times Yearly	Interviewees (%)
0	93.40
1	2.64
2	1.83
3	1.32
4	0.94

Source: Echevarría, 1971: 14, 15.

Table 6.3   Relation of the Head of the Rural Family to the Local Priest

Relation	Interviewees (%)
Has never seen him	53.10
Knows him by sight	36.74
Has no relations with him	1.94
Considers him a friend	5.43
Considers him a personal friend	2.38

Source: Echevarría, 1971: 15.

Beginning in the 1930s, the relations of caciquism gradually lost strength in rural areas as a result of the struggles of the sugar proletariat (James, 1974; Ibarra, 1992). The revolutionary measures of the Grau-Guiteras government and the mobilizations of the populist Auténticos and the Communist Party helped to raise the consciousness of the rural workers. The populism of Grau San Martín, based on the social gains achieved in 1933 under the pressure of the masses, emboldened a considerable part of the farm population and agricultural workers to vote independently of the dictates of the rural caciques in the elections of 1944. The perseverance of Communist leaders of the stature of Jesús Menéndez encouraged the rural proletariat to liberate themselves gradually from their links to the caciques of the landowning class and from their dependence on the sugar companies' stores. At the same time, the struggle of rural Communist leaders against the spreading land expropriation, particularly in the period 1934–1958, contributed to a growing awareness among the rural population, especially in the province of Oriente, of the land-grabbing nature of the large landowners and sugar companies (Regalado, 1973). Freed in great measure from the dominance of rural landowners and caciques and uninfluenced by the conformist predications of the church, broad sectors of the rural proletariat and farm population were prepared to embrace any revolutionary movement that undertook the liberation of the class.

The years 1933 to 1957 were definitive for the Cuban rural proletariat. As I have pointed out (agreeing with Pierre Vilar), the decisive factor in the change of attitude of social groups and classes was their abrupt impoverishment or enrichment rather than their poverty or wealth in itself. What, then, were the conjunctural changes that took place in the relatively stable income structure among the diverse groups and classes? The salaries of the rural proletariat had stabilized at a low level from 1927 to 1953. The social movements that convulsed the rural regions of the country between 1927 and 1930, the general strike of 1933 and the creation of soviets at sugar mills, the strike for differential pay in Las Villas in 1955, and, finally, the 1957 incorporation of the rural proletariat and farmers into the rebel army in Las Villas and Oriente reveal a *structure* (the impossibility or incapacity of the rural proletariat to withstand drastic reductions in their real salaries in cases of restriction or inflationary processes) and a *conjuncture* (the same restriction or inflationary process accompanied by the consequences already mentioned).

The index of the volume of real salaries in the industrial sugar sector from 1937 to 1957 shows an almost imperceptible increase between 1937 and 1947, with relative stagnation from this last year up to 1951 and, following the giant harvest of 1952, a marked drop during the next five-year period of 1953–1957. In absolute numbers, this means that salaries in the industrial sugar sector dropped by $22 million from 1953 to 1957 compared to 1948–1952. Salaries of agricultural workers in the sugar industry in 1953–1957 declined by $138 million compared to the preceding five-year period. In that period, which culminated with the constitution of the guerrilla fronts in Oriente and had one of its decisive moments in the December 1955 strike of sugar workers in Las Villas, the rural proletariat saw its living standard drastically reduced following a period of relatively stable low income. For 1948–1952, the average salary of the worker in the sugar industry (including both the agricultural and industrial sector) dropped, relative to 1953–1957, by $6.26 monthly—from $24.66 to $18.40, or 24.6%. Not only did the average individual real salary diminish but the large landowners (hacendados), protected by the Auténtico governments and the Batista dictatorship, systematically subtracted a considerable part of the sugar differential.

From the end of the 1940s, it was clear that the hacendados, in collusion with national labor leaders, were withholding pay for days not worked because of overproduction. Jacinto Torras revealed the extent of the losses in earnings suffered by the sugar workers during the Auténtico governments. Table 6.4 illustrates the rising tendency in the number of unpaid days.

During these six harvests, the workers lost more than the equivalent of one and a half harvests in wages through the reduction of time

Table 6.4 Loss of Salary Due to Shortened Sugar Harvests, 1942–1950

	Average Daily Production (in bags)	Duration of Harvest (in days)	Duration Harvest Should Have Lasted (in days)	Difference (in days)
1942	284,952	81	81	—
1946	339,508	80	95	15
1947	369,143	106	137	31
1948	389,465	104	142	38
1949	401,969	87	123	36
1950	413,043	90	130	40
Total		548	708	160

Source: Torras, 1985, vol. 2: 247.

worked. Torras estimated that the losses in salaries reached $72 million in those years. In this way the sugar differential and the guarantee clause won by labor struggles led by Jesús Menéndez were snatched away by the landowners during the Auténtico governments. Even the presidential decree requiring the maintenance of hygienic conditions in workers' living areas at sugar mills was systematically violated. During the second dictatorship of Batista, the gains of the sugar proletariat met the same fate. After the Batista coup, the payment for overproduction was subtracted from the workers' earnings, a practice the proletariat called *el intensivismo*. Henry F. Holland, assistant secretary of state, declared before the Finance Committee of the U.S. Senate in 1956 that the Cuban government estimated that the sugar restriction had diminished the salaries of sugar mill workers by 13% and that the take-home earnings at the end of the harvest had been reduced by another 27% (U.S. Senate, Finance Committee, 1956: 19–21).

The process of concentrating sugar mills and stepping up cane grinding resulted in the dismissal of 25,000 to 36,000 workers between 1940 and 1958 and dozens of unpaid days because of overproduction, with the unconditional backing of the governments of Prío and Batista. Records show that some 28 million *arrobas* of cane were ground daily from 1936 to 1958. From 1940 to 1948, 30 million to 39 million were ground, and from 1950 to 1958, 41 million to 47 million. The progressive increase in industrial productivity meant fewer days of pay for the workers, thanks to the complicity of the country's governments. By the 1950s, the harvests had been reduced by one month for every three. At the same time, U.S.-owned sugar companies published their balances: They had obtained profits two or three times greater in 1955 than the preceding year, despite a harvest that had been reduced by 350,000 tons.

The indices of real salaries in the sugar industry for 1937–1958 as well as their levels in the different provinces of the country allow some interesting observations. After a slow and painful ascent of real salaries, the return to a situation much like that of 1933–1938 confronted workers in rural areas not only with the prospect of regression to an economic plane they had supposedly left behind but also, after Batista's coup d'état, with the disappearance from the political and social horizon of any possible solution to the difficult conditions they endured.

The indices of apparent consumption of goods indispensable to workers (food, electricity, transport, housing) clearly show the drop in living standard in 1927–1949 compared to the period of relative well-being and international economic growth from 1898 to 1928, coincident with the last expansive stage of the sugar industry. All the food and other basic necessities increase progressively in the first period and decline constantly in the second. The low indices of per capita consumption in this period were caused not only by the low levels of income for 1925 to 1949 but also by the quantitative growth of the permanent army of unemployed.

From 1905–1909 to 1925–1929, the consumption of basic foodstuffs seemed to maintain the same pace as demographic evolution, but although population growth slowed in the two following decades (the 1930s and 1940s), consumption declined. In those twenty years, per capita consumption of flour and beans tended to diminish, as did that of other basic products. Only the consumption of beer grew rapidly, which seems logical, since rates of alcohol consumption tend to rise among undernourished populations. Energy consumption and the use of transport, too, went down.

To find out how the living conditions of the rural masses were affected, I investigated the level of consumption of protein-rich foods, basic to rural people in Cuba: tasajo (jerked beef or horse meat) and dried codfish. The per capita consumption of these products could be quantified with considerable precision from the quantities that were imported each year and recorded in the government's foreign trade statistics. National production of tasajo could also be quantified in one five-year period of the 1930s and in another of the 1950s. According to various estimates, 90% of all imported dried cod and tasajo was consumed in rural areas; the index I use is the index of apparent consumption of these foods among the rural masses. The consumption of essential foodstuffs by the rural population dropped throughout the twenty-year period from 1905–1909 to 1925–1929 and again from 1925–1929 to 1953–1957 (this last five-year period was included to determine the level of protein consumption during those critical years and confirm the tendency evident in the earlier periods). In the first period, from 1905–1909 to 1925–1929, total consumption of dried cod and tasajo declined by 14 pounds per capita per year, from 52 to 38 pounds. In the time frame from 1929 to 1953–1957, in which income was relatively stable at very low levels, the drop in protein consumption was still greater: Consumption of dried cod and tasajo decreased by 26 pounds per capita annually in this period. The deterioration in the food ration was extraordinarily acute, dropping to 11.9 pounds per year, that is, scarcely 0.6 pounds of dried cod and 11.3 pounds of tasajo per capita per year.

It might be thought that the decline in the consumption of these basic foods resulted from their replacement by other sources of protein, but the contemporary surveys and other accounts of levels of nourishment suggest no foodstuff that replaced dried cod and *tasajo*. If any substitution of certain products for others took place in those periods, it was that of dried cod for *tasajo*, which accentuated still more the shortage of protein in the diet of the rural proletariat and farmers and testifies to the situation of economic helplessness of the rural population. In fact, *tasajo*, which had a much higher protein content than dried cod, was more expensive, so the rural proletariat and the impoverished farmers came to depend more on the latter. In 1905–1909 Cuba imported almost 42 million pounds of *tasajo*. In 1953–1957 this amount had dropped below 1.7 million pounds. The displacement of *tasajo* by cod began to appear in 1925–1929. The information provided by the Economic Commission for Latin America tends to confirm the general reduction in per capita consumption in a series of countries of the continent between the 1920s and the 1940s. Statistics elaborated on the basis of imports and local production, although easily quantifiable, are always suspect, but as Dudley Seers points out, when many such statistics tell the same story in such a vivid way, the story can be much more readily believed than any estimate or statistical calculation.

The survey carried out by the ACU among rural workers of every region of the country in 1956–1957 backs up at least some of my statistical estimates on nourishment in rural areas. The survey did not include the mountainous regions of Oriente Province, the scene of the first battles of the rebel army led by Fidel Castro, but had it been carried out there, the nutritional indices and living standard of the population it would have indicated would probably have been even more alarming.

According to this survey, the index of malnutrition was 91%. Although rural workers should have received a daily quota of 3,500 calories, the real daily caloric intake did not exceed 2,500 calories. Only 4% of those interviewed said they regularly ate meat; less than 1% reported eating fish, .1% eggs, and only 11.2% milk. Just 3.3% of the agricultural workers consumed bread, 7% cornmeal. Root vegetables made up 22% of the rural diet, but the primary source of nourishment was rice, supplying 24% of the total diet, almost as much as beans (23%). Sugar made up some of the caloric deficit.

The survey further found that 14% of the workers either suffered or had suffered from tuberculosis, 13% from typhoid fever, and 36% from intestinal parasites. A total of 31% had had malaria. These diseases were closely related to the lack of education among the rural population (according to the survey, 34% of the agricultural workers were illiterate), poor housing conditions (dirt floors, latrines, overcrowding), and lack of medical attention (ACU, 1972: 188–214).

Family budgets constitute another important index for measuring the tendencies observed in this period. The study of salary in relation to the domestic budget of poor farm families and rural workers reveals a permanent imbalance between expenditures for food and other expenditures from 1933 to 1958. A 1934 Foreign Policy Association survey of 113 families in the province of Oriente with an average monthly income of $41 found that 57.4% of the family budget went toward food. A similar study by the ACU in 1956–1957 noted that rural families in Cuba devoted as much of their income (69.1%) to food as did the most poverty-stricken Asians (55–75%). Obviously, this distribution contrasts notably with that of farmers in Europe, the United States and Canada, who allocated only 30–45% of their family budget for food.

Nelson's 1945 study, in contrast, shows a proportion of the domestic budget devoted to food (49.7%) closer to the European, U.S., and Canadian percentage. But 1945 was a year of prosperity for Cuba. As Nelson states: "For the Cuban economy in general, . . . the war brought prosperity. Demand for its principal product, sugar, was insatiable, and unemployment fell to low levels, although it by no means disappeared. Wages rose to the highest levels in history" (Nelson, 1950: 216).

Another explanation for the reduction in the part of the budget devoted to food in the rural homes was the high proportion of families of proprietors and tenants Nelson's team visited in comparison to families of agricultural workers. Of 742 interviewees, 76.3% were proprietors, tenants, and sharecroppers, and only 23.7% were salaried workers—a skewed sample. The agricultural census of 1946 found that 57.1% of the rural population were rural proletarians and 42.9% farmers. According to the survey by Pollitt, 49.4% were salaried proletarians and 30.4% farmers. It is logical, then, to assume that Nelson's investigative team interviewed primarily farmers whose income level was higher than that of rural laborers, even though the salaries that the latter received that year were relatively high. In only two municipalities of the nine in which rural workers predominated was it shown that the percentage of income devoted to food was equivalent to that given in the 1934 survey of the Foreign Policy Association and the 1956 survey of the ACU: In the municipalities of Florida and San Juan y Martínez, where housing was provided by the company for which they worked, 118 rural proletarians declared that they spent annually from $597 to $1,156 for food, that is, from 69.5% to 70.6% of their domestic budget.

All this tells us that the fundamental expenditures of Cuban farmers and rural workers were on food, since their earnings were so scarce that they could barely cover other elementary needs. Of the three surveys mentioned here, only the 1945 survey reveals a certain relief from expenditures for food, and this coincides with a brief time in which real salaries had reached a higher level.

The birthrate, fertility rate, and rate of net reproduction for the years 1899–1958 tell us much about living conditions in Cuba during this period. Birthrates in the three decades from 1899 to 1929 fell from 44.6% to 32.9%, a drop of 11.7% (Coliver, 1969). This decline was closely related to the relative bonanza that accompanied the expansion of sugar production in the first thirty years of republican life. In the three subsequent decades, however, from 1930 to 1959, the birthrate fell by a mere 1.2%, indicating that living conditions did not improve. From 1960 to 1975, natality declined by 9.4% in only fifteen years, a sign of the progressive improvement in living standards, including health care, following the triumph of the Cuban revolution.

The rate of net reproduction reflects still more precisely the relation between vital statistics and improvements in living standards. Following an increase in fertility and reproduction rates in the period immediately after the war of 1895, the longer-lasting economic factors began to bring about their steady decline until 1929. The net rate of reproduction diminished from 1.56 to 1.40 between 1907 and 1931 as a consequence of the rise in the standard of living. In contrast, with the fall in living conditions of the mass of the population between 1931 and 1953, the net rate of reproduction increased from 1.40 to 1.43.

The assertion that Cuba was a small bourgeois country in the sociological sense was true of the 1930s, but the description no longer applied once the process of proletarianization accelerated among the broad intermediate strata of the urban and rural population. Nevertheless, this process does not necessarily lead to the formation of a working class in the basic sectors of industry, construction, and transport large enough to represent a quantitative majority among all classes making up a nation. The formation of a modern, majority proletariat required a previous process of industrialization. In the 1950s Cuba was no longer a small bourgeois country, nor was it a proletarian country. It was a proletarianized country. Proletarianization, accompanied by a considerable demographic increase coincident with a depressive economic cycle but without prior industrialization, contributes to the creation of antagonism between relations of production and productive forces. In these conditions broadly based revolutionary movements with a national and social orientation may arise.

The participation of the urban and rural proletariat in the revolutionary movements of the 1930s and 1950s poses one of the most important historiographic problems of the republican period. Cuban historians have not questioned the leading role of the working class in the overthrow of the Machado dictatorship. The general strike of August 1930 cleared the way for the coup d'état carried out on September 4 by noncommissioned army officers and soldiers. The August strike, like the others that had preceded it during the Machado administration, had been based strictly on class demands. The economic-corporative attitude of the proletariat tended to separate it from the middle classes and their demands of a popular national character. Although the strike movement created the necessary conditions for the overthrow of the dictatorship, the country's labor leaders at no time sought a leading role with respect to the subordinate classes of the population. The exclusively proletarian positions inculcated in the working class by anarchist leaders during the first decades of republican life were not overcome once socialists and Communists acceded to the leadership of the proletariat. In fact, during the 1930s these leaders endorsed a policy of class against class, in which the nonproletarian sectors of the population and the middle class, erroneously identified with the dependent bourgeoisie, were considered rivals (Roa, 1982; Soto, 1977). The dogmatic and sectarian line imposed after the Sixth Congress of the Communist International and its Caribbean Bureau laid the foundation for the hostile attitude of Cuban Communists vis-à-vis the revolutionary Grau-Guiteras government. This policy also placed them in direct confrontation with the middle classes, which, though conscious of evils of U.S. imperialism, clung to their class interests and privileges, insofar as they still maintained a relatively stable position in society. In other words, neither the representatives of the proletariat nor those of the middle classes had a conception of the preponderant role they should play, uniting and leading the people toward achievement of their national demands, or of the mutual concessions that needed to be made to cement national unity. Referring to the dimensions of the popular mobilization and the passions that had been aroused in the course of the brief revolutionary period of the 100-day Grau-Guiteras government, the U.S. authors of the book *Problems of the New Cuba* (Foreign Policy Association, 1935) wrote prophetically that when the nationalist tendencies of the Cuban middle classes merged with the socialist tendencies of the working class, the result would be a social revolution that would put an end to U.S. hegemony in Cuba.

Nevertheless, in 1933 the sectorial, economic-corporative interests of the working class and the middle class tended to predominate over the interests of society as a whole. And the sectorial interests of these classes, represented by their short-sighted ideologues and leaders, frustrated the realization of the national-popular, antiimperialist revolutionary project of the 1930s. Conditions for the unity of the Cuban people were not yet ripe.

The decisive process of proletarianization of the 1940s and 1950s contributed to a progressive deterioration of the defensive sectorial positions of the working class and the middle class. At the same time, many of the corporative demands and claims of the working class of the 1930s had been satisfied, to the point that Cuban workers in general enjoyed the best salaries and the most progressive social legislation in Latin America. But in factories with fewer than twenty workers all over the island, where proletarian organization was weakest, the fear of layoffs and the steady decline in real wages had the effect of mobilizing the workers against the dictatorship of the 1950s. In the interior of the country, what brought about unity from the beginning was a national-popular movement in which the people were represented, not as classes and not as a result of the autonomous organizing power of any of these but as a consequence of the collective aspirations of all the people. Thus, the workers did not participate in strike movements as such, that is, as a class aspiring to power, but as individuals, as an integral part of the people in their struggle against the dictatorship. The sugar workers' strike of December 1955, which originated in concrete class demands for payment of the differential wage, became a political strike against the dictatorship, led, significantly, by the student leader José Antonio Echeverría. The strikes called by the leadership of the July 26 Movement in September 1957, April 1958, and January 1959 were also political strikes in which workers participated as a part of the people, not as a class. The working class, consequently, did not play a vanguard, predominant role in the sense of leading the rest of the people against the dictatorship through their own class organizations, by themselves and for themselves. As the historian Vania Bambirra has pointed out, adhering to the postulate of Rosa Luxemburg, "It is not the mass strike that produces the revolution; it is the revolution that produces the mass strike" (Bambirra, 1979: 67–68).

The revolutionary situation among each of the classes that made up "the people" was the effective cause of the calls for strikes. Thus, exhortations for political strikes against the regime were issued by the national-popular revolutionary vanguard, not the worker vanguard. And the attempts to carry out a general strike in September 1957 and April 1958 were successful only in the towns of the interior but failed in Havana, fundamentally because of the differences in living conditions.

The destabilizing and deeply perturbing effect of the process of proletarianization created similar revolutionary conditions within the middle class, hard hit by the closure of small businesses and industries, leading to its mobilization against the dictatorship in the 1950s. The creation of a broad proletarianized sector tended to dissolve the strictly sectorial, class interests predominant during the 1930s. The threat of unemployment and recession and the progressive loss, at the hands of the dictatorship, of their historical social conquests mobilized these classes as a whole in the critical conjuncture of the 1950s. It was no longer a matter of each of these popular classes' making strictly class demands, as in the 1930s, but of their closely uniting in a national-popular front, confronting the dangers of the depressive economic cycle and the reactionary restoration of dictatorship. In these circumstances, a united political front that called for the overthrow of the dictatorship was born. The various classes accepted the minimal program of national-popular demands of the revolutionary organizations without making separate, special claims. What mattered, above all, was to overthrow the dictatorship that had tried to reverse the social gains of the Cuban people. The formulation of particular economic-corporative demands was left for a later moment.

Finally, since the urban working class, as a quantitatively small sector of the people, could not direct the national-popular movement, it was obliged to follow the lead of the majority. Nevertheless, the relatively privileged sectors of the working class, entrenched in and clinging to their particular interests, lagged behind with respect to the popular movement of opposition to the Batista dictatorship.

7

The Marginalization
of Women

In the slavery-based Cuban society of the nineteenth century, there were few "respectable" jobs for women and few "decent" women who worked for a wage or participated in paid activities. In the second half of that century, almost all university studies were closed to women, while in Europe and the United States women prepared themselves for all types of professions. The Cuban men of the times believed that women could only be seamstresses, laundresses, or in the best of cases teachers. Poor women had no alternatives. In the slavery-based society, as in the capitalist, rural women were expected to perform numerous tasks on the farm. The same attitude prevailed in the working-class home. Meanwhile, women of the dominant class devoted themselves to paying activities only when these were related to the family inheritance; widows administered businesses, plantations, and haciendas of their deceased husbands.

Beginning in the 1870s, some women found employment in commercial establishments and offices. They also began to find work in the tobacco industry in the less well paid jobs. The great majority devoted themselves to the traditional occupations of their sex and were ill paid in the marginally productive activities in which they were engaged. The abolition of slavery brought about the transformation of thousands of domestic slaves into servants paid absurdly low wages.

Women's work in the first decades of the twentieth century was still confined essentially to the home, as domestic servants or housewives. Until the 1950s women generally were admitted only to those occupations that were a social projection of household tasks. As Larguía and Dumoulin have pointed out, "It is not by chance that they are allowed to enter the textile and garment industries, the food and pharmaceutical industries, and the broad branch of services as nurses, manicurists, primary school teachers, secretaries, waitresses, and in the archetypical role of servant for any type of work" (Larguía and Dumoulin, 1973).

A principal observation for understanding the treatment meted out to women is that of Jürgen Kuczynski: Women occupy a status of pariah similar to that reserved for discriminated ethnic groups. Larguía and Dumoulin have given an apt description of the essence of women's exclusion: "The pariahs, as a whole, compose a second stratum within the working class that fulfills an important function for the system. Ill paid, they reduce the average wage, and their status constitutes a threat to the other workers, who could be replaced or fall to a lower wage level. Thus, discrimination of women helps to depress workers' wage." Of course, the specifics of the situation of women in Cuba and other underdeveloped countries of Latin America were linked to their role as part of the abundant labor reserves on which the capitalism of backward societies depends to force factory workers to produce more.

One of the most reliable indices for measuring the economic growth of countries of dependent capitalism is the incorporation of women into the workforce. In Cuba from 1899 to 1943, only 8.8% to 10.2% of women were occupied in moneymaking activities or sold their labor. Significantly, the proportion of black women employed in production dropped from 18.2% to 11.8%, which meant a decrease in absolute numbers from 48,767 to 44,982. Many of the new work opportunities opened to women during the period of the republic were limited to the service sector and especially employment in commercial establishments, a sphere in which black women were particularly discriminated against. The majority of job opportunities in this sector were monopolized by white women of the middle class; white women of humble extraction increased their presence in the labor sphere primarily in industries and manufacturing shops in the large cities. In this way their participation in the manufacturing sector grew from 16.6% to 19.6% between 1899 and 1943.

Essentially, women were admitted into the labor sectors traditionally occupied by men because of the desire of employers to depress wages. A survey carried out by the National Economic Council from May 1956 to April 1957 reveals that Cuban women of all ages received the lowest wages. Women between fourteen and twenty-four years old were particularly exploited on the basis of their lack of work experience. Of this group, 87.1% received less than $75 per month, whereas 82.6% of males of the same age group received this pay. Overall, 71.1% of working women earned less than $75; only 60.5% of males earned less than this amount. The industries that opened their doors to women for the purpose of reducing wages thus preferred young women ignorant of their labor rights. This study shows a sustained increase in the tendency to employ young black women. In 1899 the cohort between the ages of fifteen and twenty-four made up only 21.7% of the total women workers; by 1953 this proportion had grown to 36.3%.

The census of women workers in the tobacco industry in 1947 shows that 47.2% of the cigar labelers who were active in the industry and 37.8% of those who were inactive at the moment of the census were between ten and twenty-five years old. Another 27.2% of those who were active and 18.5% of the inactive were between twenty-six and thirty-five years. Significantly, 87.3% of the labelers were white, 10.7% were mestizas, and 2% were black.

One of the most notable differences between the work situation of white women and black women was in the relative discrimination of black women occupied in domestic service and in agricultural labor. From 1899 to 1943, their participation declined from 61.8% to 44.3% in domestic service and from 10.4% to just under 4% in sugarcane and other agricultural cultivation. At the same time, black women moved to jobs in urban industries, in which their participation rose from 10.3% to 36.3%, and professional services, where it grew from 1.1% to 12.9% in the same period.

These changes in the labor situation of black women provide evidence of their decision to escape the servile work traditionally associated with slavery by becoming part of the urban proletariat and entering professional activities. The emigration of black farmers and rural proletarians to cities, a process that followed the abolition of slavery and intensified with the establishment of the republic, allowed the urban industrial and commercial bourgeoisie an opportunity to contract cheap labor that kept wage levels low. It was under these circumstances that black women joined the ranks of the urban proletariat.

Racial discrimination, nevertheless, restricted the access of black women to the spheres of shops and offices. The presence of black women in this sector grew only from 0.3% in 1899 to 2.5% in 1943. Meanwhile, the representation of native white women in domestic service declined from 54.4% in 1899 to 15.2% in 1943. Despite the reduction in the number of white and black Cuban women in this sector, by 1953 the absolute number of domestic employees had grown to 20,723. Because the census for that year does not give statistics by race, it is impossible to determine the breakdown. Nevertheless, the employment of white women between 1899 and 1943 increased by 6.6% in commercial activities, 23.5% in professional services, and 18.7% in urban industrial activities.

The proportion of women workers by province confirms some of the tendencies already mentioned. The industrial and commercial development reached by the city of Havana from 1899 to 1953 enabled thousands of women emigrants from the countryside to find employment in the capital. Thus, the proportion of women in industrial production and commerce in Havana in this period grew from 12% to 22.9%. As a result of the war of 1895, the activity of tobacco plantations and the tobacco industry in Pinar del Río dwindled notably, as reflected in the census of 1899, which registered the lowest proportion of women working all over the island: 4.8%. In 1953, 25.3% of workers employed in agricultural and industrial activities linked to tobacco were women, the majority in Pinar del Río, which had the highest proportion of women workers among the economically active population in the entire republic. This employment in the rest of the provinces lagged behind Havana and Pinar del Río. Scant industrial development in Matanzas, Camagüey, and Oriente meant that the participation of women in the labor force in these provinces increased only slightly: in Matanzas by 1.3%, in Camagüey by 2.0%, and in Oriente by 7.3%.

Another variable that allows us to evaluate the situation of women in the social structure is literacy. According to census figures, in 1899, 70.4% of black women above ten years of age and 51.5% of white women of the same age could not read. Forty-four years later, 23.3% of black women and 19.8% of white women were illiterate. The educational advances of Cuban women, slowly and painfully achieved, were in great measure the result of women's desires for higher status in a society dominated by male values. Learning to read and write broadened prospects for thousands of women and helped them acquire consciousness of the subordinate positions they held within the family and at work, but it did not break down the barrier that separated them from men.

In 1899, 47.4% of white men and 51.5% of women above ten could not read, but the highest rate of illiteracy existed among black men, where it reached 73.8%, and among black women, at 70.4%. The authors of the census of 1899 explain this distinction by noting that men worked more in the country than in the city and that the opposite was true of women. Of course, this explanation did not take into account the need for black men to start working at an earlier age than black women. Progress in literacy among both men and women came about largely because of black families' concern for the cultural advancement of their descendants.

Aside from women's limited steps toward integration into certain sectors of production and raising their cultural level, the basic structural fact of this historical stage is that the proportion of women active in the workforce from 1899 to 1953 rose from only 8.8% to 13.7% of the female population over fourteen years of age, which numbered 1,376,672 women. Of these, 73.8% devoted all their time to domestic work in the home.

The socialization of women, their full integration into work and social life, remained an inaccessible and remote ideal in those years. Restricted to the narrow limits of the home, women could not participate in political and social decisions of the time. Although they shared with men the great aspirations and desires for national and social liberation, the privatization of their work in the home considerably reduced their possibilities of political and social action. The domestic labor of women determined in a fundamental way the direct reproduction of the workforce as well as the education of the new generation and the economic maintenance of the working-class home, yet the sociologic and economic theories in vogue did not consider this work the creator of economic, social, and cultural values. Thus, the subordinate role of women in society was justified, their essential contribution in the home, basic cell of the economic-social tissue of society, ignored. Their presence outside the home therefore had a passive and marginal character. Nevertheless, their will to distance themselves from work traditionally considered servile and their growing integration into the proletariat and intellectual activities showed that slowly and imperceptibly women were becoming aware of the social compartmentalization to which they were subjected. In the critical conjunctures of the 1930s and 1950s, the progressive attitude of women was translated into belligerent militancy in the feminist movement and the revolutionary vanguard. Signs that the traditional status of women was beginning to change were the approval of a divorce law in 1917 and the repeal in 1930 of article 437 of the penal code, which had permitted a husband to kill an unfaithful wife. On November 12, 1929, a law was introduced into the senate stipulating a minimum daily salary for women in industry amounting to $1.20. Although a militant feminist movement existed during the 1920s, these laws were passed by men in congress as a concession to women (Stoner, *From the House*, 1991: 83–99).

Decree law 589, passed October 19, 1934, recognized for women "equality in the right to work . . . with the exceptions established in the present law, with the right to receive, for the performance of similar work, the same salary or wage as a man." Among the exceptions were night work and dangerous or unhealthy occupations. The right to vote was conceded to women by a law of congress under Machado in 1931, but the Marxist Labor Union of Women opposed the dictatorship's manipulation of this demand of the feminist movement.

Feminists believed that "in spite of having approved women's right to vote, the Chamber of Representatives is frankly hostile to feminine demands. . . . When Cuba has a legitimate government, we will support the vote for women. We don't want a hollow right. We want to be free in every sense" (Domínguez Navarro, 1971: 223).

No preliminary study of social structure is possible without taking into account the situation of the strata that were discriminated against because of race or sex. The position in the social structure of these excluded strata was determined by class structure. It was not a matter, therefore, of attributing a role of exploiter to men or of considering women incapable of carrying out given functions but of evaluating to what extent the subordinate situation of these strata was the result of a policy of the ruling classes. If this link existed, then the liberation of women would lie in their complete integration with full rights and duties into a new society. Obviously, for this to happen it was essential to eliminate the petty domestic economy that kept women secluded at home.

In the conditions of growing unemployment and scant industrial development inherent in neocolonial society, the seclusion of women in the home acquired a more generalized character in backward and dependent societies than in developed capitalist countries. Discrimination against women was justified by the lack of work opportunities in the country, but the proportion, relative to men, by which they gradually incorporated themselves into productive work showed that they had always been the object of discrimination in access to such work. Of course, even when developed capitalist societies could hypothetically solve the problem of women's employment, that would not by any means signify women's liberation, since they would continue to be exploited as workers.

The situation of discrimination against the black population grew out of the old racist practices of the colonial slaveholding society and the deficient process of integration following the creation of the republic. The full incorporation of the black population into society, a right it had earned during the country's wars of independence, was impeded by racist political leaders and the domination of the dependent bourgeoisie and U.S. financial capital. Thus, the segregation of blacks, like that of women, was a product of the policy of the ruling classes and deeply rooted tradition. Inasmuch as the discrimination against both women and blacks affected close to 70% of the citizenry, it constituted one of the most significant phenomena deriving from the social structure. The black population was harder hit than the white by the increasing unemployment and the process of proletarianization. As lower-middle-class and black families sank further and further into poverty, young women found themselves obliged to seek the most diverse forms of employment to help balance the economic situation at home.

The issue of women's role in society and civil rights equal to those of men was first presented by Ana Betancourt de Mora at the Guaimaro constitutional convention, held during Cuba's first war of independence (1868–1878). In the same way that Cuban men had emancipated slaves, she said, they were bound to liberate women and "dedicate their generous souls to women's rights." Her reason for expecting this new attitude was linked to the fact that "women who today and in wartime are their sisters of charity, even while they are denied their rights, will tomorrow be men's exemplary companions" (Sarabia, 1970: 55). The Cuban patriots at the Guaimaro convention, however—believing that women had reaffirmed their social role by joining the Cuban liberation army, thereby proving that they were faithful to their husbands and fathers—saw no need for the representation of women separate from that of men, and so the convention did not address the question of women's rights. During the Ten Years' War (1868–1878), the community of Cuban émigrés had aided the Cuban revolutionary cause through its numerous organizations, including women's clubs in New York and New Orleans. The principal women's club was founded by Emilia Casanovas de Villaverde to raise funds for the cause of Cuban independence.

Toward the end of Cuba's third war of independence (1895–1898), of 299 clubs of Cuban émigrés in the United States working for Cuban independence, forty-nine were women's revolutionary organizations. Like the men's organizations, they collected money and bought weapons, medicine, and clothes for the Cuban liberation army. According to historian Paul Estrade, nowhere else in the world (except in Scandinavia) could women assemble, deliberate, organize themselves, and vote as the Cuban women émigrés did in their clubs. In October 1896 the leaders of the women's club Daughters of Liberty petitioned the Cuban revolutionary government to give women the right to vote in the future republic, but the Patriotic Council at Key West, which was asked to transmit the petition, said that it did not have sufficient authority to act on the matter. With that the issue apparently died (Estrade, 1986: 16–20, 33). The Cuban constitution promulgated in 1901 did not alter the legal colonial status of women: They were denied the right to the equal civil status in society that they had earned during thirty years of struggle, fighting side by side with men, against Spanish colonialism and for Cuban independence.

Women played an important role in their country's wars of

independence as active collaborators of their fathers, husbands, and brothers on diverse political fronts in the émigré community and in the urban clandestine movement and rural battle areas of their homeland. They also assumed roles as heads of family in the hard and uncertain conditions imposed by the war that took tens of thousands of men away from their homes, as they were deported, exiled, or joined the Cuban liberation army. These circumstances changed the status of women, heightening their prestige in Cuban society. Motherhood brought power, not the devalued servility it had meant in the old patriarchal family. The new link between mothers and sons increased women's centrality and authority in the Cuban family. Women's power as heads of family while men fought for independence was based on their effective autonomy in this new situation. The process of socialization that took place within Cuban families made women the subject of a new cultural type of relationship. From then on, women not only transmitted traditions to their descendants but created values. They endured the hardships of war, clandestine activities, and emigration because of their respect and submission to the patriarchal head of the family, but as they consecrated and sacrificed their lives to their husbands and descendants, they were giving birth to a new type of family. At the same time that they reproduced the old values of the patriarchy, they made clear their aspirations for a different relationship to men that generated in women the capacity to transcend their status as a subordinate gender group through a feminist ideology and project.

Historians have asked themselves why Cuban women did not demand their rights during the first two decades of the republic and why Cuban men did not concede them the rights they had so clearly earned. According to historian K. Lynn Stoner, Cuban statesmen believed the building of a new nation demanded above all order and tranquility. The executive and legislative branches of government were concerned primarily with "matters of statehood and determining ruling order." The first Cuban governments had to cope with separating church and state, secularizing education, providing jobs for a needy middle class, pacifying the marginalized black population, and defending itself from armed interventions by the United States. Women's issues thus "remained peripheral to the building of a new state" (Stoner, *From the House,* 1991: 34). But the postponement of women's claims did not depend only on the attitudes of Cuban statesmen and legislators. Women shared the concerns of men about the state of affairs in the republic. But the decisive motive behind their inaction seems to have been that they were obliged to confront a precarious economic situation within their homes similar to what they had experienced in the past. The domestic economy in most homes was as unstable as before, and women again had to assume the responsibility of bringing up their children, whereas men were primarily concerned with finding work. This complex situation restrained women from demanding a revision of existing patriarchal relations within the Cuban family. By the 1920s the increasing loss of patriotic ideals seems to have worsened the position of women in their families still further as men demanded more power and showed constantly less respect for women. The novels of Carrión, Loveira, Ramos, and Castellanos bear witness to the growing disintegration of Cuban families and the fragile situation of women during the critical decade of the 1920s.

At the beginning of the twentieth century, however, men had facilitated the integration of women into teaching, one of the most influential professions in society, since teachers and professors exert a profound impact on the ideological outlook of the new generations. Recognizing women's natural influence on children, many leaders supported the entrance of women into teaching, thus helping them to regain the prestige they had won in the revolutionary past. Soon women virtually monopolized the profession. From 1899 to 1943, the number of women teachers grew from 1,502 to 16,780. By 1953 the total had reached 34,845. In 1899 women constituted 56% of all teachers and professors; by 1919 the proportion reached 72.8%. In 1943 it was 70.6% and in 1953, 81%. This was by far the occupational category in which women most consistently increased their participation. Nevertheless, the presence of women also rose steadily in other white-collar jobs (professionals, clerks, and employees), from 2,401 in 1899 to 11,079 in 1919 and 61,352 in 1943. These working women made up an articulate and powerful group that would lead the struggles to change the status of women in the 1920s and 1930s. Although the number of black women in teaching grew steadily, the profession was represented mainly by white women. The leaders of the feminist groups were also white women from the middle class, distributed fairly evenly among the different tendencies in the Cuban political spectrum. This augmented their influence among the most diverse and antagonistic political groups, which enabled them to push ahead the feminist cause. Meanwhile, middle-class white leaders represented the demands of women workers. What they sought for black and poor workers, however, was help, not power or representation (Stoner, *From the House*, 1991: 171). The birth of the feminist movement is closely related to the creation of the Feminine Club on July 3, 1917, under the presidency of Emma López Oña and the secretaryship of Pilar Jorge de Tella. On April 1, 1918, feminist leader Carmen

Velacorado de Lara, director of the literary magazine *Aspiraciones*, expounded to the Cuban congress the justice of women's claims to the right to vote in Cuban electoral processes (Primelles, 1955: 463–465).

Soon, the Liberal and Popular political parties were campaigning for women's suffrage. As it became clear that their adversaries were going to be currying women's favor in the elections, male politicians co-opted the feminist demand for women's right to vote. In the difficult 1920s, politicians began to bargain for women's support at the same time that new organizations appeared on the political and social stage, with industrialists, students, workers, and women advancing their claims for the first time, forcing traditional and new political groups to heed them.

In 1918, with the only organized opposition that of the Catholic church, a law authorizing divorce was passed. The Cuban press, with the exception of *Diario de la Marina*, supported the law without reserve. In the senate the vote was ninety to ten in favor and in the chamber of representatives sixty-three to seventeen. Most Cuban politicians were either nonreligious or influenced by Freemasonry, which contradicted church doctrine on the divorce question.

Behind those reforms was the pressure of the growing feminist movement of the 1920s. By that time the feminists had organized two congresses, in 1923 and 1925, attended by the most important politicians, including the heads of two national political parties, Alfredo Zayas and Gerardo Machado, the latter of whom was not yet the bloody dictator he was to become. Although Machado promised at the 1925 congress to favor women's demands, he later left the question up to congressional decision, washing his hands of the controversial issue.

In the revolutionary 1930s, women played a vanguard role, a circumstance that helped to bring about reforms and that arose from women's will to work with men, not against them, demanding their rightful share in society. In order to change patriarchal authority by degrees, they pointed out that Hispanic patriarchal values stressed the obligation of men to care for women and children. In contrast to radical American and European feminists, Cuban women did not challenge men's authority but joined men in order to strengthen the values of womanhood. According to the patriarchy, women should be the inspirers of men's attitudes, not an ungovernable driving force.

By the 1940s Cuban legislation on women's rights (divorce, maternity, and equal civil rights) was among the most advanced in the Western world. Even some leftist feminist leaders in the 1940s were optimistic about the trend toward improvement in gender relations.

They admitted that the 1940 constitution granted women equality with men in the home and were pleased that a few women held high political positions. But these achievements did not mean that women had attained true justice. The great majority of women continued to be subject to the restrictions that had been imposed on them in the past. In some measure, then, it was of little help to them that Cuba had enacted such progressive legislation regarding women, since they were deprived of most of their supposed rights both in their places of work and at home. Cuban women may have had the right to receive the same pay as men for the same work, but most did not have a job or received the lowest pay if they did.

8

Race and
Social Stratification

The existence of a policy tending to isolate Afro-Cubans from the principal decisions affecting the nation initially became evident during the first U.S. intervention, with the establishment of a new armed forces institution to replace the Cuban liberation army. As the census of 1899 indicates, of 4,824 soldiers and police, 794 were black. In the 1907 census only 1,178 of the 8,238 members of the armed forces were black. By 1917 the composition of the army varied slightly; of 16,238 soldiers and police, 4,200 were black. Although 60% of the soldiers of the Cuban liberation army were black, they were prevented from taking part in the new republican institutions until 1959. From the time of the first U.S. intervention, Cuban authorities sanctioned such old customs and racist practices as not allowing blacks or mulattos to stroll in the parks of some towns and cities, attend certain theaters or artistic performances, enter certain hotels and recreation centers, and so on. It was extremely difficult for black students to enter the University of Havana: In 1899 only 6% of the country's professionals were black; in 1907, 7%; and in 1919, under 12%.

In the same way that white Cubans were discriminated against in the workplace in favor of Spaniards, white workers were favored over black workers. The colonialist policy of excluding blacks from jobs in clothing stores, shoe shops, jewelry shops, and eating establishments was maintained. Any contact between the well-to-do and blacks was avoided in elegant establishments. This discrimination was applied as well in administrative and technical jobs in U.S. companies, telephone and telegraph companies, electric companies, sugar mills, and so on. Most employees in public offices of the state were also white. The hardest and worst-paid jobs, meanwhile, were reserved for the black population. Aside from certain artisanlike occupations in which they had traditionally worked since the colonial era (as bakers, carpenters, tailors, blacksmiths, laundresses, shoemakers) and work-ing-class activities in which they had mastered some processes of pro-duction (as in cigar making), the work assigned to blacks was always the most menial. There was, for example, a high proportion of blacks among urban bakers and construction workers, and stevedores were almost exclusively black. The rural proletariat, the most exploited in the country, was also made up essentially of blacks.

The division enshrined in Cuban society by neocolonial racism could have created a consciousness of a national group or of a nation apart as did the revivalist movement headed in the United States by Marcus Garvey, which won tens of thousands of followers among black men and women who saw an escape from their dire situation through a return to the African continent. In Cuba, however, the strong links of solidarity created among the people in the course of their epic struggles for national independence withstood the racist practices designed to disintegrate Cuban society. A movement known as the Independents of Color, although it represented a breakdown in national solidarity provoked in great measure by the system of racism, had the same aims as those for which the founders of the nation, from Céspedes to Martí, had fought: to give blacks the same rights as whites.

The black and mulatto petty bourgeoisie who formed these "col-ored" societies, contributed still further to their own social compart-mentalization, though the societies attracted as well the most enlight-ened of the marginalized ethnic groups. The economic situation of the black petty bourgeoisie scarcely mitigated the discrimination directed against it. In receiving different treatment, it was subjected to a more refined form of discrimination, with the aim of keeping it separated from the rest of the black population. The higher earnings of its members and their relative independence from exploitation by the dependent white bourgeoisie made their existence more endurable.

From 1898 to 1958, the black working population moved away from jobs linked to agriculture and mining toward a tertiary sector, increasing their representation in professional services, especially in transport and commerce. Black workers also reduced their presence in industry and domestic service but to a lesser degree than the groups previously mentioned. Thus, from 1899 to 1943 their repre-sentation in urban industries declined from 41.5% to 35.9% and in domestic service from 50.3% to 46.9%; in agriculture and mining it fell from 33.8% to 23%. The number of black workers in transport and commerce rose from 9.5% to 22.9%. By 1943, 44.2% of these workers were employed in construction, the occupational sector in which they were most represented. Table 8.1 shows black representation in the basic occupational groups. The concentration of black workers in construction and domestic and personal services stands out clearly, as does their lesser presence in occupations related to banking, finances, commerce, professional services, government, and communications, where white workers were preferred.

Table 8.2 shows the racial component within occupational levels. Black workers are a clear minority among professionals, urban proprietors, managers, high-level employees, owners, and administrators of farms. The almost equal representation of blacks and mulattos compared to whites among some groups of skilled workers is the result of their preponderance in artisan occupations (carpentry, mechanics, etc.) since colonial days, when white workers considered physical labor a disgrace because of its association with work performed by slaves. Their greater number among unskilled laborers is due to the fact that the classification includes construction, in which the representation of the black working population was very high. The same compartmentalization is seen in Table 8.3, based on data from the census of 1943, in which those surveyed were asked if they were proprietors, self-employed workers, or simply workers. The difference in

Table 8.1 Population Structure in the Economy by Race, 1943

	Whites (%)	Blacks (%)
Agriculture, cattle raising, fishing	77.0	23.0
Mining	67.0	33.0
Construction	55.8	44.2
Manufacturing and machine industries	64.1	35.9
Transport and communications	77.1	22.9
Commerce	84.1	15.9
Banking and finance	90.8	9.2
Domestic and personal services	53.1	46.9
Recreational and similar services	60.3	39.7
Professional services	85.5	14.5
Government	80.7	19.3
Diverse services	72.0	28.0
Unclassified industry and commerce	73.5	26.5
Total	74.1	25.9

Source: Census of 1943.

Table 8.2 Population Structure, Occupation, and Race, 1943

	Whites (%)	Blacks (%)
Professionals and semiprofessionals	81.8	12.2
Farmers and farm administrators	77.2	22.8
Owners, managers, and high-level employees	84.9	15.1
Office-workers, salespeople, and similar	84.0	15.9
Skilled workers	58.5	41.5
Unskilled workers	63.8	36.2
Protection-service employees	80.1	19.9
Personal-service employees	66.1	33.9
Agricultural workers	73.3	26.7
Total	74.1	25.9

Source: Census of 1943.

Table 8.3 Population Structure by Percentage of Proprietors, Workers, and the Self-Employed, by Nationality and Race, 1943

	Proprietors (%)	Workers (%)	Self-Employed (%)
White Cubans	8.1	43.4	48.5
Black Cubans	4.9	43.4	51.7
White foreigners	18.0	32.0	50.0
Black foreigners	11.1	26.5	62.4

the proportion of proprietors in the various ethnic groups is important, since the absolute number of these was considerable. The percentage distribution of the labor force according to monthly income by race in 1943 reveals the subordinate position of blacks on the wage scale and as independent producers. With respect to unemployment, Table 8.4, compiled from 1943 census data, gives a clearer idea of how this affected black workers.

The situation of the rural black population did not differ significantly from that of the urban black population. According to the census of 1899, of the areas cultivated on working farms 40.7% were owned and 44.2% rented by whites, making a total of 84.9% of farms occupied by whites (see Tables 8.5 and 8.6). Black farmers owned only 2.8% of the farms and rented 8.2%. By 1931, areas cultivated on

Table 8.4   Employment, by Nationality and Race, 1943

	Employed (%)	Unemployed (%)
Cubans		
White	73.97	26.07
Black	68.75	32.25
Foreigners		
White	75.60	24.40
Black	70.77	29.23

Source: Census of 1943.

Table 8.5   Percentage of Area Cultivated by Whites Versus Blacks as Landowners and Tenants, 1899 and 1931

	% Cultivated Area	
	1899	1931
Whites		
Owners	40.7	50.4[a]
Tenants and sharecroppers	44.2	42.5
Blacks		
Owners	2.8	4.6[a]
Tenants and sharecroppers	8.2	2.7

a. Includes administrators.
Sources: Census of 1899: 555–556; Census of 1931: 37.

Table 8.6   Number of Farms Cultivated by White Versus Black Owners and Tenants, 1899 and 1931

	Number of Farms	
	1899	1931
White owners	13,898	37,815
White tenants and sharecroppers	29,737	29,334
Black owners	3,092	5,297
Black tenants and sharecroppers	11,247	4,950
Mixed occupation	2,737	—
Total	60,711	77,396

Source: Census of 1899 and 1931.

farms by whites had risen to 92.9%, of which 50.4% were cultivated by owners and 42.5% by tenants and sharecroppers. The participation of black farmers, both Cuban and Antillean, in cultivation of the land had diminished to only 7.1% of the areas, of which 4.6% were cultivated by owners and 3.7% by tenants and sharecroppers.

The percentage of cultivated surface held by white owners increased by 39.7% from 1899 to 1931, whereas the surface cultivated by black owners increased by only 1.8%. The surface cultivated by white tenants and sharecroppers declined by 1.7%; that cultivated by black tenants and sharecroppers declined by 5.5%.

Some results of the census of 1899 have been criticized because of the state of confusion regarding property that supposedly existed at the end of the war of 1895. The figures can be corrected only after close examination of the original records. The census of 1931 is in my view as reliable as other calculations carried out in the republican period; its conclusions are congruent with previous and subsequent census results. In any event, what is important for a study of the situation of blacks in the labor force is that the results of both the census of 1899 and that of 1931 concur in showing the underprivileged situation of the black farmer relative to that of the white farmer.

Another source of information is the rural investigation carried out by sociologist Lowry Nelson of the U.S. Department of State in 1946. But as a number of scholars have shown, this study does not accurately represent the critical situation of the rural masses. Nevertheless, Nelson's chart of the distribution by race and type of land occupancy in 1946 coincides with the Cuban censuses in making it clear that the black population scarcely had access to ownership of the land (see Table 8.7).

Table 8.7   Occupation Distribution of 734 Cuban Farmers, by Race, 1946

Type of Occupancy	Total		White		Mulatto		Black	
	Number	%	Number	%	Number	%	Number	%
All groups	734	100.0	642	100.0	47	100.0	45	100.0
Proprietors	182	24.8	166	25.9	13	27.7	3	6.0
Tenants	212	28.9	199	31.0	9	19.1	4	8.0
Sharecroppers	167	22.8	134	20.9	18	38.3	15	33.3
Laborers	173	23.6	143	22.2	7	14.9	23	51.1

Source: Nelson, 1950.

Nelson himself, after pointing out some limitations deriving from the sample he used—such as the fact that the sample areas were selected primarily by the type of cultivation as well as the small number of blacks and mulattos registered in the regions—emphasized its validity in suggesting that landownership was as common among mulattos as among whites. Proportionally, there were many fewer tenants and more sharecroppers among mulattos compared to whites. The black group was concentrated fundamentally in the categories of sharecroppers and rural proletarians, in which they surpassed whites. All these data testified to the growing proletarianization of blacks in the rural areas of the country. With the abolition of slavery, Cuban blacks, unlike Brazilian blacks or blacks of the southern U.S. Cotton Belt, did not become sharecroppers but were obliged to sell their labor. The critical economic situation endured by the black population had a particularly severe impact on its mortality rate, as indicated in Table 8.8.

The extent to which Afro-Cubans felt excluded during the first decades of neocolonial life was demonstrated not only by the existence of political organizations such as the Independents of Color and the societies exclusively for blacks and mulattos that were founded in the nineteenth century but also by their reluctance to accept values, norms, and institutions of Hispanic origin, alien to those of their original culture. The degree of political and cultural integration of blacks into the new republican society can be measured in large part by their acceptance of the cultural patterns that guided family life in neocolonial society. Legal recognition of descendants and marriages sanctioned by law were cultural and institutional mores of European origin that the black population ignored in the first decades of the twentieth century, then gradually accepted as they became convinced that doing so promised positive social

Table 8.8 Proportion of Deaths per 1,000 Inhabitants, by Race, 1907–1943

	Whites	Blacks
1907	15.30	19.50
1919	9.17	19.46
1931	9.48	12.12
1943	9.50	11.65

Sources: Census of 1919: 255; Census of 1931: 286; *Boletín Oficial de Salubridad y Asistencia Social,* 1943–1944, vol. 41.

consequences for children and spouses. Until well into the 1940s, blacks did not recognize to the same degree as did whites the convenience of these norms of family life and until then abided by the values of their original culture.

According to the censuses, the proliferation of illegitimate children increased tenfold among whites and fourfold among blacks between 1899 and 1943, with an equal proportion of illegitimate children for both races in the latter year. Thus, 126,090 illegitimate black children were recorded for 1899, 68.1% of the total; the figure for white children was 58,940, or 31.9% of the total. In 1943, however, the percentage of illegitimate children was approximately the same for both races, with 606,951, or 50.3% of the total, among whites and 600,500, or 49.7% of the total, among blacks. The proportion of Afro-Cubans legally married or united by common consent varied significantly between 1899 and 1943. In 1899, 28% of black couples were legally married and 72% united by common consent; in 1943, 84.6% were reported as legally married and only 15.1% united without legal sanction.

The black population further showed its desire for integration into republican society by embracing education. Between 1899 and 1943, the percentage of literate Afro-Cubans rose from 28% to 67.4%. The white population increased its participation among the literate sectors of society by 25.9% from 1899 to 1943, whereas the black Cuban population increased its presence in these sectors by 39.4% in the same period. Thus, in 1943 the literate black population reached 67.4%, and the literate white population totaled 72.6%. The relation by province between the literate white and the literate black population in 1943 is shown in Table 8.9. Apparently, the regional variations in this respect were the result of educational opportunities and the treatment accorded the black population in the different provinces. In any event, Afro-Cubans showed a tendency to improve themselves

Table 8.9   Percentage of the Literate White and Literate Black Populations, by Province, 1943

	Pinar del Río	Habana	Matanzas	Las Villas	Camagüey	Oriente
Literate whites	63.1	81.5	75.7	70.9	73.1	65.2
Literate blacks	60.4	80.0	77.6	72.9	61.7	57.9

Source: Census of 1943.

similar to that of whites and to become a part of society with equal cultural conditions.

Following the abolition of slavery and the subsequent founding of the republic of Cuba, the Afro-Cuban population declined in the western region of the island, as agricultural workers set the pace for the general west-to-east population shift that accompanied the transfer of the greater part of sugar production to the provinces of Oriente and Camagüey. Thus, from 1899 to 1919 the proportion of blacks decreased in the western provinces of Pinar del Río, Matanzas, and Las Villas and increased in the two above-mentioned eastern provinces. The crisis and stagnation that began in 1928 brought about a reversal in Afro-Cuban migration trends, as black workers from Oriente and Camagüey increasingly migrated to Havana (Schwartz, 1979).

Some scholars believe that the quantitative increase in the number of blacks working in different professions and occupations by 1943 revealed their effective economic integration into society. They do not take into account, however, the proportion of blacks to whites in the different occupations or how many of them had stable employment. In fact, their employment rate decreased from 1899 on. The 1943 census reported 31% of blacks and 25% of whites unemployed. The census tables did not register underemployment within the black population. Cuban scholars have calculated that some 80% of blacks were either unemployed or underemployed—that is, they were proletarianized. The increasing number of Afro-Cubans without jobs did nothing to create a working-class mentality in the proletariat, nor did the low wages earned by blacks help to promote their self-esteem. Whereas 88% of blacks received wages lower than $60 a month, 79% of whites were in that wage category.

The segregation and marginalization of blacks contributed to the division of the Cuban people from 1898 to 1933. Thus, in the first two decades of the twentieth century Cubans of Spanish descent and those of African descent took separate paths. The crisis of 1933 brought them together again. It also introduced on the Cuban historical stage urban and rural masses with clear classist demands (Portuondo, 1979). In other words, the Cuban nation, created by the struggles of Cuban patriots in the nineteenth century, was on its feet again. The union of its various racial constituents made possible the building of the Cuban nation.

The numerous racial conflicts that arose during the 1930s reveal the tensions aroused by the gradually changing status of blacks. At the same time that their aspirations drove blacks to rebel against old discriminatory practices, the fears of the white authorities led them quickly to repress any signs of discontent. As blacks and mulattos fought for equality of opportunity and treatment, antagonisms mounted. Their competition for social positions threatened the country's traditional relationships in which nonwhites were expected to "know their place."

At this time, and in view of the fact that blacks had taken part in the struggles against the oligarchic Machado regime, a cultural movement arose that expressed their deepest feelings. The *negrista* literary movement was founded by Ramón Guirao, José Zacarias Tallet, Emilio Ballegas, Alejo Carpentier, and Nicolás Guillén, and its sociological rationale was supplied by the scientific research of Fernando Ortiz and Lydia Cabrera. The most distinguished musicians of the time, Rolando García Caturla and Amadeo Roldán, also joined the *negrista* movement, whose important role in Cuban culture from 1925 to 1935 stimulated the rise of blacks in Cuban social and political life.

The peculiar way in which blacks participated in the revolutionary movement of the 1930s, expressing their demands both as workers and as part of the Cuban people, as blacks as well as Cubans, gives evidence of their diverse conflicts in society. Cuban blacks were confronted by a threefold contradiction: They were subject to discrimination as a racial minority, to exploitation as members of the working class, and to marginalization as members of the unemployed, proletarianized masses, isolated from the country's productive forces. They were by far the most rejected, exploited, and marginalized group in society. Nevertheless, the most relevant aspects of black participation in the 1930s were their demands as members of the working class and as blacks. By that time, the emigration of blacks from the provinces to Havana had increased considerably, and blacks took part, mainly in Havana, in voicing their economic claims. By 1943 more than one-third of all Afro-Cubans employed in manufacturing and 45% of those working in the building industry lived in the capital. Thus, the demands for more recognition, higher wages, and better working conditions that characterized the workers' movement in the 1930s and 1940s were backed by Afro-Cubans as members of the working class (Schwartz, 1979).

The most prominent union leaders in the 1940s and 1950s were Jesús Menéndez, Lázaro Peña, and Juan Taquechel, who were well known and admired not only as champions of workers' rights but also as Afro-Cuban leaders. Their commitment to their unions did not lessen their popularity, and they gathered many adherents during electoral campaigns. In general, the Afro-Cubans voted for black candidates at election time, but many were bribed or coerced to vote for caudillos. As Cuban society moved away from a *caudillista* to a populist political foundation, blacks abandoned their traditional political affiliations to join the populist parties and the minority Communist Party.

Afro-Cuban representation in congress increased in the populist era. In 1904, of sixty-three congressmen, only four were blacks; in 1945, of 131 congressmen, seventeen were blacks, although the proportion of blacks in the Cuban population decreased from 32.2% in 1899 to 25.2% in 1943 (Helg, 1995: 128; Pérez, 1988: 306). By 1945, moderate Jorge Mañach, liberal Carleton Beals, and Communist Juan Marinello concurred that the majority of the Cuban population was racially and culturally mixed.

The 1940 constitutional convention responded to the changes that had taken place in Afro-Cubans' political status. The proceedings and minutes of the convention reveal that the most progressive constitutional articles were conceived and approved by the populists and the Communist Party, with the opposition of the traditional liberal and conservative *caudillista* parties. According to the leftist intellectual Raúl Roa, "The new political parties, in particular, the Auténticos, Communists, and Abecedarios, imposed their progressive doctrinal orientations as far as political, economic, racial, and cultural matters were concerned" (Roa, 1982: 71). When article 23, forbidding racial discrimination, was debated at the 1940 constitutional convention, the populist Auténtico and Communist vote assured its passage without alterations. In the 1950s Afro-Cubans, still little represented in the best-paid jobs, were condemned mostly to poorly paid and less prestigious employment. Black workers who obtained good jobs and salaries in large industries and the public service sector followed the attitude of that privileged proletarian strata, whereas those who worked in small manufacturing and craft industry shops, finding themselves unemployed most of the time, joined their fellow workers in the revolutionary movements.

In general, in the 1950s blacks participated in the revolutionary movement not as blacks or as workers but as a part of the humblest strata of the revolutionary masses. Rather than making special class or racial claims, they joined the popular movement inspired by the revolutionary program of the July 26 Movement and of the Revolutionary Directorate that promised economic benefits to the lower strata of the population. The populist character of political alignments, not based on strictly class or racial demands, encouraged Afro-Cubans to support the revolutionary movement as a part of the people, not as workers or as blacks. They opposed the Batista dictatorship because of its reactionary, antipopulist nature and joined the revolutionary movement because of its progressive character. They were thus strongly represented in the revolutionary movement, especially in the rebel army in Oriente Province.

9

Generations in Conflict

One of the most dramatic issues in the social history of republican Cuba is that of the relation between the generations and the social structure. Traditional historiography has limited itself to formulating some generalizations about the subject, lacking a sociological foundation and a quantitative base. At the same time, a reductionist conception of Marxism has served to invalidate the very concept of generational analysis. Ironically, it was Marx, one of the first social scientists, who defined the role of generations in history. According to Marx: "History is no more than the succession of generations, each one of which exploits the materials, capital and productive forces transmitted by those who have preceded it; that is, on the one hand, it continues the preceding activities in completely different conditions, while on the other, it modifies the preceding circumstances by means of a totally different activity" (Marx, 1965: 47). Of course, Marx is referring here to the innovative essence of the generations in relation to the history of production, but what he postulated with respect to the economic structure of society is perhaps even more applicable to the actions of the generations on the superstructural plane, where transformations frequently acquire a more abrupt and radical character.

The role that has been attributed to the generations in the republican historical process has given rise to a variety of conceptual errors and misunderstandings. On the one hand, the role of protagonist has been assigned to the generations in isolation from social determinants. On the other hand, their part in history has been radically impugned with the argument that only classes fulfill a transforming function in society. Only by taking into consideration that the generation is above all a historical category, whereas the class is essentially a sociological category, can we elude this dilemma. Nevertheless, both

153

the generation and the class are complementary analytical categories in the diachronic and synchronic processes of society.

Recent studies have helped clarify the relations between generation and class. Generational conflicts, according to this new perspective, constitute "a metamorphosed form" of class conflicts. In reality, the generational conflict cannot be reduced to or identified with the class conflict. It is therefore necessary to analyze the social self-determination of the generations in their historical specificity.

Positivist and Hegelian historiography, inspired by the works of its founders, was interested only in the political and literary generations and disdained examining the so-called material generations, constituted by the totality of the individuals who are born, live, and die at a given time, since their study was the responsibility "only of statisticians." Unlike Marx, who established a dialectical relation between the sectors making up a generation, the positivist scholars stressed the distinction between the thinking generation and the material generation (Portuondo, 1981: 39–46).

Among the most important questions concerning the period 1898–1958 are how the new generations exerted an influence on the country's workforce and how many of them did not find work. Thus, in 1907 some 242,114 young males were between fifteen and twenty-five, a cohort that constituted 34.4% of men of working age. Of these, 16,578 (6.8%) had no paid occupation. Of this last group, 9,683 attended school, leaving only 6,895, or 2.9% of the total, without paid employment. According to the census of 1919, some 259,590 males reached the ages of fourteen to twenty-five that year, 44,364 (17.2%) of whom had no paid occupation. Of these last, 23,258 were students, which meant 21,106 (8.1% of the total) were without jobs. Altogether, the young men in this age group represented 28.6% of the male workforce.

The census of 1931 showed that some 300,574 males made up the group between the ages of fourteen and twenty-five, or 30% of the men of working age. Approximately 87,846 had no paid occupation. Of these, some 17,892 were studying, leaving some 69,954 without paid jobs, 23.2% of the total (though this census was made in the dead season, when juvenile unemployment tended to be higher). In the census of 1953 (carried out in the harvest season), 593,007 young men between fourteen and twenty-four years of age were recorded, of whom 184,958 had no paid occupation. Of the latter, 102,802 were students, so that 82,156, or 14% of the total, were unemployed. The young men in this age group represented 21% of the male workforce.

To repeat, then, the young men without paid employment reached 6,895 in 1907, 21,106 in 1919, 69,954 in 1931, and 82,156 in

1953. A human contingent was progressively formed that had no access to work and faced common problems. The percentage of unemployed among the group of young men reaching working age in 1907 was 2.9% of the total; in 1919, 8.1%; in 1931, 23.2%; and in 1953, 14%. The decline in the percentage of unemployed youth in 1953 with relation to 1931 is explained by the fact that in contrast to the others the census of 1953 was made in the harvest season and classified young men only between the ages of fourteen and twenty-four years, not between fourteen and twenty-five. Another point to be considered about the census of 1953 is that a considerable number of persons who worked without receiving remuneration appear together with those who did receive wages in the column "working with or without pay." Because this does not allow us to determine the number of young men without a paid occupation, as we were able to do in the other censuses, we can assume that the percentage of young men without paid work was considerably higher than the 14% figure we reached by taking into account only those who, according to the census, "were not working last week," were "working without pay for a relative," or were "looking for work" (Census of 1953: table 43). Finally, the unemployment created by the sugar restriction had not reached the dimensions in 1953 that it would have in the following years.

These estimates give us an idea of the particularly acute way in which unemployment among young people increased over the years. These figures show the demographic and economic bases of the generations that followed in the first fifty years of republican life and suggest the access to jobs of the different age groups. The relative peace in the first decades of the century is explained in part by the stability in work opportunities for young people. In the critical decade that culminated with the revolution of 1933, the new generations found no such secure place in neocolonial society. The active participation of youth in the student and social struggles of the 1930s and 1950s is due in great measure to the lack of work stability for these generational groups.

The survey by the National Economic Council from 1956 to 1957 underscores the dimensions of unemployment in the 1950s. The tables, by ages, of this survey give an exact image of the differences between the economic and social situation of the young generation of workers and that of the preceding generations. The difference in monthly earnings between the young men of fourteen to twenty-four years and those of other age groups reveals the instability that affected the younger group. According to this survey, in the group from fourteen to twenty-four years, 83.6% received less than $75; in the group from twenty-five to thirty-four years, 58.8%; in the group from thirty-five to forty-four years, 58.2%; and in the group forty-five years or older, 55.2%.

The differences in occupational status—the permanent or temporary character of work—of the various age groups further reflect the precarious situation of youth. Using the data from table 46 of the census of 1953, I determined that those who had worked from forty to fifty-two weeks of the year were to be classified as permanent workers, whereas those who had worked fewer than forty weeks of the year were to be considered temporary workers. In this way, I found that of the workforce between fourteen and twenty-four years, 65.2% had been temporary workers in 1952 and only 34.8% had had permanent jobs. For those between twenty-five and thirty-four years, 54.7% had temporary jobs and 45.3% permanent employment. In the age group from thirty-four to forty-four years, 53.5% had temporary work and 46.7% had steady work the greater part of the year. Finally, of those between forty-five and forty-nine years of age, 51.6% had worked on a temporary basis and 48.4% had had permanent employment.

Estimates of the high levels of unemployment and underemployment after the end of the worst of the economic recession in 1957 reveal the enduring nature of the employment crisis in Cuba. Conditions did not improve much because of the steady growth of the Cuban population, which expanded at an annual rate of 2.5%. An estimated 50,000 young men reached working age every year after 1956, a great many of whom could not find new jobs. Thus, between 1956, when economic recuperation began, and 1958, only 8,000 new jobs were created in industry; at the same time about 150,000 young people joined the labor force (Seers, 1964). A total of 26.5% of the Cuban labor force was unemployed or underemployed. In 1955 the developed capitalist country with the highest index of unemployment and underemployment was Germany, with 10.2%, followed by Denmark, with 8.7%; Sweden, 5.1%; the United States, 5%; Canada, 3.8%; Australia, 0.4%; the United Kingdom, 0.2%; and Belgium, 0.1%.

Although estimates of underemployment are still more indicative of the unstable work situation of young people in comparison to adults, these indicators reveal the insecure labor situation of the country's workforce as a whole, its situation of helplessness in the face of the cyclical phenomenon of lack of work. Another important index of the economic impotence of the new generation is the statistics on worker emigration to the United States. According to a report the U.S. vice consul supplied to a journalist of the magazine *Bohemia*, the number of Cuban immigrants to the United States registered a significant increase between 1952 and 1956. More precise information comes from the U.S. Secretary of Commerce, which puts the number of Cubans who emigrated to the United States in 1945 at 2,172. In 1956 the number reached 14,953. To these figures must be added the thousands of young people who traveled to the United States as tourists and remained there working illegally. The importance of these contingents of clandestine workers was evaluated at the time by Segundo Ceballos, Pino Santos, and other scholars, who estimated that from 40,000 to 50,000 young people above the age of eighteen emigrated to the United States each year. During the 1930s some 10,000 Cubans resided in New York, and a similar number lived in Tampa. In the 1950s, 150,000 Cubans were living in the United States (Pérez, 1990: 208).

I underscore the importance of these facts not only as an index of the general situation faced by youth but also as a massive phenomenon that gave rise to the formation of a large community of young workers abroad that contributed economically and politically to the preparation of expeditions, combatants, and arms shipments to the island in the years of the insurrection.

But other evidence suggests the awakening of revolutionary consciousness in the country's proletarianized youth. The intensive character of capitalist production demands the incorporation of large contingents of strong young workers, to whom the hardest and most intense labor has traditionally been assigned in factories, shops, and work centers in general. The labor unions dominated by Mujal had no interest in responding to the problems created by the presence of a new generation of workers, whom they regarded as fortunate to have found work at all. The overwhelming majority of young workers, underemployed as temporary workers, as we have seen, were not considered deserving of the benefits won by the historical struggles of the working class. Thus, young proletarians, finding little help in working-class organizations, tried to channel their political and social anxieties into the revolutionary organizations of the new generation that were confronting the dictatorship.

The subjective situation of secondary and university students made them especially sensitive to the crisis in the country. Thousands of young people from the most diverse social backgrounds were concentrated in centers of secondary education and the universities over a period of eight to ten years. The creation of universities in the provinces of Las Villas and Oriente in the late 1940s and early 1950s made it possible for young people from poorer social strata outside the capital to begin higher studies, though not without considerable

financial strain. Despite this progress, the increase in student population did not correspond to an increase in work possibilities after grad-
uation.

The degree of "mass concentration" and the organization of the
educational process in modern secondary institutions and universities
led the social scientist Korobeinikov to compare these centers to
industrial enterprises, taking into account the degree of socialization
and the proximity of the students over a long period (Korobeinikov,
1979: 128, 129). In any event, the intermingling of students of diverse
social origins in the different educational centers over a prolonged
time in which they were not yet linked organically to the class structure generated fraternal links that were reinforced, in the Cuban
case, by their common negative vision of the social disorder and the
critical situation of the country in the 1950s: the dictatorship, unemployment, political corruption, and the betrayal of national interests
by the preceding generation. Be that as it may, this common viewpoint was not due to the suppression of differences in class outlook,
which maintained their validity, but to the prevailing historical circumstances.

The relative provisional release from class structure also affected
numerous young people of bourgeois extraction, who, still in the
stage of intellectual formation, did not feel committed to the immediate needs of their class and instead felt attracted to the most
advanced ideas, at the same time sharing the critical attitude of their
fellow students toward the society that had been molded by their
elders. In turn, in the face of the economic, political, and institutional crises affecting society—especially, the country's small producers,
merchants, and professionals—a majority of the young people from
the middle classes felt disinclined to inherit the class positions of
their parents or their attitudes toward the dispossessed classes. On
the contrary, many identified ideologically and emotionally with
those classes and felt obliged to struggle for their advancement.
Although this affinity with the most exploited classes was generally of
a spontaneous or sublimated character, this did not impede the establishment of a community of interests among the classes. Forging such
links was seen as a way to renew the deteriorated political leadership
and to avoid conflicts among the different generations present on the
political stage.

The coup d'état of Fulgencio Batista on March 10 thus coincided
with the emergence of this new generation into national life. The
composition of this new political group has been the subject of considerable discussion. Probably the most sensible approach is to recognize the heterogeneous character of the revolutionary youth organi-

zations. The revolutionary vanguard was made up not only of proletarianized young people but included others from petty bourgeois,
peasant, and proletarian backgrounds who had stable employment.
Also prominent in this generation were the country's students, who
could foresee a future, at the end of their studies, without jobs. The
isolation of the proletarianized sector from the nation's class structure and from relations of production—as it was not organically integrated into any class and adopted different attitudes according to the
way in which it was affected by the economic situation, encouraged its
identification with the classes most affected by neocolonial domination.

The proletarianized youth, whether unemployed or only occasionally employed, felt overlooked in neocolonial society. The same
sentiment was harbored by young workers with stable employment
who were nevertheless threatened by unemployment. Thus, whether
unemployed or employed, descendants of petty bourgeois families,
peasants, or workers, young people tended to identify with each other
in the face of a situation that closed off their horizon. Whatever their
social background, they united in the revolutionary organizations in
the 1950s. An old Arab saying offers a deep sociological insight:
"Young people are more the children of their era than of their parents." In this sense, they respond above all to the determinations of
the situation in which they are obliged to live and not to those arising
from the class condition of their progenitors.

The role of youth in the crises of the 1930s and 1940s should also
be studied in the light of their political and social actions. Certainly,
in the 1930s young people assumed a vanguard role in opposition to
the Machado dictatorship and in the Grau-Guiteras revolutionary government, a regime defined as a "youthocracy" (*efebocracia*) (Roa,
1982: 60). The young politicians who represented the generation of
the 1930s returned to power with the electoral triumph of the
Auténticos in 1944, but the growing corruption and demoralization
of that party provoked a division in its ranks and the formation of a
new political party, the Cuban People's Party, led by Eduardo Chibás,
who proposed to clean up Cuban political life.

At the same time, the Ortodoxo Party attracted the new generation that burst onto the national political stage in the late 1940s and
early 1950s, raising their hopes with its program of social justice and
national self-determination. The young revolutionaries of the 1950s
participated in the intense Ortodoxo political agitation among the
masses, becoming imbued with the ethics expounded by Chibás.
According to a survey carried out by Raúl Gutiérrez in May 1951,
Chibás recruited the majority of his followers from among the

country's youth: 40% of those who said they would vote for Chibás for president were between twenty and twenty-nine years old; 32% were thirty to thirty-nine; 23% were forty to forty-nine; and only 15% were fifty or older (Gutiérrez, 1951: May). The Ortodoxo Party was unquestionably the party with the broadest base among the country's youth. As the young generation confronted crises brought on by the process of proletarianization, they flocked to the party that offered the best possibilities for change.

10

City Versus Countryside

Urban-rural relations involve distinct classes and layers of society. In the countries of dependent capitalism, the countryside is disproportionately subordinated to the city. The hypertrophy of the social structure occasionally gives rise to two major poles: the capital and the rest of the country. Wealth and political power are concentrated in the large cities; poverty and cultural backwardness are concentrated in rural areas and small towns.

In Cuba in the 1950s, the differences between Havana and the rest of the country had become extreme. In that period 60% of the country's physicians and 62% of the dentists worked in the capital. Havana had one hospital bed for every 195 inhabitants, while Las Villas had one for every 1,333 inhabitants and Oriente one for every 1,870; the capital boasted 80% of all hospital beds, whereas only one hospital existed in the rural zones (Torras, 1985, vol. 2: 357; Del Toro, 1974: 250, 251). The houses in urban zones usually had electricity (87%), running water (82%), and indoor toilets (95%). The capital surpassed the cities of the interior by a large margin in these indices: Although Havana residents made up only 26.3% of the total population, they lived in 52% of the urban homes with electricity, 60% of those with running water, and 65% of those with indoor toilets. In contrast, people in the countryside lived in flimsy houses without water (85%), indoor toilets (54%), or electricity (93%).

The other face of the prosperous metropolis was that of its impoverished workers and unemployed. In the capital, 10% of homes lacked running water, 6% indoor toilets, and 26% a bathtub or shower. These were generally found in the neighborhoods of indigents that began to appear in the 1930s as a result of migratory waves from the provinces (or "from the interior," as the residents of Havana called it). Conditions similar to those of shantytowns prevailed in the

161

tenement houses of slum areas. A survey made by Juan Chailloux
found that 80% of the capital's unemployed lived in dilapidated collective dwellings (Chailloux, 1945: 124). In slum dwellings the average number of inhabitants per indoor toilet was thirty-six. The average number of persons living in each room was five, and it was
common to find rooms inhabited by ten or twelve persons. Chailloux
estimated that the city held 2,000 tenement houses where 20,000 persons lived in conditions of overcrowding and absolute lack of sanitation. Meanwhile, another 20,000 persons vegetated in the shantytowns in a still more depressing situation. Of the 2,038 slum dwellers
Chailloux interviewed, 21% were domestic servants, 21% skilled workers, 13% day laborers, and 7% street vendors. The majority of these
tenants were occasional workers, and 36% stated that they were
unemployed.

In 1953, 11.6% of the country's illiterate were concentrated in
urban zones and 47.1% in the countryside. The educational level in
Havana, on the contrary, had risen as a result of the development of
commercial and industrial activities in the city. School registration in
the capital reached 74% of the school-age population. Only 7.5% of
Havana's inhabitants were illiterate. The percentage of illiteracy in
the provinces, including the rural population of Havana Province,
ranged from 19.2% in Matanzas to 35.3% in Oriente. Havana also
had 60% of the island's secondary school graduates, 50% of the graduates of vocational schools, and almost 70% of the university graduates (Pérez-Stable, 1988: 44).

The class structure also differed notably between Havana and the
rest of the country. The economically active population above fourteen years of age in the capital included 20.6% of persons employed
in industry, 6.2% in transport, and 6% in construction—sectors composed chiefly of the working class—whereas 42% grouped in services
and 18% in commerce represented essentially the middle classes.
Nearly 50% of the country's industry was concentrated in Havana. In
the rest of the country, 15% of the economically active population
was employed in industry, 4.3% in transport, and 2% in construction,
making up the working class (primarily urban), whereas only 13%
worked in services and 9% in commerce, constituting in broad terms
a middle class. Meanwhile, 54% of the economically active population
in the countryside labored in agriculture.

The growing unemployment favored the creation of a variety of
occupations in the informal sector that could not be defined as proletarian or forms of self-employment. Thus, between 1943 and 1953 the
number of domestic servants doubled and that of street vendors
increased ten times more than that of the working population. The

numbers of shoe shiners, news vendors, car washers, parking lot employees, and others increased twofold or threefold without being registered in the census. Many wandered about aimlessly without work and some without motivation; many were crippled, maimed, or ill, living on public welfare and private charity. More than 5,000 beggars walked the streets of Havana (Pérez, 1988: 304). Such was the outcome of the slow rhythm of growth, which compelled numerous men and women to devise all kinds of odd (and often degrading) jobs as the only escape from unemployment. Even many ex-members of the petty bourgeoisie tried to find jobs in factories.

The most notable difference in the occupational structure of the capital consisted in the disproportionate tertiary sector (60%) compared to the rest of the country (22%). The enormous number of employees in the commercial and service sectors identified Havana as the capital of an underdeveloped country. The differences in the proletarian sector of industry, transportation, and construction, comprising 34% of the economically active population of the capital and 23% in the rest of the country, were less marked. (It must be kept in mind, however, that the percentage of persons employed in the proletarian sector appeared greater than it really was, since the census of 1953 was carried out in the harvest season.)

The Keynesian policies of the Batista regime, which tended to increase public spending in the capital, exacerbated the existing inequalities. Construction undertaken in the capital from 1952 to 1956 made up 79% of that carried out in the entire country. Twenty-story buildings and luxurious avenues appeared in the capital. One illustrious traveler, Jean-Paul Sartre, visiting the city in 1959 wrote that "this outbreak of skyscrapers had only one meaning: it revealed the tenacious refusal of bourgeois savings to industrialize the country" (Sartre, 1961: 68).

In reality, it was not a matter of a refusal but of a tendency to follow the path of least resistance in the face of growing U.S. industrial investments on the island. These, in fact, were occasionally associated with local entrepreneurs, which brought about a slight increase in industrial production in the 1950s. The number of industrial clients, that is, industries and factories that paid the Cuban Electric Company for their consumption of electricity, grew by a factor of 1.15 from 1952 to 1957 (Kuczynski, 1973: 90–129). During those years, 149 industries, representing 73% of all the industrial investments in Cuba, were established or projected for establishment in Havana. During 1956 and 1957, however, the unemployment rate in Havana was 11.8%; the national average was 16.4%. Unemployment in the capital tended to grow as a result of the considerable immigration from the rest of the country, so that the indices of unemployment do not accurately reflect to what extent Havana workers were affected.

In conformance with Agreement 21 of 1944 decreed by the National Commission of Minimum Salaries, urban workers received a wage of $2 daily and rural workers $1.60, but the agreement specified the possibility of reducing wages 20% in provincial cities and capitals, 30% in towns, and 40% in farm areas. Workers in the capital were not affected by these reductions.

The agreement of February 15, 1958, established $3.30 as the minimum daily wage in Havana, $3.10 for cities in the rest of the country, and $2.90 in rural areas. The concentration in the capital of the majority of industries and the central organs of public administration determined in large measure the existing wage imbalances. Thus, 41% of the total salaries paid in 1948 were disbursed in the capital; in 1952, 52%; and in 1958, 63%. The survey made in 1956 and 1957 by the Coordinating Investigation Commission on Employment showed that 51% of the labor force of Havana received a monthly income above $75; in the rest of the country only 26% of the workers reached that level. Table 10.1 shows the lower cost of food in the capital.

The census of 1953 provided evidence of significant disparities in rents by tenants with low, medium, and high incomes. In urban zones all over the country, a larger proportion of tenants paid rent of less than $10, whereas in the province of Havana, a considerably higher number of persons paid more than $25. Table 10.2 shows the marked contrast in this index.

The distribution of the domestic budget found in surveys made in the 1950s reveals the imbalance between income groups in the city compared to the countryside. These samples show, in the first place, the deficit in the domestic budget of the families of agricultural

Table 10.1   Index of Food Costs, National Versus Havana, 1954–1957

	National	Havana
1954	234.1	213.3
1955	229.2	205.9
1956	229.2	208.3
1957	236.3	214.5

Note: Base year is the second quarter of 1937.
Sources: Boletín Informativo del Consejo Nacional de Economía, October 1955: 238; May 1957: 302.

Table 10.2   Monthly Rent for Urban Housing, Havana Versus Other Cities, 1953

Rent	Urban Zones in Havana Province		Cities and Towns in Rest of the Country	
	Persons	%	Persons	%
Up to $10	77,114	30.69	97,059	57.65
$10–$25	85,679	34.10	48,302	28.69
More than $25	82,852	32.95	16,491	9.71
Not declared	5,690	2.26	6,584	3.95
Total urban dwellings	252,335	100.00	168,436	99.96

Source: Census of 1953: 302, 303.

workers and urban workers of low and middle incomes in the city of Havana. Table 10.3 illustrates the situation.

Perhaps most significant in Table 10.3 are the differences in income spent on food. The percentage of food expenditure of the poor Havana family constitutes approximately the mean of the percentage of this expense for the other two families. Nevertheless, the real cost in pesos of the food ration of the poor family in the capital is closer to that of the family of the agricultural worker. Thus, its

Table 10.3   Estimate of Family Budget, Rural Versus Urban Workers, 1950s

Type of Expenditure	Agricultural Worker's Family[a]		Urban Worker's Family (Low Income)[b]		Urban Worker's Family (Middle Income)[c]	
	Pesos	%	Pesos	%	Pesos	%
Housing	0.86	1.7	10	13.2	48	16.2
Clothing	7.80	15.5	6	6.7	31	10.5
Food	34.87	69.1	49	54.0	118	40.0
Services	3.87	7.3	16	18.0	44	14.8
Other	3.75	6.4	8	9.0	55	18.5
Total	51.15	100	89	100	286	100

a. Family of agricultural worker with average income of $51 in 1957.
b. Havana family with average income of less than $83 in 1955.
c. Havana family with average income of $250–$333 in 1955.
Source: Del Toro, 1974: 266, 267.

expenditure for food is about $14 more than that of the rural family and $66 less than that of the middle-income Havana family. If we take into account that the agricultural worker frequently had a small plot for growing vegetables and raising fowl or pigs, we can conclude that the differences were not so pronounced.

Although expenditures for food took up the largest part of the domestic budget for each of the three groups of families, for the urban families rent was also a major expense. The percentage of families who paid rent of less than $10 gives an idea of the dimensions of the poverty existing in Havana: A total of 77,114 persons, or 30.6% of all families in urban zones of Havana, lived in such low-rent housing. In 1952, a prosperous year, 60,000 eviction cases were handled in the courts of Havana alone, despite a rent-freeze. In 1914, 23,695 such cases were tried; in 1926, 27,812; and in 1930, during a national crisis, 55,102 (*Anuario de Estadística Judicial,* 1917; Comisión Nacional de Estadísticas y Reformas Económica, 1926 and 1931).

Consumption levels in the country reflected further existing differences. The consumption boom that took place in the capital, stimulated by the compensatory spending behavior among the middle- and high-income sectors, created a false impression of widespread prosperity. In reality, only the middle class, the worker aristocracy, and certain highly paid skilled workers shared any kind of wealth. The 1953 census revealed that 28% of all radio receivers, 43.8% of TV sets, and 64.5% of refrigerators in the country belonged to Havana residents. Registrations of private automobiles doubled between 1948 and 1952 and tripled between 1953 and 1957. Residents in the capital owned 62.7% of the automobiles and 76.8% of the country's telephones. At the beginning of the 1950s, Cuba imported $45 million in durable consumer goods (electric fans, blenders, etc.), and from 1956 to 1958 the annual average was $68 million. A considerable part of the increase in goods went to the capital (57%) (U.S. Department of Commerce, *Investment in Cuba,* 1956: 191).

As mentioned earlier, the working class in urban zones outside Havana could count on only occasional employment. Unemployment and work insecurity led to discontent and revolutionary nonconformity among these Cubans. And in contrast, relative job security for other workers often instilled in them a passive attitude.

Table 10.4 shows the incidence of underemployment in the capital and in the cities and towns of the rest of the country. As the table shows, the situation of underemployment or occasional employment tended to be more prolonged and generalized in the rest of the country; permanent employment was more frequent in the capital. In absolute numbers, 373,312 more persons in the rest of the country

Table 10.4   Weeks Worked in Urban Zones, Havana Versus Other Cities, 1953

	Percentage of the Population That Worked		
	Less Than 30 Weeks	31–49 Weeks	All Year
Urban zones in Havana Province (including the capital)	54.4	5.7	39.9
Urban zones in the rest of the country	58.7	6.4	34.9

Note: Individuals above fourteen years.
Source: Census of 1953: table 47.

had casual, or occasional, employment than those in Havana, and 24,107 more persons in the capital had permanent work.

The authors of the 1957 survey by the ACU stated that "Havana is enjoying extraordinary prosperity, while the rural areas, especially the salaried workers, are living in an incredibly stationary, poverty-stricken, and desperate condition." An independent social investigator, Segundo Ceballos, described the extremes of the city-countryside disparity as follows: "The contrast between Havana and the countryside reflects the profound imbalance between the rent captured by the high levels of urban capitalism and the slow and scarce circulation of money in the countryside. Calculated in terms of sweat, Havana has cost the rural people millions of dollars" (Ceballos, 1953: 54). It was not the population of Havana that was to blame for the situation but rather the capitalism of the metropolis and U.S. financial capital. Those responsible for the poverty in the rural areas and for the impoverishment of a sector of the working middle class of the capital were the local bourgeoisie, many of whom resided in the beautiful and modern residential neighborhoods of the capital. Around 1953 there were 3,500 owners of luxury residences and mansions, each with a value of more than $20,000. These Havana residences accounted for 86% of the homes of that value on the island.

The economic, social, and demographic contrasts and imbalances I have analyzed in this chapter tend to explain why—unlike the 1930s, in which the proletariat of the capital constituted the epicenter of the revolutionary movement—the revolutionary role in the 1950s was assumed by the urban and rural proletariat in the rest of the country. But a complete historical explanation of this process demands an evaluation of the path followed by the proletariat of the capital in the period 1934–1958.

Following the overthrow of the revolutionary Grau-Guiteras government in 1934, the struggles of the working class had earned it greater occupational stability and higher wages. Nevertheless, these conquests had stimulated an economist current within the class and in many of its leaders. The leadership of the Communist Party criticized this tendency on occasion, inasmuch as it affected not only the working class but even labor leaders and cadres of that party. The unionist mentality was common among the reformist labor leaders grouped in the populist Auténtico Party led by Grau San Martín. With the Auténtico Party in power, the submissiveness and venality of the reformist labor leadership, headed by Eusebio Mujal, became manifest. Although the ascent of Auténtico unionists to positions of power in the CTC was the work of governmental and gang violence, and worker-employer relations from that time on were marked by corruption and capitulation to government policies, some reformist leaders managed to attain a certain prestige by satisfying demands of an economist character. The numerous mediations of the Auténtico governments in worker-employer conflicts were aimed at avoiding spontaneous or Communist-led strikes and protest movements by partially satisfying specific, limited worker demands, designed to strengthen the position of Mujal in the unions. The election of Auténtico labor leaders in work centers became virtually a precondition necessary to ensure that the Ministry of Labor would show some favor to the workers in their conflicts with employers. Despite the growing demoralization of the Mujal group, its reformist orientation succeeded in penetrating the working class. Nor did the apolitical positions of a broad sector of workers prevent the proletariat from taking part in the political struggle against the growing corruption, loss of prestige, and surrender to Washington of the Auténtico administrations and the CTC leadership.

In the 1940s Havana had become the political pulpit for the vibrant sermons of Eduardo Chibás and the base for the persevering activity of the Communists within the unions. The popular patriotic orientation of the political campaigns of Chibás and the efforts of the Communist Party to raise class consciousness among the working class helped to undermine the power of the political machinery. The partisan elections of 1950 illustrated the changes that had taken place in the political awareness of the working classes. The candidates for representatives from the province of Havana with the largest number of votes were the populist Ortodoxo orator José Pardo Llada, with

70,000 votes, and the Communist labor leader Lázaro Peña, with 32,675 votes. Although the Communist Party lost electoral strength in the last reorganization of 1950 as a consequence of government repression and the anti-Communist campaigns unleashed by the mass media, the anti-Yankee campaigns of Chibás and his support for strongly felt popular demands attracted a considerable number of Communist Party followers to the Ortodoxos (Gutiérrez, 1950, 1951).

Persecuted and excluded from the unions, first by the Prío and then by the Batista regime, Communist labor leaders and other opposition parties found it extraordinarily difficult to mobilize workers in the capital against the dictatorship. At the same time, the division among opposition labor leaders—a reflection in part of the rivalries among the political parties—was an obstacle to the unity and mass struggle expounded by the Communists in the hope of repeating the events of 1933, when the explosion of a general strike overthrew Machado.

Added to these difficulties was the fact that the centers of power in Cuba were concentrated in the capital: the ministries and central organs of public administration; the bulk of the country's repressive forces, the army and police; and the large newspapers and radio and television stations, owned by the dependent bourgeoisie yoked to the illegal regime. The power of coercion and ideological dissuasion of this bloc tended to restrain the actions of the working population.

But the people made their presence felt in one way or another, as in the mass meetings to denounce the Batista regime called by groups such as the Federation of University Students (FEU). Thousands of young workers and unemployed in the capital took part in torchlight marches; the funeral for the student Rubén Batista; the demonstration of December 9; the five-minute work stoppage of December 14, 1955; and other actions of opposition to the dictatorship organized by student leaders. The only authorized mass meeting was that held at the Luz Docks, where 50,000 to 60,000 Havana residents protested against Batista's coup d'état of March 10.

Between 1952 and 1957, partial strikes with political implications were carried out in the capital by bakers, bank employees, and workers of the H. Uppman and Partagás tobacco factories, but they did draw participants from other sectors. The struggles of the working class achieved broader participation and intensity in the rest of the country, where the abrupt decline in the standard of living and growing unemployment led to strikes of the railroad and transport workers in Oriente and Camagüey, shoe industry workers in Manzanillo, henequen workers in Matanzas, cigar and tobacco workers in Cabaiguán (who declared five towns of Las Villas Province "dead cities"), and agricultural and industrial workers of several sugar mills in various provinces. In 1955 the movement culminated in the sugar strike of Las Villas that was transformed into a political strike under the leadership of José Antonio Echevarría, president of the Federation of University Students, and led to the revolutionary takeover of several towns and destruction of means of communication.

From the beginning, all classes in the city of Santiago de Cuba demonstrated against the dictatorship. When Grau San Martín visited the city during the presidential campaign of 1954, the residents of Santiago poured out into the streets to demand the resignation of the dictator and the liberation of the young people who had attacked the Moncada garrison.

A 1956 report of the Popular Socialist Party on unions led by its militants or by workers who supported unity among the organizations pointed up the difficulties they faced in the capital. Of the eighty-two unions led directly by Communists, only twenty, or 12% of the total, were in the capital. In the provinces of Las Villas and Oriente, in contrast, the Communists controlled 31% and 29%, respectively, of the total number of unions. Altogether the Communist unions and those that similarly advocated unity totaled some 300, although the report did not include complete data for Oriente and Las Villas Provinces. Of the 2,000 unions in the country, those led by the Communists and unitarians constituted only 15%. The report reflected the harsh conditions, under police repression, in which union and political activities of the worker opposition had to be carried out, as well as the extremely complicated situation prevailing in the capital (Instituto de Historia del Partido Comunista y de la Revolución Socialista de Cuba, 1980, vol. 2: 319, 320).

The revolutionary vortex began to move imperceptibly toward the eastern and central provinces, where the protests of students and young workers began to assume the character of clandestine revolutionary organizations. Meanwhile, at the University of Havana, a forum for the nonconformity of the new generation, thousands of young people from all classes joined the March 13 Revolutionary Directorate under the leadership of Echeverría and the FEU. Following the directorate's assault on the presidential palace and the death of Echeverría, the organization focused its efforts on the creation of a guerrilla front in Las Villas, where the protests of workers and farmers were mounting. The major historical merit of Fidel Castro, as the leader and organizer of the July 26 Movement, lay in his having recognized from the beginning the potential for starting a movement in the provinces that would revolutionize the country.

During the 1930s, the historical initiative had been assumed by the labor and student movement in Havana. The most numerous contingents of the proletariat, deprived of the rights and historical gains won by the working class in industrialized countries, were concentrated in the capital. The economic crisis that had descended on the country beginning in 1929 and reached a critical point in 1933 dramatically reduced the real income of workers, a situation the Machado regime failed to alleviate. Lacking work stability, victims of a massive wave of layoffs that raised the number of idle workers in the capital to 40,000, and their real income dwindling, the proletarians of the city decided to play for high stakes, carrying out the general strike that overthrew the dictatorship.

In contrast, during the 1950s the struggles of the proletariat in the capital had won for it relative job security and the highest earnings of all Latin American countries. Workers in Havana were not inclined to lose their hard-won right to work and higher wages in impetuous, risky actions. Unlike the rest of the island, where unemployment had affected broad sectors and the majority of workers had no hope of finding jobs, the capital had been favored by investments in construction and new industries that had created thousands of jobs, and unemployment had been less severe.

An axiom of the class struggle was proven: The threat of unemployment exerted a stronger coercive force upon the workers than its actual realization. At the same time, the surveillance and repression of the labor opposition, including Communists and leaders of other tendencies, were carried to extremes in Havana, where the greater part of the dictatorship's repressive forces and the Mujalist hierarchy were concentrated.

It must also be kept in mind that during the 1950s the real earnings of workers in the capital did not deteriorate as sharply as they had in the provinces. Social scientists who dismiss this influence on skilled workers' attitudes, assuming instead essentially their revolutionary nature, in effect deny the impact of economic cycles on the behavior of the working class (Okunieva, 1988: 95, 96, 101). In Cuba the revolutionary events of 1895–1898, 1929–1933, and 1952–1958 have coincided with a steep drop in the real incomes of the working classes. Workers' attitudes fluctuate with their fortunes. Although other factors are at work as well, it is not the case that the political culture thrusts certain workers into a vanguard role in struggles against dictatorships. Highly paid skilled workers are not somehow "less revolutionary" or privileged or blind to the evils of capitalism and the need for socialism. But workers who are victims of both an abrupt decline in their real earnings and job instability tend to become aware of the need to undertake decisive action against the enemies of their class and to place themselves in the front ranks of the struggle. This was evidenced in Cuba by the growing participation of workers in the hinterland in protests against the Batista regime and by the lag in Havana workers' participation.

It should also be taken into account that during the 1950s the rest of the country had proportionally more underemployed and unemployed workers, whereas the capital had more permanently employed workers. Job instability seems to be one of the most powerful factors in the determination of workers to assume an active vanguard role. According to Zeitlin, workers whose employment was of a nonpermanent, casual character tended to identify more closely with the Communists before the revolutionary triumph of 1959 and with subsequent realizations of the Cuban revolution (Zeitlin, 1967: 56–64).

Finally, the large number of employees in the private and state sector (60%) in the population of the capital was an obstacle to mass action against the dictatorship. Contrary to its relative insignificance in Santiago de Cuba and other cities of the interior, the tertiary sector had great impact in Havana. A considerable part of this sector, with middle and high incomes, tended to adopt the values of the consumer society that was artificially created in those years. López Segrera gives a vivid description of the way in which the labor aristocracy and these petty bourgeois sectors working in services and commerce benefited from the Havana oligarchy as they provided them with goods and services. In other cities these strata of the population supported the revolutionary projects of the July 26 Movement and the Revolutionary Directorate, but in the capital they were likelier to adopt apolitical attitudes or to clamor for an agreement between the government and the bourgeois opposition that would restore constitutional normalcy. In Havana, however, the proletarianized youth, students, groups of professionals, and the sectors of the middle class and the proletariat with low and middle incomes joined the revolutionary organizations of the new generation. The heroic vanguard of the July 26 Movement, the Revolutionary Directorate, and the Communists kept the resistance alive in the capital using various forms of struggle.

The failure of the general strikes in Havana, called by the July 26 Movement in 1957 and again in 1958, proved that the necessary conditions for the working class to act had not yet been created. Certainly, the proletariat of the capital had greater experience and class consciousness, but it did not have an integral awareness of its role in the popular struggles. Thus, its delayed incorporation into the struggle impeded it from exercising a more active influence on the course of events. Nevertheless, it was the organized labor movement in the capital that delivered the final blow to the dictatorship. After the failure of the April strike, the labor leaders of Havana organized and united, following Castro's calls for unity from his base in the Sierra Maestra. The will to overcome existing divisions was translated into a systematic and persistent effort in every work center. The creation of the National United Workers' Front (FONU) prepared conditions for the Havana skilled proletariat at last to assume a vanguard role. By the end of 1958, workers of the capital were ready to respond to the call for a general strike against the maneuvers of General Cantillo. Beginning in 1959, the skilled workers of Havana and the rest of the country were in the front ranks, together with other strata of workers and the middle class. Their class awareness, sense of organization, and labor discipline enabled them to play a key role in production, technical and cultural improvement, and the defense of the country.

Some indices of the standard of living in the Latin American context seem to deny the existence of objective conditions for a revolutionary process, despite evidence of the growing impoverishment of the rural population, certain sectors of the urban working class, and the proletarianized masses. The historiography that seeks to refute the revolutionary process presents indices indicating a supposed state of well-being to demonstrate that conditions for a social revolution did not exist in Cuba in the 1950s. According to this thesis, the revolution should have taken place in the most poverty-stricken countries of Latin America, not in Cuba.

Indeed, in the 1950s, the island enjoyed the second highest per capita income of the South American continent. Average income in Cuba reached $374 in 1957, second only to Venezuela, with $857. Only Mexico and Brazil surpassed Cuba in number of radio sets (one for each 6.5 inhabitants). The island ranked first in TV sets (one per twenty-five inhabitants) and in number of telephones (one for each thirty-eight persons), newspapers (one copy per eight inhabitants), automobiles (one per forty persons), and railroad miles per square mile (one for each four). It was estimated that 58.2% of homes had electricity. In 1953, 76.4% of the Cuban population could read and write, surpassed only by Argentina (86.4%), Chile (79.5%), and Costa Rica (79.4%). Average food consumption in Cuba was exceeded only by that of Argentina and Uruguay. Cuba held third place in number of persons per medical doctor (1,000), again surpassed only by Uruguay (860) and Argentina (760). In 1952 the island had the lowest infant mortality rates of Latin America (25.1%), followed by Argentina (24.7%) and Uruguay (18.5%). These statistics would seem to confirm the thesis of a prosperous Cuba, on the road to industrialization and economic independence. As I have shown, however, Cuba's relatively high overall indices in the Latin American context were due to the high standard of consumption enjoyed by Havana compared to other large Latin American cities. Havana was in fact one of the three most expensive cities in the world. Thus, the higher incomes of the Cuban middle classes and the labor aristocracy in the capital were absorbed in great measure by the galloping inflation of the 1940s and the 1950s. At the same time, the Cuban rural scene was as poor and backward as that in the rest of Latin America and Asia. The social precariousness and instability of the middle class and the proletarianized sectors were more acute than among their counterparts in Latin America. As we have seen, those classes and strata in Latin America were relatively quiet and composed, subject to firm links of dependence. Thus, general statistics do not disclose the critically weak spots of the island's social structure or the low standard of living and instability of the rural masses, the impoverished strata of the middle classes, and the proletarianized sectors.

As the historian Louis A. Pérez Jr. has pointed out, the apparent prosperity in Cuba relative to the rest of Latin America masked a diversity of social tensions and frustrations that extended throughout the society. The links of economic dependency on the United States, no less than psychological links, helped to create totally unrealizable expectations among Cubans (Pérez, 1990: 227). At the forefront of the tensions were fears of losing or not finding employment, being evicted, falling ill and not receiving medical attention, racial discrimination, and inability to pay the cost of children's education. Cuban workers simply wanted job security, not the living standard of the labor aristocracy. Since the Cuban working class had a high educational level compared to that of the rest of Latin America as well as a history of struggle that had helped to raise its standard of living and had opened its eyes to the possibility of a more just society, at the same time that it found itself threatened by unemployment and poverty, it could identify itself with a popular and national revolution. In any event, there was sufficient social instability and poverty in Cuban society to mobilize 90% of the population in support of a revolutionary project. The thesis that revolutionary processes arise only from extreme situations of poverty does not take into account the level of social consciousness the classes that participated in the revolutionary process in Cuba had reached. It further fails to consider that it is not long-lasting, stagnant poverty but abrupt, steep changes in the level of living that usually give rise to social transformations.

11

Social Change and Political Transformation

One of the most relevant historiographic problems in the study of the process of proletarianization is unquestionably the relation between the evolution of sugar production from 1898 to 1958 and the rate of population growth. Table 11.1 shows the unequal growth rates of these two factors in that period.

Table 11.1 Relation Between Growth in Sugar Production and Population Growth, 1898–1958

	(1)	(2)	Growth (2/1)	(3)	Growth (3/2)
	1898–1907	1919–1928		1949–1958	
Sugar production (tons)	7,030,248	44,900,430	6.4	55,216,728	1.2
	1898	1928		1958	
Population (inhabitants)	1,572,792	3,693,000	2.3	6,255,931	1.7

Sources: Moreno Fraginals, 1973, vol. 3: 46–48; Alienes, 1950:52.

As can be seen, sugar production increased 6.4 times in the ten-year period 1919–1928, compared to its growth in the ten years from 1898 to 1907, whereas the population grew only 2.3 times in the whole period between 1898 and 1928. Hence, during the expansion of the sugar industry in the first three decades of the republic, sugar production grew at a rate approximately three times greater than did the population, thus accounting for the relative prosperity and

175

stability of the period, despite the drain on national surpluses by the mechanisms of neocolonial domination. In the following period, 1928–1958, the recession in the sugar industry inverted this relation, with sugar production growing only 1.2 times as the population grew 1.7 times.

Simply stated, these estimates indicate that the years between 1898 and 1928 were years of growth, as expansion in sugar production outpaced demographic growth; in contrast, in the period from 1928 to 1958 the development of the sugar industry was arrested at the same time that demographic growth surpassed economic growth. In this context of limited work opportunities, the increasing demand for jobs could not be met, leading to a disproportionate jump in unemployment and underemployment.

To this situation, negative enough in itself, must be added the fact that the beginning of the period of stagnation in the sugar industry coincided with the onset of one conjunctural crisis (1928–1934) and culminated with another (1953–1957). Within these short spans, the inflationary process intensified the social instability of the period, marked by growing unemployment and low real incomes for workers. Thus, unemployment and the deterioration of living standards reached a climax during these periods of crisis. The brief period from 1928 to 1934 was characterized by a drastic reduction in nominal salaries, protested in numerous strikes for higher wages. During those turbulent years, the process of proletarianization apparently did not reach the levels it would attain in the 1950s. In contrast, the short span from 1953 to 1957 was marked by a reduction of real salaries resulting from a rise in the cost of living and growing unemployment. The highly paid industrial sectors of the working class, protected by legislation that guaranteed them relative job security, felt the effects of the inflationary process on their income but did not feel sufficiently threatened to confront the regime. Thus, these critical periods provoked two revolutionary crises that instigated two different class and institutional mobilizations as well as two different strategic conceptions of the taking of power.

From 1927 to 1958, Cuba showed little progress. Consumption statistics for Latin America reveal that the drop in the per capita level of nourishment in Cuba in that period compared to the three preceding decades was more abrupt and longer lasting than in most other Latin American countries. The most significant fact in this context is that Cuba was the only Latin American country in the twentieth century whose rate of growth in the value of its exports declined from 1930 to 1950 compared to the three preceding decades, that is, from 1899 to 1930. The remaining Latin American countries, whose development, like that of Cuba, depended on the export sector, registered notable growth in their export trade from 1930 to 1950 compared to the first three decades of the century. The fall in the rate of Cuban exports from 1927 to 1957, coincident with an unfavorable international price cycle, together with the short recession of 1953–1957, triggered the revolutionary crisis (Cardoso, 1979: 174–184).

The significance of this process can be appreciated more precisely in the Latin American context. Of all the countries of the area, Cuba had the highest percentage of persons obliged to sell their labor (72.1%), with the exception of Chile (72.5%). The difference between these two countries lay in the fact that the process of proletarianization in Chile was accompanied by a certain level of industrial development.

Self-employed persons on the island represented only 24% of the economically active population. On the rest of the continent, the proportion of self-employed individuals was reported as follows: Brazil 28.1%, El Salvador 25.7%, Guatemala 38.9%, Haiti 42.5%, Mexico 40.7%, Nicaragua 25%, Panama 36.5%, Paraguay 36.5%, the Dominican Republic 38.4%, and Venezuela 27.3%. Only Colombia (23.7%), Argentina (6.8%), and Costa Rica (10.9%) had a lower proportion than Cuba in this important aspect of social structure (Unión Panamericana, Instituto Interamericano de Estadísticas, 1956).

In Cuba the large number of individuals obliged to sell their labor included not only the working class but also the proletarianized masses that made up the industrial reserve army registered in the censuses as occasionally employed, underemployed, or unemployed. In no other Latin American country did the phenomenon of proletarianization reach the magnitude it attained in Cuba. Thus, the island appeared in the statistics of the North American Institute of Statistics of the Pan-American Union as the country with the second highest proportion of its economically active population defined as workers. Most of these, however, were not stable workers but unemployed or underemployed persons. The high proportion of self-employed among the economically active populations of the majority of Latin American countries gave these countries a high degree of social stability. In Cuba, in contrast, the mass of unemployed and occasional workers did not venture into self-employment in the same proportion as occurred in the majority of Latin American countries, depending for their subsistence instead on the precarious demand of the labor market. This situation resulted in a high degree of instability on the Caribbean island, as a large percentage of those Cubans without work had no source of income during the "dead season" or in the period in which they were jobless.

Cuba was also third among the Latin American countries with the lowest percentage of the economically active population working in agriculture—that is, it was one of the least agriculturally developed. It likewise had the third highest rate of urbanization. This factor was highly significant, since most of its population did not live under the conservative rural traditions or hegemonic direction of its landowning class, as did the majority of inhabitants of Latin American countries (*Revista Interamericana de Ciencias Sociales*, 2, vol. 3, special number, 1964: 93, 205).

It is difficult to draw a comparison of unemployment during the periods of expansion (1898–1928) and recession (1928–1958) of the sugar industry, as no direct information exists on this score in the censuses and statistical records of the first period. But some scholars of the period (Cuban Economic Research Project, 1965; Mesa Lago, 1972) agree on the detrimental effects of unemployment in those first decades. Because individuals reported as "without a paid occupation" according to the category used in the first censuses of 1907 and 1919 included housewives, students, and the physically handicapped, the authors of the Cuban Economic Research Project rightly concluded that unemployment before 1930 "was not a serious problem." At the same time, the demand for Caribbean field hands in the sugar industry beginning in 1910 offered evidence that the labor market was saturated and that very little unemployment existed in the country's rural zones. The economy was in an expansive phase, with considerable investments in the sugar industry and in the transport sector, contributing to the absorption of labor. World War I appears to have created a slight rise in unemployment, but in general terms economic growth seems to have satisfied the existing demand for jobs. One way to investigate employment trends is to measure the percentage of the population reported as employed by the censuses of 1907, 1919, and 1931. As mentioned, in these reports the unemployed and underemployed were grouped together with those not included in the labor force (housewives, students, internees, and the physically handicapped) in the category "without a paid occupation," making it impossible to calculate the totals of unemployed and underemployed. Nevertheless, the evolution of the percentage of the employed population in relation to the labor force should suggest the unemployment situation. The percentage of employed persons with respect to the population of working age declined as follows: According to the census of 1899, it constituted 64.9%; in 1907, 61.9%; in 1919, 57.2%; in 1931, 53.7%; and in 1943 it was 35.8%. The abrupt drop between 1931 and 1943 in the percentage of the employed population must reflect to some extent the increase in unemployment during the depression of the 1930s and 1940s.

In 1943 the proletarianized sector—that is, the unemployed and underemployed—greatly surpassed the primary, secondary, and tertiary sectors in both quantity and proportion of the labor force. Whereas the unemployed and underemployed totaled 492,537 persons (32.4% of the labor force), the secondary sector was composed of 220,491 persons (14.5%), the primary of 397,708 (26.1%), and the tertiary of 410,115 (26.9%). If we take into account that the secondary sector was made up in large measure of the urban working class, the tertiary of the urban middle class, and the primary of agricultural workers and peasants, we can appreciate the weight and importance of the proletarianized sector in the overall social structure. The proletarianized sector acquired constantly greater importance, whereas the urban middle class, which because of its dimensions and participation in the economic activities of the country from 1898 to 1928 had shaped the class structure as a whole, tended to lose force. At the same time, the urban working class remained stationary during the period of stagnation between 1928 and 1958, with only a slight gain in its numbers.

The persistence of unemployment in the depressive cycle of the sugar industry is evidenced by the following facts. The minimum unemployment rate in the 1956–1957 survey (9% in February–April 1957) was very close to the unemployment rate registered by the 1953 census (8.4% in January–March). The maximum unemployment rate in the 1956–1957 survey (20.7% in August–October 1956) was very close to the unemployment rate registered by the 1943 census (21%, taken in July–September of that year). Those findings led conservative economic historian Mesa Lago to affirm that "although different methods were used in 1943, 1953, and 1956, the conclusion seems to be that unemployment did not improve in all those years" (Mesa Lago, 1972: 25). According to the data of the 1943 census, there were in absolute numbers some 443,283 unemployed and underemployed men that year, a figure that reached 673,455 men who had worked fewer than forty weeks in the year prior to the census of 1953 and were in a situation of unemployment or underemployment and 631,000 men who were in a similar situation in 1956–1957 (*Boletín Informativo del Consejo Nacional de Economía,* 1958). These figures give an idea of the growing mass of proletarianized Cubans, unemployed and underemployed, who in the 1940s and 1950s made up more than 30% of the workforce and whose position in the social structure was defined by their separation from relations of production—that is, they could not strictly define themselves as belonging to any class. Some partial estimates of the social structure of the Latin American countries reveal that in the 1950s and 1960s none of those agrarian countries, characterized by a high proportion of peasants and self-employed persons, had the high percentage of unemployed that existed in Cuba, a country midway between agrarian backwardness and incipient industrialization. Thus, several censuses carried out in Latin American countries in 1965 showed an unemployment rate ranging between 5% and 10% of the labor force.

A number of European historians and sociologists have studied the phenomenon of Cuban proletarianization from the point of view of intense processes of disintegration, fragmentation, destabilization, and destruction of the social structure (Sabbatini, 1968; Blackburn, 1963). These studies, however, have not distinguished the paths that led to proletarianization. Although they have emphasized that the phenomenon should not be interpreted mechanically or in strict economic terms, they have reduced it to the crisis and ruin of the petty bourgeoisie, or middle classes. This sector, however, was only one of several that made up the proletarianized masses. The appearance of this phenomenon in the first half of the twentieth century was the result not only of the proletarianization of the petty bourgeoisie but also of the existence of a growing permanent army of the proletarianized, individuals from the middle classes, the peasantry, and the proletariat who found themselves subjected to a more or less prolonged situation of unemployment or underemployment. This group included young people of diverse social origins who reached working age only to find it increasingly difficult to obtain employment or any habitual or stable economic activity. The lack of stable social integration resulted in a lack of precise ideology, making them susceptible to ideas of the most dissimilar origin—hence the need to define this sector conceptually as an independent social category, marginalized from relations of production and differentiated from the classes from which they came originally.

Of course, the absence of a defined class consciousness in the proletarianized masses did not keep them from having an acute awareness of their precarious situation, so that they were prepared to take part in the first favorable subversive option that presented itself. They were thus at least as disposed to revolutionary action as the workers or the exploited peasants.

The tense process of proletarianization that had taken place in the cities and the countryside since the 1930s obliges us to define the sociological type that the proletarianized individual represented. The sons of farmers, petty bourgeois, or urban workers who find themselves employed or underemployed most of the time cannot consider themselves farmers, petty bourgeois, or proletarians. They may have the ideas of a farmer, a petty bourgeois, or a proletarian, but they lack an integral conception linked to a class condition, to a given social practice. In other words, they lack the experience of being organically linked to production in a stable way, as farmers, petty bourgeois, or workers. Their belonging to this nebulous region does not imply that those who are employed and those who are unemployed or underemployed most of the time think and behave socially alike, independently of their class origin. The young who are employed, unemployed, or underemployed project themselves in society and behave differently according in part to the education they have received within their families. Thus it is necessary to define the social condition of the hundreds of thousands of proletarianized young people of farmer, petty bourgeois, or proletarian extraction who made up the social base of the revolutionary vanguard throughout the entire country in the 1950s. Only in this context is it legitimate to speak of a new generation, as some Marxist social scientists have correctly pointed out (Moskichov, 1979).

Independently of their social background, the numerous contingents of young people who could find no place in the neocolonial society of the 1950s united and organized throughout the country, at first spontaneously and later under the leadership of those involved in the attack on the Moncada garrison, aimed at overthrowing the pro-U.S. tyranny of Fulgencio Batista. This fact alone is of enormous importance and presupposes the existence of a common social structure that led them to organize themselves beyond the most immediate class determinations. Basically, what served as a common link for the new generation arising from the middle classes and the proletariat was the structural fact that the threat of unemployment, social insecurity, U.S. interference in Cuban domestic affairs, betrayal of national interests by traditional political parties, and the absence of liberties and rights hung over them all equally. Still not entirely integrated into production and hence into class relations, the country's youth responded to this conjunction of social and political considerations by uniting organically in the revolutionary vanguard. As a result, the most active foci of discontent were found among the youth.

The most significant aspect of this process of proletarianization was that a majority working class, quantitatively and qualitatively essential and capable of leading the people in their struggle against the dictatorship, could not arise ipso facto. No process of class decomposition leads immediately to the formation and crystallization of a new class. For a modern and dominant proletariat to be born from the massive process of proletarianization that took place in Cuban neocolonial society, the country would have had to have been previously industrialized. When a process of this nature and dimension occurs under the effects of depressive economic cycles, the pauperized nonproletarian masses and the proletarianized masses, unable to integrate themselves organically into the social structure, are likely to organize themselves under the leadership of a generational vanguard and to initiate a movement against the power of the dependent bourgeoisie and financial capital that can culminate in a social revolution. This new type of revolution Lenin differentiated from the classical democratic-bourgeois type of revolution, designating it democratic-revolutionary with a national-popular base. And although this type of revolution still had a bourgeois character and could not be termed proletarian, its driving force was not the bourgeoisie but the most exploited strata of the population. Lenin had foreseen as well the possibility that genuine democratic revolutions could evolve toward socialism. A true democratic-revolutionary movement, too, implied the struggle for socialist transformations: "The problem always comes down to the same thing: domination by the bourgeoisie is incompatible with a true democracy, authentically revolutionary. In the 20th century, it is impossible to be a revolutionary democrat in a capitalist country if one is afraid of moving toward socialism" (Lenin, 1960, vol. 25: 347).

The social base of the Cuban revolutionary movement in the 1950s, led by a vanguard of proletarianized youth, students, and workers, should not have opposed an evolution toward socialism. Perhaps the explanation for the early failure of the revolution of 1933 was that the fundamental social base of that democratic-revolutionary movement was a petty bourgeois mass. The intensive process of proletarianization that I have described had not yet taken place. The most relevant note of that revolutionary process was that the antiimperialist, socialist discourse of Antonio Guiteras did not materialize in a political party or revolutionary movement capable of putting his ideas into practice in the 1930s and 1940s. The ideas of Guiteras would survive only with the triumph of the Cuban revolution.

Although the Guiteras revolutionary project was rooted in a long-lasting structure of Cuban society—the historical conflict between the United States and Cuba and the aspirations of the lower classes to a new society—the cadres of the revolutionary movement he created were co-opted by the charismatic, populist leadership of Grau San Martín and proved incapable of remaining united and organized in the period of revolutionary ebb. With the death of Guiteras, Grau San Martín, at the head of the revolutionary movement of 1933, symbolized the revolutionary changes that took place during his mandate. Thus the Guiterists were attracted to and absorbed by the hegemonic populist Auténtico Party, which after its leader's death represented the possibility of continuing the revolutionary movement. In contrast to radical and democratic movements that respond to constantly fluctuating circumstances, the Communist Party, by appealing to workers' historical demands for a better standard of living, was thus able to survive politically.

During this period the antiimperialist ideas of Guiteras were not rooted in a revolutionary mass organization, whereas the Marxist ideas of Carlos Baliño and Julio Antonio Mella constituted a unifying element among the working class. Organized opposition to the neocolonial system by the middle classes seems to manifest itself in specific critical moments; that of the working class is evidently structural but tends to assume economist forms. The message of the Cuban Communists to the working class and the sugar industry remained essentially the same throughout the 1940s and 1950s. A considerable sector of the working class proved to be faithful to its historical commitments and to the men who had devoted their lives to defending its rights. The Communist Party retained its members in the large industries and in the sugar industry, as an investigation by the U.S. sociologist Maurice Zeitlin (1967) revealed. At the same time, although its errors isolated it from the nonproletarian masses, that is, from the greater part of the population, the party leadership remained essentially intact.

A survey carried out in mid-1964 in twenty-one large and medium-sized industries all over the country made clear the extent to which Communist union leaders had contributed to the awakening of social consciousness in this sector of the working class—above all, among the workers between the ages of forty-four and sixty, who had been witnesses to and participants in the struggles of the Communist Party to improve the living conditions of the proletariat in the 1930s. It should be pointed out, however, that this was the best-paid sector of the working class.

In urban factories, 30% of the workers had been party members or sympathizers before the triumph of the revolution in 1959; in the sugar industry the figure was 41%. Among the workers surveyed in the country's largest factories, a majority expressed Communist sympathies or were party members. The majority (54%) of the skilled workers in factories employing more than 1,000 workers were Communists (Zeitlin, 1967: 157–184).

That the large groups of revolutionary vanguards of the Guiteras movement and other antiimperialist organizations were unable to create an independent organization and became absorbed in part by the hegemonic national-reformist group of the Auténtico Party by no means signifies that their revolutionary potential had been exhausted. The painful and bitter experience that the betrayal of the ideals of the 1930s by the governments of Grau and Prío represented for many revolutionaries did not stop them from joining the struggle against the dictatorship of Batista or the new battles that the Cuban people would fight for their genuine and definitive independence following the revolutionary triumph of 1959.

Another factor that prevented the national-revolutionary vanguard from finding its true path after the death of Guiteras was the division created by the class policy put into practice by the Communist Party during the course of the 1933 revolution that condemned the Grau-Guiteras government. When an alliance of the Communist Party with the revolutionaries and reformists of the 1933 revolution was being forged in 1937, the more conservative elements of this latter tendency, led by Grau San Martín, revived the earlier conflicts and rivalries of the brief revolutionary interregnum of 1933, thwarting efforts to unify the groups and classes objectively opposed to neocolonial domination. As Carlos Rafael Rodríguez has recognized, some aspects of the policy of alliances of the Cuban Communists between 1938 and 1944 "prevented the full exercise of their influence on important student sectors and other zones of the urban petty bourgeoisie." As Rodríguez also pointed out, these contradictions were still influential in the sentiment of these social classes between 1952 and 1959, "obstructing at that time as well actions of political leadership by the Communists" (Rodríguez, 1979: 94). This breach widened still further as the Communists opposed the insurrectional line adopted by Cuban youth during the 1950s. Of course, the determining factor in the revolutionary ebb of the middle classes was the fact that they still maintained a relatively stable position in society and had not yet entered upon the process of economic deterioration that led to the growing proletarianization of the 1950s.

The fundamental revolutionary forces among the Cuban people from 1930 to 1940, the proletariat and the middle classes, were split by dogmatic conceptions imported from the European proletariat that did not fit the Cuban reality. Since the process of decomposition and crisis of the class structure had not yet reached its apogee, the ideas and practices capable of forging unity among the fundamental classes of the people did not appear. In the prevailing conditions, the Communist Party could not take advantage of the protest movement of the middle classes. By the end of the 1940s and the early 1950s, the portion of these classes that the party had been able to attract and maintain within its sphere of influence was considerably reduced, and the Ortodoxo Party captured the votes of a majority of those who remained (Gutiérrez, 1950–1951).

The unity forged in the 1960s was the work of the historical awareness and willingness to change by the revolutionary vanguards, which implied a criticism of old attitudes, tendencies, and forms of struggle. New relations were also made possible by the individual characteristics of the different historical personalities who knew how to direct the movement, especially Fidel Castro. At the same time, the advance and consolidation of the revolutionary movement would have been inconceivable without the student movement in the period following the assault on the Moncada garrison. The student movement created the subjective conditions for the armed insurrection of the country's youth and unemployed workers. Without the selflessness, generosity, and spirit of sacrifice of leaders of the stature of Frank País, José Tey, and Félix Peña in Santiago de Cuba and José Antonio Echeverría and Fructuoso Rodríguez in Havana, the conditions for developing the revolutionary movement that followed the landing of the *Granma* would not have been created. In turn, the most powerful stimulus for these opening battles and for the independent organization of the island's youth was the discourse of men such as Rafael García Bárcena and, above all, the example of the Moncada leaders headed by Fidel Castro.

Because they were not themselves organically linked to relations of production, the students and other youth were inclined to join other classes of the population in their struggle against the dictatorship. Over all of them hung the threat, once their studies ended, of unemployment and recession. Both their intellectual level and the historical tradition of struggle by such student leaders as Mella and Trejo led the youth without a future in the neocolonial society to organize themselves. The methods of struggle they employed were in consonance with their social situation. Unable to organize or direct the struggles of the working class and to participate in the military conspiracies being hatched by the Auténtico opposition or the electoral processes of the regime, the young people turned to street demonstrations and began to prepare for armed struggle. The ideology of the students, like that of the proletarianized youth, cannot be identified with that of the petty bourgeoisie, linked to production and commercial activity. Youth and student leaders were not proposing to defend the interests of that class but the general rights of the people, trampled by the tyranny. The petty bourgeoisie as a class was

characterized at first by its passivity; the students, in contrast, confronted the dictatorship with physical opposition and assumed
responsibility for organizing the armed struggle.

Many diverse tendencies could be found among the youth of the
period, determined in part by social origin. But their identification in
general with the needs of the working class, with workers' protests
against the high cost of transportation and the standard of living,
defined their orientation in the country's political and social struggles. At the same time, in given centers of secondary education such
as the schools of arts and occupations and in some high schools,
those of proletarian origin predominated. Still more important in
this sense is that the leaders of petty bourgeois origin showed themselves capable of "surpassing in their lifetime" the "solutions" posed
by "their material interest and social situation"—that is, they rose
above the petty bourgeois solutions presented by the historical
moment, as they adopted the social revolution expounded by the
Moncada leadership. Thus, their general orientation in the 1950s
should be defined as popular-national, not as petty bourgeois. Their
unselfish attitude in defense of the people's interests as well as their
lack of identification with the narrow interests of petty bourgeois calculation do not define the youth leaders who formed part of the revolutionary vanguard in the struggle against the dictatorship as representatives of that class. In the course of the struggle, their integration
into the guerrilla forces alongside the rural proletariat and farmers
and into the clandestine movement in the cities merged their aspirations with those of the laboring class of the population (García
Olivera, 1979; Rodríguez Loeche, 1976; Chomón, 1969; Lupiáñez,
1985).

In any event, we underscore that what was determinant in the attitudes of the students was not social origin but their alignment with
the fundamental classes of the people as they situated themselves in
the front ranks of the popular national vanguard. Historical testimonies point out that the membership of organizations founded by
Frank País was composed essentially of young unemployed persons,
students, teachers, and workers between the ages of fifteen and twenty-five, who came from the humblest sectors of the proletarian neighborhoods of Santa Barbara, Martí, and Sueño and proletarianized
strata of employees and artisans of the city of Santiago de Cuba. The
research of Gladys García (1998) on the July 26 Movement in
Matanzas confirms these conclusions, as does the research of Julio
García Olivera.

Unlike the Directorate of University Students (DEU) of the
1930s—which did not create a movement or a clandestine organiza-

tion involving the humble strata of the population but later backed up the military movement carried out at the Columbia military barracks September 4 and prepared a democratic-bourgeois program— the first organizations of País and the July 26 Movement had a primarily popular-national base and it was democratic-revolutionary and antiimperialist. The petty bourgeois mass of the DEU and the ABC of the 1930s had still not been subjected to the generalized proletarianization of the 1940s and 1950s and was therefore unable to advance further along the road to revolutionary transformation than what was achieved in 1933.

With Batista's first coup d'état, engineered by Jefferson Caffery, the revolutionary possibilities of the DEU were practically exhausted, as the Auténtico governments subsequently demonstrated. The Ortodoxo Party, in contrast, never transcended the populism of a democratic-bourgeois project. This was the fundamental orientation imparted by its leadership despite the democratic-revolutionary orientation of its younger members.

In *La historia me absolverá*, the degree of importance that Fidel Castro conceded to the diverse strata and classes of the people susceptible to being incorporated into the revolutionary movement is suggested by the order in which he enumerates them:

> As far as the struggle is concerned, we call "the people" those *six hundred thousand* Cubans who are without work, wishing to earn their bread honestly without having to emigrate from their homeland in search of sustenance; those *five hundred thousand* rural workers who inhabit miserable *bohíos* [thatched huts], who work four months of the year and go hungry the rest, sharing their poverty with their children, who have not one inch of land on which to plant and whose existence would move any hearts not made of stone; those *four hundred thousand* industrial workers and laborers whose pension funds have been embezzled, whose benefits are being snatched away, whose homes are the wretched rooms of tenement buildings, whose salaries pass from the hands of the bosses to those of the moneylenders, whose future is pay cuts and layoffs, whose life is eternal work and whose only rest is the tomb; those *one hundred thousand* small farmers who live and die working on land that is not their own, forever looking at it with sadness, as Moses looked at the promised land and dying without ever managing to own it, who like feudal serfs must pay for the use of their parcel of land by giving up a portion of their products, who cannot love it or improve it or plant a lemon or orange tree because they never know when a sheriff will arrive with a rural guard to evict them from it; those *thirty thousand* teachers and professors, who are so devoted, dedicated, and necessary to the better destiny of our future generations and who are so badly treated and badly paid; those *twenty thousand* small businesspeople weighed down by debt, ruined by the crisis and harangued

by a plague of grafting and venal officials; those *ten thousand* young professionals: doctors, engineers, lawyers, veterinarians, educators, dentists, pharmacists, journalists, painters, sculptors, etc., who leave school with their degrees, anxious to work and full of hope, only to find themselves in a dead-end street, with all the doors closed and where no one hears their pleas and demands. (Castro, 1963)

Fidel called for the unity of all the people without excepting any strata or class. His relation was with the national-popular bloc in its entirety, without privileging any sector. It is unquestionable, from the order in which he listed them in his historic manifesto, that he was fully aware of which of the forces were most capable of contributing a greater quantitative potential to the revolutionary movement.

Thus he spoke first of the 600,000 unemployed, then of the 500,000 rural proletarians, the 400,000 industrial workers, the 100,000 small farmers, the 30,000 teachers, the 20,000 small business-people, and the 10,000 professionals. In his description of their situation, the shadow of unemployment and proletarianization looms over these sectors. There are 600,000 Cubans "without work," 500,000 rural proletarians who "work four months of the year," 400,000 industrial workers whose future is "pay cuts and layoffs," 100,000 small farmers who "never know" when they might be evicted, 30,000 teachers "badly treated and badly paid," 20,000 small businesspeople "ruined by the crisis," and 10,000 professionals who are in "a dead-end street." The critical situation all these classes face is more a matter of the threat of losing their means of livelihood, of being cut off from the means of production, that is, of becoming proletarianized (if this has not already occurred) than it is of their low standard of living. Castro had not made a statistical study of the country's censuses nor pinned down precisely, from a quantitative standpoint, the vagaries to which the diverse social strata and classes were subjected, but he had studied them and knew the dominant phenomenon that determined the instability of the whole system. He was aware that these strata and classes were susceptible to being revolutionized in favor of a minimum program of social revolution. To this effect, he based the organization of the revolutionary vanguard of the July 26 Movement on young proletarianized urban workers, students, and youth, the sectors that had demonstrated the greatest combativeness until that moment, and later created a guerrilla group made up of rural proletarians and farmers in the Sierra Maestra. With the guerrilla movement consolidated, the Moncada leadership set forth a policy of alliance with the urban working class and with the middle class. It was thus that the leadership of Castro and his comrades of the

Moncada group was established, by means of which the hegemony of Marxist ideas was expressed.

In the Moncada program, not only was the so-called national bourgeoisie excluded from the classes making up the people but all the demands and vindications of this class were ignored. What is more, the program presupposes the expropriation of the industrial bourgeois class by posing that 50% of their profits should form part of the earnings of the working class. The original position with respect to this class changed around 1957, following the conversations the Moncada leadership held in the Sierra Maestra with Raúl Chibás and Felipe Pazos, representatives of the national bourgeoisie.

As Faustino Pérez accurately pointed out, the bourgeoisie did not participate in the revolutionary process as a class, although a certain number of individuals joined it, motivated by the idea that "this is finished, the situation is very bad and later something else will take its place, so let me keep on the good side of both God and the devil" (Pérez, F., 1969: 79–80).

Various other testimonies of the era have amply proved that the fundamental social base of the rebel army was made up largely of rural proletarians and semiproletarians. A study of the historical documentation—records of the rebel army and other sources—would be necessary to determine more precisely its members' different social rank, age, social and regional origins, and so on. The composition of the revolutionary vanguard up to the landing of the *Granma,* made up of proletarianized young people, students, and workers according to contemporary accounts, can also be quantitatively analyzed from the records of participants in clandestine activities and from surveys similar to those described.

The social origin, situation in the social structure, and so on of militants of the Popular Socialist Party and other opposition organizations might be examined as well. In these investigations, the use of rigid categories such as worker or petty bourgeois should be avoided in order to define the great proletarianized mass quantitatively and determine its proportion in the ranks of revolutionary organizations.

The results of the present historiographic study of Cuban social classes clash with the hypotheses formulated by historians of the republican period concerning the hegemonic role played by given classes or social groups in the formation and structural transformation of Cuban neocolonial society. In fact, I was able to reach certain conclusions in the course of my investigation mainly because I set myself the task of exhausting the sources, insofar as possible, from which other researchers had departed in their dealing with the subjects that have been the object of my analysis. Since the perception of specific aspects of social structure—their greater or lesser coherence or maturity—has been the foundation on which historians and social scientists have based their hypotheses about the hegemonic role of classes and groups, to the degree that I have realized an integral empirical study of the diverse economic, demographic, and social sources of the age, I shall have contributed to the posing of new historiographic problems related to the republican period prior to 1959.

Humans are the result not only of the set of biological, economic, demographic, social, and cultural determinations that influence them but also of what they think they are. They can be mistaken. The image that they form of themselves may be erroneous, but they will always try to act in consonance with it. Separation from the productive process can be felt as destiny, as a permanent condition. When those separated from production (marginal workers, unemployed, underemployed) reach numbers in the thousands or tens and hundreds of thousands, we are face to face with a new demographic, social, and human reality.

Is the young, proletarianized, unemployed son of a worker, small manufacturer, small merchant, or peasant also a worker, small merchant or proprietor, or owner of a parcel of land? Does the worker without work, the ruined urban petty bourgeois, the small farmer thrown off his land, whose situation of permanent separation from production or chronic or eventual unemployment is prolonged for three, four, five, or more years, think or continue to think like a worker, like a small proprietor, like a peasant, or does he feel like a declassed person, an excluded individual? How does he fit into the social structure? To what class does he belong? What is his permanent place? One is not proletarianized for a few months or a year; this situation can become a permanent social condition, a *destiny*, for hundreds of thousands of persons. Sociological surveys show that proletarianized individuals, as their situation is prolonged, consider themselves permanently declassed, excluded from the large social groups (Galich, 1978: 7–17, 214–240, 250–254; Alvaro Estramina, 1989: 211–243).

Beginning in 1899 the proletarianized sector grew unceasingly year after year. The army of permanently unemployed therefore did not respond to a crisis but to the structure of neocolonial plantation society. The decline in the percentage of the employed population in relation to the population of working age from 1899 to 1953 gives us an idea, albeit imprecise, of the progressive growth of the proletarianized sector of neocolonial society.

Does not this rootlessness, this permanent instability of the proletarianized person, condition a mentality, an experience of work, a social and ideological identification different from that of the worker, a full-time factory employee, and the stable petty bourgeois? Hence, the need to ask ourselves about the ideas, or rather the predominant ideology, of the proletarianized masses. Which are the ideas that circulate most frequently and intensely in that sector—those of the working class, those of the petty bourgeoisie, or those that correspond to a condition of rootlessness or alienation? Whatever the answer, the most important thing is that the attitudes of the proletarianized sector tend to differ from those of the steady, stable sectors of the proletariat (or working class), the petty bourgeoisie, and the peasantry—therefore the need and importance of studying this sector as a differentiated formation with relation to the classes that constituted the people in neocolonial society. It is true that the proletarianized person is often a transitional type between the petty bourgeois and the peasant on the one hand and the proletarian on the other, whose evolution tends to extend over time. At other times, the proletarianized person comes from a working-class family and delays several years in finding fixed occupation as a worker, artisan, small merchant, or the like in the informal sector. At still other times, the change from one social category to another occurs rapidly. In situations of prolonged economic crisis, the condition of unemployed or only occasionally employed tends to have a lasting character.

Of course, in neocolonial plantation societies, in which demographic growth is accompanied by an atrophy in production, unemployment increases progressively and tends to become permanent. In Cuba the unemployed population of working age increased in relation to the overall population of working age in each of the censuses carried out from 1899 on. Table 11.2 illustrates indirectly the intense process of proletarianization that took place from the beginning to the middle of the twentieth century. The slight decline shown in the census of 1953 is due to the fact that this count, unlike the others, was made in the harvest season, but the sample of the National Economic Council of 1957 confirms the tendency of the process of proletarianization to grow steadily and to become a permanent characteristic of the plantation society, or of neocolonial plantation capitalism.

Although the pundits and ideologists of Cuban neocolonial society denied the existence of a permanent economic and institutional crisis and even posed a kind of capitalist takeoff in the 1950s in an effort to present the revolutionary transformations of the 1960s as the result of an aberration of political consciousness, the most

Table 11.2   **Percentage of Unemployment Among Those of Working Age,**
1899–1957

	% of Unemployed Population of Working Age
1899	37.5
1907	42.5
1919	45.1
1931	49.1
1943	53.2
1953	48.5
1957	55.0

Source: *Cuba Económica y Financiera*, May 1960: 7.

representative personalities of the dictatorship and of the traditional political opposition of the time were deeply concerned about the direction that the country's demographic and economic evolution had taken. In a televised roundtable on unemployment held February 23, 1953, on CMQ-TV, high officials of the regime agreed concerning the critical situation facing the country. José Abalos, the economic adviser of the National Economic Board, stated that the economic crisis and the much-debated problem of unemployment were the results of "a structural fault and a given economic structure whose framework is not susceptible to change without carrying out major reform efforts, efforts that may be structural and that would be very long-range." In turn, the hacendado Amado Aréchaga was inclined to think that "unemployment will be dangerously accentuated in the coming years." The dictatorship-backed labor leader, Samuel Powel, revealed that according to the statistical calculations of the CTC, "some 25,000 young people between eighteen and twenty-five years of age enter the torrent of unemployment in the country each year." For the union leader, the situation was genuinely critical and alarming, since these young people tended to "become types who repudiate society, the constitution of 1940, as well as all constitutional ideals because they have no solution, no possibility of solving their problems."

The engineer Amadeo López Castro, president of the Commission of National Development, stated that "thirty years ago, there was practically no unemployment visible in the country," but as the population increased and the sugar industry had "reached its limit" the situation had been aggravated. The problem was such that even when "in general Cuban public opinion has, until now, throughout every change in leaders, considered this problem as secondary . . . it is a capital problem that must be faced and . . . all Cuba has to attack it frontally and put all its efforts into finding a solution." López Castro affirmed, "There may be no case in America more dramatic than that of Cuba."

Solutions to the problems those officials described could not arise from among that group. Although López Castro idealistically recommended creating several work shifts in the sugar industry and having the government discreetly promote the cultivation of rice, he admitted that Cuba could not seek self-sufficiency with a view to creating new sources of jobs without transforming structures of neocolonial domination, which impeded this type of solution. In the television debate, the employers' representatives pronounced themselves in favor of compensated layoffs as the best way to activate investments and increase sources of jobs, whereas the union leaders proposed that the government reduce the taxes that burdened the industrial bourgeoisie.

Gustavo Gutiérrez claimed "the discovery of a phenomenon that has enormous importance for the political stability of the nation— namely, that the behavior of the curve of political stability is mainly shaped by the lack of employment opportunities" (*Boletín Informativo del Consejo Nacional de Economía,* 1958: 21–23). Although there is a clear link between unemployment and political stability, this axiom does not apply to every district of the country. Mesa Lago has shown that the provinces affected by the insurrection were not necessarily the ones with the highest rates of unemployment (Mesa Lago, 1972: 26). The comparisons between the number of unemployed in each province and the total population in the same province shows that rates of relative unemployment were highest in Matanzas and Las Villas, followed by Camagüey and Oriente and, finally, Havana and Pinar del Río. It is generally admitted that Matanzas, Pinar del Río, and Camagüey were comparatively peaceful. However, the concentration of the largest absolute number of young men, students and unemployed, in the populous provinces of Oriente, Las Villas, and Havana contributed to the leading revolutionary role of these provinces. Since the largest groups of discontented, jobless, and marginalized youth were in these regions, they tended to organize themselves into revolutionary vanguards. Unemployment and revolutionary attitudes were closely related, as Zeitlin's sample of Cuban workers reveals. The workers who experienced unemployment and underemployment most often during the 1950s were the ones who joined the revolutionary movement from its beginning (Zeitlin, 1967).

Similar declarations were formulated at that time by representatives of the traditional political opposition, such as Cosme de la Torriente and José Miró Cardona. They claimed the mediating actions of the Society of Friends of the Republic sought to avoid above all a repetition of the events of the 1930s in which the political process could take on a revolutionary aspect. In this sense, the economic crisis, with its high levels of unemployment and the general decline in real wages, as well as the notable participation of proletarianized youth in the revolutionary struggle, presented a threat, in the opinion of these ideologists, that an antiimperialist revolution with socialist elements could be knocking at the door (Ibarra Guitart, 1994). These judgments, together with the statistical documentation reproduced in this study, deny the veracity of the Panglossian views apropos of a supposed period of prosperity and the rise of bourgeois hegemony.

Although investigations based on the archives of clandestine combatants have not been published, a survey made in the 1950s among militants of the July 26 Movement in the humble, marginal neighborhood of Chicharrones, one of the epicenters of the revolutionary movement in Santiago de Cuba, revealed a human and social reality that cold statistics of unemployment were incapable of transmitting. After conducting hundreds of interviews, excerpts of which are reproduced in his book, the historian Rigoberto Cruz arrived at conclusions similar to those I have reached from my analysis of the statistics and the sociological samplings carried at the time. According to Cruz, the population of Chicharrones was not composed of "indigents—they still had possibilities of survival. The group was composed of unemployed or very poorly paid workers, teachers, technicians of various specialities, and even professionals displaced from their jobs by the traditional movements of government employees that took place during the changes of government."

Cruz described the situation of labor instability affecting the inhabitants of the neighborhood: "Very few . . . had continuous work that allowed them to attend in a stable way to their basic needs. Some paid-by-the-day agricultural work of short duration; sporadic work in construction or another sector, always for a brief time; at best a job in the Ministry of Public Works or Public Health subject to instability in pay, the loan sharks, and the constant anxiety provoked by the feeling of being adrift, the victim of political maneuvers, made up the labor panorama of that neighborhood." The situation of Chicharrones was not unique but was repeated in every city of the country, as the declarations of the clandestine combatants of the time tend to confirm. "All that need, all that shared poverty, all that longing for justice in a medium that was clearly unjust and moreover illogical, repeated throughout the length and breadth of the country, was the cultural broth in which the germ of our present revolutionary process violently developed" (Cruz, 1982: 1–4).

The proletarianized sector of Cuban neocolonial society takes on a life of its own as an entity differentiated from the petty bourgeoisie and the working class when we evaluate it in a broader historical and sociological context. After a careful revision of part of the extensive bibliography devoted to social structure, I discovered in the work of Henri Lefebvre judgments that in a certain sense approach the empirical results and conceptual formulations of my study (Lefebvre, 1973: 112, 134–135, 161). Apparently drawing on the opinions of Arnold Toynbee concerning the existence of a proletariat opposed to the imperial powers in the ancient world, the French sociologist formulated a hypothesis in which he distinguished conceptually the colonial proletarianized sectors from the working class and from the petty bourgeoisie of the First World. Lefebvre affirmed that worldwide economic growth provokes not only inequalities of development but also the decomposition of social relations, that is, impoverishment and marginalization surrounding the nucleus of the working class, which tends to remain relatively stable and integrated:

> Beside the working class, a gigantic proletarianization takes place as a result of this vast decomposition with new conflictive elements. If we define the proletariat by its lack of juridical and practical links with the means of production, proletarianization touches the entire world: proletarianization of the middle classes, of white-collar workers, of ruined farmers not integrated into production, in every different type of country, in Latin America, for example, in the urban peripheries. A vast proletarianization of the world that contrasts with the bloc of the working class that remains there, solid. Plus youth; plus the intellectuals, for those whose knowledge does not establish direct links with the means of production; plus the negroes; plus the immigrant workers. Enormous proletarianization corresponding exactly to the original Marxist notion, that is, the notion of classes separated from the means of production, charged with negativity, capable, under given conditions, of a struggle to the death to change everything. (Lefebvre, 1973: 134–135)

What Lefebvre defined as the proletarianized world approaches very closely my definition of proletarianized sectors or proletarianized youth, opposed to the notion of an everlasting, ideally integrated and stable working class, organically linked to the means of production. The main distinction is that the proletarianized individual (that is, the proletarianized middle-class worker or youth in my definition) would be separated from the means of production by "juridical or practical links" and constitute an antagonistic sector "charged with negativity" with respect to the capitalist system, whereas the working class, according to Lefebvre, is a sector "integrated or capable of being integrated" into the capitalist system. This possibility of integration, as Lefebvre prudently pointed out, would have only a "momentary or conjunctural" character or valid value. Although in the Cuban case given sectors of the working class, especially the very highly paid industrial proletariat of the capital, seemed inclined to "integration" with the Havana oligarchic bloc (as López Segrera asserted), the working class as a whole, including its sectors in the capital, constituted one of the bases of the national popular movement.

Finally, Lefebvre included youth, blacks, and immigrant workers without explaining the reasons for their appearance in the processes of world proletarianization. It should be kept in mind that these groups are among those most susceptible to losing or not finding employment in capitalist societies: youth, independently of its proletarian or petty bourgeois origin, because they reached working age when the majority of jobs are already taken; blacks because of their condition as a stratum that is discriminated against ethnically and from the standpoint of labor; and immigrant workers because they are often temporary or emergency workers who are admitted into a country for the purpose of dragging down salaries and performing occasional, ill-paid work.

The process of proletarianization, inasmuch as it affects each and every one of the social and ideological structures, can be considered, in the view of Georges Gurvitch (1970), as an expansive social phenomenon with a global character. In that sense, historiographic interpretation should beware of reductionist, mechanistic, and economic valuations of this type of process. The perceptions and attitudes of social groups and structures not directly involved in the processes of proletarianization can be radically transformed by these, without a direct effect on their status or internal structure. Thus, for example, the fear of proletarianization among large sectors of the stable petty bourgeoisie and students, without regard to their social origin, can determine substantial changes in their ideology and political positions. It is not strange, therefore, that stable groups and strata of the middle class frequently adopt attitudes similar to those of the directly proletarianized sectors. In other instances, the fear of proletarianization among stable portions of the working class or middle classes leads them to assume conservative positions, opposed to that of the proletarianized sectors. Fear of the dangers and instability that these processes imply in neocolonial societies of dependent capitalism also determines changes of policy by the oligarchic bloc. In this way the Keynesian policy of carefree spending adopted by Batista can be seen as the response of the dictatorship to the new situation created by the process of proletarianization and the recessive economic cycle of the 1950s.

The structural transformations implied by these processes in a certain sense conditioned the premises of the social revolution of the 1960s. The differences between the revolutions of the 1930s and the 1960s correspond in large measure to the changes effected in the social structures of the country. The economic crisis of the 1930s paved the way for the formation of a petty bourgeois vanguard, marginalized by imperialist penetration but fearful of proletarian aspirations. These middle sectors, although ignored and subordinated by the relations of neocolonial domination, still maintained a position of relative stability, unthreatened by a process of disintegration. The growing proletarianization in the 1950s, in contrast, led to the creation of a vanguard composed primarily of the proletarianized youth of working-class, petty bourgeois, or peasant origin, together with young workers, small businesspeople, and professionals who saw themselves seriously threatened by the impact of the recessive economic cycle and unemployment.

Nevertheless, just as the Cuban revolution cannot be conceptualized as a "worker," "petty bourgeois," or "peasant" revolution, neither can it be defined as a revolution of the country's proletarianized youth. To the extent that the role of each of these classes in the course of events was irreplaceable, the revolutionary process can be defined only in terms of the whole. Thus, the revolution was, above all, a national-popular revolution.

In order to differentiate the Cuban revolutionary process from other processes with similar characteristics, it is necessary to return to its ideological program and discourse. The definition of the diverse revolutionary projects of the new generation as those of an unfinished social revolution of socialist orientation and with a popular national base seems to be correct. It must be seen as a revolution not defined as socialist but merely having that orientation, inasmuch as the tendency favored by its leaders required the existence of auspicious conditions that would appear only in the 1960s. Its original nucleus, its vanguard, was constituted by young people totally or partially cut off from relations of production. The original intention of its leaders was to structure it on the popular sectors where the major foci of discontent were found among the country's youth. This can be easily verified in the sources of the time (in the court records related to revolutionary actions, in the archives of the repressive forces of the dictatorship, in the archives of the associations of revolutionary combatants, and so on).

One of the first manifestations of the intention to create a revolutionary vanguard from among the youth of humble origin appears in the declaration of Fidel Castro concerning the new stage that opened with the March 10 coup d'état of Batista. The positive element in the new situation was that the revolution "opened the way to merit; to those who have valor and ideals and are sincere, to those willing to expose their bare chests and raise high the standard." To that end, "to correspond to a revolutionary people, a revolutionary leadership [is needed], young and of popular origin, arising from the people, with Cuban roots" (*El Acusador*, August 16, 1952: 2).

Castro's awareness of the abyss between the new generation and the Cuban bourgeoisie is expressed in lines written in December 1953 during his imprisonment on the Isle of Pines. Evoking the memory of his comrades who fell in the attack on the Moncada garrison, he asked, "How many remember them at this moment? . . . What do the sorrow of the homeland and the mourning in so many homes matter to the rich and fatuous who fill the salons of society? For them, we are only rash youth, perturbers of the existing social paradise." Referring to the reaction the Moncada revolutionary project had provoked among traditional politicians and the Cuban bourgeoisie, Castro wrote, "With such an awakening of a new revolutionary generation, it was logical that all the socially privileged and all the political hierarchies would feel mortally threatened."

The extent to which a generational consciousness existed among the Moncada combatants in the sense that they identified with a group without commitments to the past and proclaimed themselves members of a new generation, not of a class or political party, can be judged from the important historical testimonies of Jesús Montané, Pedro Miret, and Raúl Castro. The poet and ideologue of the "generation of the centenary," Raúl Gómez García, author of the manifesto of the attack on the Moncada garrison, identified the country's youth as the protagonists of a social revolution in the making: "The youth of today, the youth of the centenary, the historical pinnacle of the Cuban revolution, have sworn to defend those rights, to raise that banner."

As significant as the generational identification of the Moncada combatants was the revolutionary project of Rafael García Bárcenas, founder of the National Revolutionary Movement (MNR), who proposed in 1952 to capture the Columbia garrison, the country's most important military stronghold, with a force composed of young people and university students. The cardinal orientation of this new generation was to carry out a revolution on its own account, independently of the traditional political parties. The ideological principles of the MNR were nationalism, democracy, and socialism. One of the most significant aspects of the new revolutionary group was that its young leaders included individuals who would later be outstanding figures of the July 26 Movement and the Revolutionary Directorate: Frank País, José Tey, Vilma Espín, Fructuoso Rodríguez, Manuel Carbonell, Armando Hart, Faustino Pérez, and others.

After the attack on the Moncada garrison and during his imprisonment on the Isle of Pines, Castro would reiterate, in the pamphlet *Mensaje a Cuba que sufre,* his intention to organize a revolutionary movement on the same bases: "If one hundred valiant young men fell in Santiago, that only means that there are one hundred thousand young people in our homeland who are also willing to fall. Seek them and they will be found, orient them and they will march ahead no matter how hard the road; the masses are ready, they only need to be shown the true route." Definitions of the role to be played by the new revolutionary generation vis-à-vis the traditional political parties appear repeatedly throughout the discourse of the Moncada leaders (Conte Agüero, 1960: 45; Castro, 1955: 81–83).

País and Echeverría, the leaders of the principal youth movements that initially and independently supported the Moncada action, also referred on their own account to the role to be played by the country's youth: organizing and mobilizing the people against the tyranny. For País, the leadership of the revolutionary movement corresponded to "an honest, valiant, and revolutionary generation" that aspired to "guide Cuba within the political, economic, and social currents of our century," since "we aspire to deeply arouse all the sectors of the country; we aspire to create revolutionary plans that put all those sectors to work in behalf of the New Motherland; we aspire to remove, overthrow, destroy the colonialist system that still prevails; sweep out the bureaucracy; eliminate superfluous mechanisms; extract genuine values; and implant, in accordance with our idiosyncrasy, the modern philosophical currents that prevail today in the world; we aspire not to apply temporary remedies but to plan, conscientiously and responsibly, the construction of the New Motherland" (Gálvez, vol. 2, 1991: 484).

The same generational resolve to carry out a profound social revolution of antiimperialist orientation infuses the words of Echeverría: "We maintain that only a profound transformation of our political, economic, and social reality can cure the evils of our country. The immediate problem for Cuba is to overthrow the usurper Fulgencio Batista and establish a democratic government, and then to under-

take the revolutionary task of solving the problem of the unemployed, of the rural people without land, of the exploited workers, of
the youth condemned to economic exile. Cuba urgently requires a
genuine revolution that rips off what Martínez Villena called in his
inflammatory verses 'the tenacious scab of colonialism'" (Factitious
Collection of the José Martí National Library).

Regional studies of the revolutionary movement tend to show the
existence of a common opinion concerning U.S. neocolonialism,
unemployment, the hegemonic crisis of the traditional political parties, the latifundia, political and administrative corruption, and the
dictatorship. Yet comparative studies reveal that the outstanding popular leaders, representatives of their generation, still did not make up
a complete ideological universe. An analysis of the content of the key
concepts of the July 26 Movement's discourse, published in the revolutionary underground press, indicates that the revolutionary leaders
did not refer to a class, stratum, cultural group, or system of beliefs
but to a new historical and social promotion, that is, they referred to
a new generation that distinguished itself from the traditional political groups by completing and crowning the unfinished revolution of
1933. In other words, the revolutionary leadership was not defined by
an articulated project based on class or by the demands and claims of
the class or group it might belong to or represent. Rather it was
defined by the critical situation the nation faced, whose solution
would lie in the realization of the popular national project of 1933,
which incorporated the demands of all the people. Thus, in the newspaper *Surco* of the Frank País Second Eastern Front and in the *Sierra
Maestra*, organ of the July 26 Movement, the revolutionary leadership
identified itself as the representative of the new generation, or of the
country's revolutionary youth, which proposed to carry out a revolution on behalf of all the people.

Regional studies could reveal significant variations in the social
composition and ideological orientation of the leaders of the revolutionary movement. Nevertheless, until monographic studies are made
of the movement on a national scale, it cannot be characterized
socially or ideologically. What seems to be beyond all doubt is the
incapacity of the classic reductionist schema of the hegemony of a
single class or social group to account for the overall historical
process. In any event, the phenomenon of massive proletarianization
of the society had a radical influence on the change in attitude of all
the social groups, to the extent of unifying the people and establish-
ing the premises for the socialist revolution. Other factors such as the
contradictions between the nation and imperialist domination, the

role of personality in history, and the heroic inclinations derived from the island's history of struggle for national liberation all contributed decisively to the consolidation of the revolutionary movement in the 1960s, but my aim has been merely to explain some social determinants of the historical process.

Bibliography

ABAD, LUIS: "La burocracia cubana," *Cuba Económica y Financiera,* no. 130, Havana, January 1937.

——: *Cuadros estadísticos y estudios analíticos de los ferrocarriles,* Havana, 1939.

——: "La burocracia en Cuba y Colombia," *Cuba Económica y Financiera,* no. 190, Havana, February 1942.

ACOSTA, JOSÉ: "Las leyes de la Reforma Agraria en Cuba y en el sector privado campesino," *Economía y Desarrollo,* Instituto de Economía de la Universidad de La Habana, July–August 1972.

——: "De la neocolonia a la construcción del Socialismo," *Economía y Desarrollo,* Instituto de Economía de la Universidad de La Habana, November–December 1973.

AGRUPACIÓN CATÓLICA UNIVERSITARIA (ACU): "Encuesta de trabajadores rurales, 1956–1957, *Economía y Desarrollo,* Instituto de Economía de la Universidad de la Habana, July–August 1972.

——: "¿Por qué Reforma Agraria?" ACU, Havana, n.d.

AGUIRRE, MIRTA, ISABEL MONAL, and DENIA GARCÍA: *El leninismo en la Historia me absolverá,* Editorial de Ciencias Sociales, Havana, 1980.

AGUIRRE, SEVERO: *La revolución agraria,* Editorial Tipografía Ideas, Havana, 1961.

ALAVEZ, ELENA: *Eduardo Chibás en la hora de la ortodoxia,* Colección Pinos Nuevos, Editorial de Ciencias Sociales, Instituto Cubano del Libro, Havana, 1994.

ALDEN, D., ed.: *Essays Concerning the Socio-economic History of Brazil and Portuguese India,* University Press of Florida, Gainesville, 1977.

ALIENES, JULIÁN: "La economía nacional de Cuba," *Directorio Oficial de Exportación e Importación, Producción y Turismo,* Ediciones Cámara de Comercio de Cuba, Havana, 1941.

——: *Economía de la post-guerra y desempleo,* Junta Nacional de Economía, Havana, 1943.

——: *Características fundamentales de la economía cubana,* Editorial del Banco Nacional de Cuba, Havana, 1950.

ÁLVAREZ DE ACEVEDO, S. M.: *La economía española en la economía cubana,* Ucar, García, y Cía., Havana, 1936.

ÁLVAREZ VÁZQUEZ, LUISA: *La fecundidad en Cuba,* Editorial de Ciencias Sociales, Havana, 1985.

ÁLVARO ESTRAMINA, JOSÉ LUIS: *Desempleo y bienestar psicológico*, Editorial Universidad Complutense de Madrid, Madrid, 1989.

————: *Juventud, trabajo y desempleo*, Ministerio del Trabajo, Madrid, 1993.

ARANDA, SERGIO: *La revolución agraria en Cuba*, Editorial Siglo XXI, Mexico City, 1973.

Archivo de Gonzalo de Quesada. Documentos históricos, Editora Universidad de La Habana, 1956.

ARREDONDO, ALBERTO: *Cuba, tierra indefensa*, Editorial Lex, Havana, 1945.

ASOCIACIÓN NACIONAL DE AMAS DE CASA (ANAC): *Estudio sobre el trabajo de las mujeres en Cuba*, n.d.

BAIROCH, PAUL: *Revolución industrial y subdesarrollo*, Editorial de Ciencias Sociales, Havana, 1969.

BAMBIRRA, VANIA: *La Revolución Cubana: una reinterpretación*, Editorial Prensa Latinoamericana, Santiago de Chile, 1979.

BARAN, PAUL A.: *La economía política del crecimiento*, Editorial de Ciencias Sociales, Havana, 1971.

BARRACLOUGH, SOLON, and ARTHUR L. DOMIKE: "La estructura agraria en siete países de América Latina," *Desarrollo agrícola*, ed. Edmundo Flores, Fondo de Cultura Económica, Mexico City, 1974.

BATISTA, FULGENCIO: *Piedras y leyes*, Ediciones Bota, Mexico City, 1961.

BAUDI, DIETER: "La planificación a largo plazo de la Cuban Electric Company," *Monopolios norteamericanos en Cuba*, Editorial de Ciencias Sociales, Havana, 1973.

BENEDETTI, MARIO: *Jóvenes de esta América*, Editora Casa de las Américas, Havana, 1978.

BERGERE, J.: "Las actitudes ideológico-políticas de los jóvenes madrileños en situación de desempleo," *Juventud, trabajo y desempleo*, Ministerio del Trabajo, Madrid, 1993.

BERGERE, J., and J. L. ÁLVARO ESTRAMINA: *Desempleo, salud, trabajo e ideología política*, Actas del I Congreso Nacional de Medicina, Madrid, 1987.

BESADA, BENITO: "Los problemas financieros en Cuba y la creación del Banco Nacional," *Economía y Desarrollo*, Instituto de Economía de la Universidad de Havana, September–October 1975.

BLACKBURN, ROBIN: "Prologue to the Cuban Revolution," *New Left Review*, October 21, 1963.

BRUNDENIUS, CLAES: *Revolutionary Cuba: The Challenge of Economic Growth with Equity*, Westview Press, Boulder, Colo., 1984.

BYRES, T. J. PEARCE, and VERENA R. STOLCKE: *Sharecropping and Sharecroppers*, T. J. Byres, Frank Cass & Co., London, 1983.

CABRERA, OLGA: *El movimiento obrero cubano en 1920*, Editorial Pluma en Ristre, Havana, 1969.

————: *Los que viven por sus manos*, Editorial de Ciencias Sociales, Havana, 1985.

CARDOSO, CIRO F. S., and HÉCTOR PÉREZ BRIGNOLI: *Historia económica de América Latina*, vol. 2, Editorial Crítica, Mexico City, 1979.

CARLSON, WILLIAM H.: *Report of Special Commissioner on Railroads*, Havana, 1901.

CARRIÓN, MIGUEL DE: "El desenvolvimiento social de Cuba en los últimos veinte años," *Cuba Contemporánea* 27, 105, September 1921.

CASTAÑEDA, CARLOS: "¡665 000 cubanos sin trabajo!" *Bohemia*, February 16, 1958 (supplement).

CASTRO, FIDEL: "Sirvo a Cuba. Los que no tienen el valor de sacrificarse," *Bohemia* 47, November 1955.
———: *La historia me absolverá,* Editora Política, Havana, 1963.
CATASÚS, SONIA: *Evolución estimada de la fecundidad en Cuba, 1900–1950,* n.d.
CEBALLOS, SEGUNDO: "Proyección y panorama de la economía cubana," *Bohemia,* Havana, July 26, 1953.
———: "Realidad social del campesinado," *Primer Forum Nacional de la Reforma Agraria,* Havana, 1959.
CEPERO BONILLA, RAÚL: *Política azucarera, 1952–1958,* Editorial Futuro S.A., Mexico City, 1958.
———: *Escritos económicos,* Editorial de Ciencias Sociales, Havana, 1983.
CHAILLOUX, JUAN M.: *Síntesis histórica de la vivienda popular,* vol. 20, Biblioteca de Historia, Filosofía y Sociología, Havana, 1945.
CHÍA GARZÓN, JESÚS A.: *El monopolio del jabón y del perfume en Cuba,* Editorial de Ciencias Sociales, Havana, 1977.
CHIBÁS, EDUARDO: "Por defender al pueblo iría a la cárcel con orgullo," *Bohemia,* March 6, 1949.
CHOMÓN, FAURE: "El ataque al Palacio Presidencial," *La Sierra y el Llano,* Havana, 1969.
CHONCHOL, JACQUES: "Análisis crítico de la Reforma Agraria cubana," *El Trimestre Económico* 30, January–March 1963.
COLIVER, A.: *Birth Rates in Latin America. New Estimates of Historical Trends and Fluctuations,* University of California, Berkeley, 1969.
COLLAZO, ENRIQUE: *Cuba, banca y crédito,* Editorial de Ciencias Sociales, Havana, 1989.
CONTE AGÜERO, LUIS: *Héroes y mártires,* Editorial Cuba, Havana, 1960.
CRUZ, RIGOBERTO: *Chicharrones, la Sierra chiquita,* Editorial Oriente, Santiago de Cuba, 1982.
CUBA: *Informe de la Administración Provisional de la República de Cuba, 1906–1907,* Imprenta y Papelería de Rambla y Bounza, Havana, 1908.
———: *Informe de la Administración Provisional de la República de Cuba, 1907–1908,* Imprenta y Papelería de Rambla y Bounza, Havana, 1909.
CUBAN ECONOMIC RESEARCH PROJECT: *A Study on Cuba,* University of Miami, Miami, 1965.
CUERVO, FROILÁN: *Cuestión agraria, cuestión obrera,* Havana, 1908.
DALTON, J. E.: *Sugar,* Macmillan, New York, 1937.
DARUSHENKOV, OLEG: *Cuba, el camino de la revolución,* Editorial Progreso, Moscow, 1979.
DE LA TORRIENTE, COSME: *Cuarenta años de mi vida, 1898–1938,* Imprenta El Siglo, Havana, 1939.
DEL TORO, CARLOS: *El movimiento obrero cubano en 1914,* Colección Pluma en Ristre, Instituto del Libro, Havana, 1969.
———: *Algunos aspectos económicos, sociales y políticos del movimiento obrero cubano (1933–1958),* Editorial Arte y Literatura, Havana, 1974.
DOMÍNGUEZ, Jorge L.: *Order and Revolution,* Harvard University Press, Cambridge, 1978.
DOMÍNGUEZ NAVARRO, OFELIA: *50 años de una vida,* Instituto Cubano del Libro, Havana, 1971.
DORADO, FRANCISCO: "La crisis de los FC Unidos de la Habana," *Fundamentos* 13, 135, June 1953.

DOS SANTOS, THEOTONIO: *El concepto de clases sociales,* Editorial Calarcá, Bogotá, 1974.

DRAPER, THEODORE: *Castro's Revolution: Myths and Reality,* Praeger, New York, 1962.

————: *Castrismo: Theory and Practice,* Praeger, New York, 1965.

DUARTE, MARTIN: *La máquina torcedora de tabaco y las luchas en torno a su implantación en Cuba,* Editorial de Ciencias Sociales, Havana, 1973.

DUCASSI, FRANCISCO: *Desempleo y falta de ventas,* Havana, 1953.

DUHARTE, RAFAEL, and RADAMÉS DE LOS REYES: *La burguesía santiaguera (1940–1950),* Editorial Oriente, Santiago de Cuba, 1983.

DUMOULIN, JOHN: "Procedencia social de los obreros de un ingenio azucarero," *Etnología y Folklore,* no. 2, Academia de Ciencias de Cuba, 1966.

————: "Extracción y absorción interna del excedente económico cubano," *Economía y Desarrollo,* Instituto de Economía de la Universidad de Havana, May–June 1976.

————: *Azúcar y lucha de clases, 1917,* Editorial de Ciencias Sociales, Havana, 1980.

————: *La regulación estatal de las relaciones obrero-patronales en Cuba, 1933–1958,* Instituto de Ciencias Históricas de la Academia de Ciencias de Cuba, Havana, 1985.

DUMPIERRE, ERASMO: *La ESSO en Cuba. Monopolio y República burguesa,* Editorial de Ciencias Sociales, Havana, 1984.

ECHEVERRÍA SALVAT, OSCAR A.: *La agricultura cubana. 1939–1966. Régimen social, productividad y nivel de vida del sector,* Editorial Universal, Miami, 1971.

ELLIOT, J. H., ROLAND MOUSNIER, et al.: *Revoluciones y rebeliones de la Europa moderna,* Alianza Editorial, Madrid, 1984.

ESPINOSA GARCÍA, MANUEL: *La política económica de Estados Unidos hacia América Latina entre 1945 y 1961,* Editorial Casa de las Américas, Havana, 1971.

ESTRADE, PAUL: *Bibliografía de temas afrocubanos.* Biblioteca Nacional José Martí, Havana, 1985.

————: *Les clubs féminins dans le Parte Revolutionnaire cubain (1892–1898).* Publications de l'Equipe de Recherches de l'Université de Paris 8, Paris, 1986.

FACTITIOUS COLLECTION, JOSÉ MARTÍ NATIONAL LIBRARY: miscellaneous clippings no. 38, mimeograph.

FARBER, SAMUEL: *Revolution and Reaction in Cuba, 1933–1960: A Political Sociology from Machado to Castro,* Wesleyan University Press, Middletown, Conn., 1976.

FERNÁNDEZ ROBAINA, TOMÁS: *El negro en Cuba, 1902–1958,* Editorial de Ciencias Sociales, Havana, 1990.

FERROCARRILES UNIDOS DE LA HABANA: *Tarifa coordinada de clases especiales no. 2,* Havana, 1945

FONT, MAURICIO A.: "Azúcar y desarrollo en Cuba, 1902–1959: Reflexiones para un estudio," paper presented at a meeting of the Latin American Association, Miami, December 1989.

FOREIGN POLICY ASSOCIATION: *Problems of the New Cuba,* New York, 1935.

FREEMAN SMITH, ROBERT: *Cuba: Laboratory for Dollar Diplomacy, The Historian* 28, 4, August 1966.

FREYRE DE ANDRADE, LEOPOLDO: *La restricción de la zafra,* Havana, 1931.

FUNG RIVERÓN, THALÍA: *En torno a las regularidades y particularidades de la Revolución Socialista en Cuba*, Editorial de Ciencias Sociales, Havana, 1982.

GALICH, MANUEL: *Jóvenes de esta América*, Colección Honda, Editorial Casa de las Américas, Havana, 1978.

GÁLVEZ RODRÍGUEZ, WILLIAM: *Frank, entre el sol y la montaña*, Ediciones UNION, Havana, 1991.

GARCÍA, ALEJANDRO: *La gran burguesía comercial en Cuba, 1898–1920*, Editorial de Ciencias Sociales, Havana, 1990.

GARCÍA GALLÓ, GASPAR JORGE: *Biografía del tabaco habano*, Departamento de Relaciones Culturales, Universidad Central de las Villas, Santa Clara, 1959.

GARCÍA GALLÓ, GASPAR JORGE, and M. MIER FEBLES: "Recuento histórico de dos décadas. Primera parte (1948–1958)," mimeograph, n.d.

GARCÍA OLIVERA, JULIO: *José Antonio Echeverría: La lucha estudiantil contra Batista*, Editora Política, Havana, 1979.

GARCÍA-PÉREZ, GLADYS: *Insurrection and Revolution: Armed Struggle in Cuba, 1952–1959*, Lynne Rienner Publishers, Boulder, Colo., 1998.

GONZÁLES DE MENDOZA, LUIS: *Revista Semanal Azucarera. (Selecciones 1935–1945)*, Editorial Bolsa de Havana, Havana, 1945.

GONZÁLES FERNÁNDEZ, DORIA: "La manufactura tabacalera cubana," *Revista de Indias* 52, 194, January–April 1982.

GRAMSCI, ANTONIO: *Cuadernos de la cárcel*, vol. 1, Editorial Era, Mexico City, 1975.

GROBART, FABIO: "El movimiento obrero cubano," *Cuba Socialista*, Havana, August 1966.

GUERRA, RAMIRO: *La industria azucarera de Cuba*, Editorial Cultural S.A. Havana, 1940.

———: *Filosofía de la producción cubana*, Editorial Cultural S.A. Havana, 1944.

———: *Azúcar y población en las Antillas*, Editorial de Ciencias Sociales, Havana, 1961.

GUEVARA, ERNESTO: *Escritos y discursos*, vol. 2, Editorial de Ciencias Sociales, Havana, 1977.

GUNDER FRANK, ANDRÉ: "¿Quién es el enemigo inmediato? Latinoamérica: subdesarrollo capitalista o revolución socialista," *Cuadernos Ruedo Ibérico*, October–November 1967.

———: *Capitalismo y subdesarrollo en América Latina*, Editorial de Ciencias Sociales, Havana, 1970.

GURRIERY, ADOLFO, and EDELBERTO TORRES SILVA: "Situación de la juventud dentro del complejo económico-social de América Latina," *Jóvenes de esta América*, Editorial Casa de las Américas, Havana, 1978.

GURVITCH, GEORGES: *El concepto de clases sociales*, Editorial de Ciencias Sociales, Havana, 1970.

GUTIÉRREZ, GUSTAVO: *El desarrollo económico de Cuba*, Publicaciones de la Junta Nacional de Economía, Havana, 1952.

GUTIÉRREZ, RAÚL: "Encuestas electorales; estados de opinión pública," *Bohemia*, June 25, 1950: 83; December 26, 1950: 75; May 20, 1951: suppl. 8–9; December 16, 1951: 16.

GUTIÉRREZ VALLADÓN, VIRIATO: *Estudios sobre el problema azucarero, 1939–1944*, Havana, 1945.

———: *El problema mundial del azúcar*, Madrid, 1952.

HELG, ALINE: *Our Rightful Share: The Afro-Cuban Struggle for Equality, 1886–1912*, University of North Carolina Press, Chapel Hill, 1995.

HERNÁNDEZ CASTELLÓN, RAÚL, and PEDRO VALDÉS SUÁREZ: *La población*, Editorial de Ciencias Sociales, Havana, 1978.
HOERNEL, ROBERT S.: "Sugar and Social Change in Oriente, Cuba, 1898–1946," *Journal of Latin American Studies* 8, 1976.
HUBERMAN, LEO, and PAUL SWEEZY: *Cuba, anatomía de una revolución*, Vanguardia obrera, Havana, 1961.
———: *Socialism in Cuba*, Monthly Review Press, New York, 1969.
HUIZAR, GORRIT: *El potencial revolucionario en América Latina*, Editorial Siglo XXI, Mexico City, 1973.
IBARRA CUESTA, JORGE: "La investigación leninista del tránsito hacia el capitalismo en Rusia," *Casa de las Américas* 10, 59, March–April 1970.
———: "La generación del cincuentenario," *Aproximaciones a Clío*, Editorial de Ciencias Sociales, Havana, 1979.
———: "La generación del cincuentenario," *Boletín bibliográfico de Educación Interna del Comité Central del Partido Comunista de Cuba*, no. 2, 1984.
———: "Los mecanismos económicos del capital financiero obstaculizan la formación de la burguesía doméstica cubana," *Islas*, no. 79, September–December 1984.
———: *Cuba: 1898–1921. Partidos políticos y clases sociales*, Editorial de Ciencias Sociales, Instituto Cubano del Libro, Havana, 1992.
———: *Cuba; 1898–1958. Estructura y procesos sociales*, Havana, 1995.
IBARRA GUITART, JORGE RENATO: *La SAR: dictadura, mediación y revolución (1952–1955)*, Colección Pinos Nuevos, Editorial de Ciencias Sociales, Instituto Cubano del Libro, Havana, 1994.
IGLESIAS, FE, and SONIA MORO: *Contribución al estudio de la sociedad cubana en 1943 y 1953. Una investigación de estructura social basado en el procesamiento de los censos*, Departamento de Historia del Instituto de Ciencias Sociales de la Academia de Ciencias de Cuba, n.d.
INSTITUTO DE HISTORIA DEL PARTIDO COMUNISTA Y DE LA REV-OLUCIÓN SOCIALISTA DE CUBA: *Movimiento obrero cubano. Documentos y artículos*, 2 vols. (1865–1935), Editorial de Ciencias Sociales, Havana, 1975–1977; 2 vols. (1865–1958), Editora Política, Havana, 1980.
INTERNATIONAL BANK FOR RECONSTRUCTION AND DEVELOPMENT: *Report on Cuba*, vols. 1–4, John Hopkins University Press, Baltimore 1951.
IRISARRI, JOSÉ MANUEL: "La moneda cubana y los problemas económicos," *Revista Bimestre Cubana*, no. 2, March–April 1931.
JAMES, ARIEL: *Banes, imperialismo y nación en una plantación azucarera*, Editorial de Ciencias Sociales, Havana, 1976.
JAMES, JOEL: *Cuba, 1900–1928. La república dividida contra si misma*, Instituto Cubano del Libro, Santiago de Cuba, 1974.
JENKS, LELAND: *Nuestra colonia cubana*, Edición Revolucionaria, Havana, 1966.
KERBLAY, BASILE, and DANIEL THORNER: *Chayanov y la teoría de la economía campesina*, Ed. F.C.E., Mexico City, 1981.
KOROBEINIKOV, A.: "Sucesión del proceso revolucionario," *La sociedad y la sucesión de las generaciones*, Editorial Progreso, Moscow, 1979.
KOVAL, BORIS: "El proletariado agrícola y su lugar en la estructura social del campo latinoamericano," *América Latina. Editorial Academia de Ciencias de la URSS, Redacción Ciencias Sociales Contemporáneas*, Moscow, 1974.
KUCZYNSKI, JÜRGEN, KARL LAMER, et al.: *Monopolios norteamericanos en*

Cuba. Contribución al estudio de la penetración imperialista, Editorial de Ciencias Sociales, Havana, 1973.

KULA, WITOLD: *Problemas y métodos de la historia económica*, Barcelona, 1973.

LABROUSSE, ERNEST, ALBERT SOBOUL, et al.: *L'Histoire sociale. Source et méthodes*, Presses Universitaires de France, Paris, 1967.

LACLAU, ERNESTO: *Política e ideología en la teoría marxista*, Editorial Siglo XXI, Mexico City, 1980.

LARGUÍA, ISABEL, and JOHN DUMOULIN: "Aspectos de la condición social de la mujer," *Casa de las Américas* 15, 88, January–February 1975.

————: *Hacia una concepción científica en la emancipación de la mujer*, Editorial de Ciencias Sociales, Havana, 1983.

LEEDS, ANTHONY, ed.: *Seminar on Social Structure, Stratification and Mobility*, Pan American Union, Washington, D.C., 1967.

LEFEBVRE, HENRI: *La survie du capitalisme*, Editions Anthropos, Paris, 1973.

LENIN, V. I.: *El problema agrario de la social democracia*, Montevideo, 1954.

————: *Obras completas*, vols. 1, 3, 4, Editorial Cartago, Buenos Aires, 1958; vol. 15, 1960.

LE RIVEREND, JULIO: "Historia económica de Cuba," *Historia de la nación cubana*, Havana, 1952.

LINDSAY, FORBES: *Cuba and Her People of Today*, Boston, 1919.

LLOYD, REGINALD: *Twentieth Century Impressions of Cuba*, Lloyds, London, 1913.

LÓPEZ SEGRERA, FRANCISCO: "Algunos aspectos de la industria azucarera cubana," *La República neocolonial*, vol. 2, Editorial de Ciencias Sociales, Havana, 1979.

————: *Cuba: capitalismo dependiente y subdesarrollo, 1950–1959*, Editorial Casa de las Américas, Havana, 1979.

LORENZO, RAÚL: *El empleo en Cuba*, Seonne, Fernández, y Cía, Havana, 1955.

LOVEIRA, CARLOS: *Delos 26 a los 35. Lecciones de la experiencia en la lucha obrera. 1908–1917*, Law Reporter Printing Company, Washington, D.C., 1917.

LUGO, EVELIO: "La industria del tabaco y sus perspectivas," *Cuba Socialista* 3, 21, May 1963.

LUPIÁNEZ, JOSÉ: *El movimiento estudiantil en Santiago de Cuba*, Editorial de Ciencias Sociales, Havana, 1985.

LUZARDO, MANUEL: "Subsidio o trabajo para los desocupados," *Fundamentos* 9, 93, November 1946.

MAGDOFF, HARRY: *The Age of Imperialism*, Modern Reader Paper Backs, New York, 1969.

MAGOON, CHARLES E.: *Informe de la administración provisional de la República de Cuba. 1906–1907*, Rambla and Bouza, Havana, 1907.

Manual of Sugar Companies, 7th edition and 34th edition, Farr, New York, 1950 and 1958.

MARQUÉS DOLZ, MARIA ANTONIA: "La burguesía no azucarera cubana ante la crisis del sistema neocolonial," thesis, Biblioteca de la Facultad de Filosofía e Historia, Universidad de Havana, 1981–1982.

————: "Intereses y contradicciones de clases en torno al problema arancelario cubano," *Santiago*, no. 72, Universidad de Oriente, Santiago de Cuba, March 1989.

————: *Estado y economía en la antesala de la Revolución, 1940–1952*, Colección Pinos Nuevos, Editorial de Ciencias Sociales, Instituto Cubano del Libro, Havana, 1994.

MARTÍNEZ ALLIER, JUAN: "El latifundio en Andalucía y en América Latina," *Cuadernos Ruedo Ibérico*, October–November 1967.
———: *Haciendas plantations and collective farms*, Frank Cass, London, 1977.
MARTÍNEZ SÁENZ, JOAQUÍN: *Por la independencia económica de Cuba. Mi gestión en el Banco Nacional*, Editorial Cenit, S.A., Havana, 1959.
MARX, KARL: *El capital*, Fondo de Cultura Económica, México, D.F., 1946.
———: *Sobre la literatura y el arte*, Editora Política, Havana, 1965.
MARX, KARL, and FREDERICK ENGELS: *Collected Works*, Progress Publisher, Moscow, 1980.
———: *Ideología alemana*, Editorial Victoria, Mexico City, 1988.
MAYO, JOSÉ: *La guerrilla se vistió de yarey*, Editora Política, Havana, 1979.
MEDEROS, ELENA: "La indigencia en Cuba. ¿Es un mal controlable?" *Cuadernos de la Universidad del Aire del Circuito CMQ*, October 1940–June 1950, Ed. Lex, May 1950.
"Memorándum de la Asociación de Entidades del Comercio Exterior de Cuba al Secretario de Estado," *Cuba Económica y Financiera* 13, 151, December 1938.
MESA LAGO, CARMELO: *The Labor Force, Employment, Unemployment and Underemployment*, Sage Publications, Beverly Hills, Calif., 1972.
MIKESELL, RAYMOND F.: "Foreign Investments in Latin America," Interamerican and Social Council, Organization of American States, Washington, D.C., 1955.
MINNEMAN, P. G.: *The Agriculture of Cuba*, U.S. Department of Agriculture, Washington, D.C., 1942.
———: "Mechanization of Cuban Agriculture," mimeograph, 1947.
MINTZ, SIDNEY W.: "Petits cultivateurs et proletaires ruraux dans la région des Caribes," *Les problèmes agraires des Amériques Latines*, Centre Nacional de la Recherche Scientifique, Paris, 1967.
MONDÉJAR, JOHN P.: "Neo-colonialism as an Economic System: Cuba, 1898–1934," Ph.D. diss., Indiana University, 1976.
MONTORO, RAFAEL: *Obras*, vol. 3, Cultural, S.A., Havana, 1930.
MORENO FRAGINALS, MANUEL: *El ingenio*, 3 vols., Editorial de Ciencias Sociales, Havana, 1978.
MOSKICHOV, L.: *La sociedad y la sucesión de las generaciones*, Editorial Progreso, Moscow, 1979.
NARANJO OROVIO, CONSUELO: *Del campo a la bodega: recuerdos de gallegos en Cuba (Siglo XX)*, Edicios do Castro, Coruña, 1988.
NELSON, LOWRY: *Rural Cuba*, University of Minnesota Press, Minneapolis, 1950.
NIN ABARCA, MARIO: "El azúcar refino y la Carta del Atlántico," *Cuba Económica y Financiera*, July 1944.
NÚÑEZ JIMÉNEZ, ANTONIO: *Geografía de Cuba*, Editorial Lex, Havana, 1962.
O'CONNOR, JAMES: *The Origins of Socialism in Cuba*, Cornell University Press, Ithaca, New York, 1970.
OKUNIEVA, M.: *La clase obrera en la Revolución Cubana*, Editorial Progreso/Editorial de Ciencias Sociales, Moscow, 1988.
ORDOQUÍ, JOAQUÍN: *Elementos para la historia del movimiento obrero*, Havana, 1961.
OSA, ENRIQUE DE LA: *En Cuba Primer tiempo (1943–1946)*, Editorial de Ciencias Sociales, Havana, 1960.
OSHIMA, HARRY T.: "The New Estimate of the National Income and

Product of Cuba in 1953," *Food Research Institute Studies,* November 1961.

OSSOWSKI, STANISLAW: *Estructura de clases y conciencia social,* Editorial Península, Madrid, 1969.

PARDEIRO, F.: "Grupos fundamentales de la oligarquía financiera norteamericana en la economía de Cuba pre-revolucionaria," *Los monopolios extranjeros en Cuba, 1898–1950,* Editorial de Ciencias Sociales, Havana, 1984.

PARTIDO SOCIALISTA POPULAR (PSP): *Las tareas de PSP en la lucha por los derechos de la población negra,* Havana, 1947.

————: *VIII Asamblea Nacional,* Ediciones Populares, Havana, 1960.

PAVÓN GONZÁLEZ, RAMIRO: *El empleo femenino en Cuba,* Havana, 1977.

PEÑA, LÁZARO: "La unidad de la clase obrera cubana," *Fundamentos* 3, 68, June 1947.

PERDOMO, JOSÉ E., and J. POSSE: *Mecanización de la industria tabacalera,* Imprenta La Milagrosa, Havana, 1945.

PÉREZ, FAUSTINO: "La Sierra y el Llano," *Pensamiento Crítico,* no. 51, August 1969.

PÉREZ, LOUIS A., JR.: *Cuba Between Reform and Revolution,* Oxford University Press, New York, 1988.

————: *Cuba and the United States: Ties of Singular Intimacy,* University of Georgia Press, Atlanta, 1990.

PÉREZ, LUIS MARINO: "La situación económica de Cuba," *La Reforma Social,* vol. 6, Havana, 1915–1916.

PÉREZ DE LA RIVA, JUAN: "Brazos para el azúcar: historia de un viejo problema," *Cuba. Comercio exterior,* Havana, March–June 1969.

PÉREZ DE LA RIVA, JUAN, OSCAR PINO SANTOS, et al.: *La República neocolonial,* vol. 2, Editorial de Ciencias Sociales, Havana, 1979.

PÉREZ-STABLE, MARIFELI: "Nationalism and the Struggle for Social Justice," manuscript, June 1988.

————: *The Cuban Revolution: Origins, Course, and Legacy,* Oxford University Press, New York, 1993.

PINO SANTOS, OSCAR: *Historia de Cuba, aspectos fundamentales,* Editora Universitaria, Havana, 1964.

————: *El asalto a Cuba por la oligarquía financiera yanqui,* Casa de las Américas, Havana, 1973.

POLLITT, BRIAN: "Estudios acerca del nivel de vida rural en la Cuba pre-revolucionaria: un análisis crítico," *Teoría y Práctica,* no. 42, 1967.

————: "Some Problems in the Enumeration of the 'Peasantry' in Cuba," *Journal of Peasant Studies* 4, 2, January 1977.

————: *Agrarian Reform and the Agricultural Proletariat in Cuba, 1958–1966: Some Notes,* Institute of Latin American Studies, University of Glasgow, Occasional Papers, no. 27, 1979.

PORTER, ROBERT: *Industrial Cuba,* Young People's Missionary Movement, New York, 1899.

PORTUONDO, JOSÉ ANTONIO: *La Historia y las generaciones,* Editorial Letras Cubanas, Havana, 1981.

PORTUONDO MORET, OCTAVIANO: *El Soviet de Tacajó,* Editorial Oriente, Santiago de Cuba, 1979.

POULANTZAS, NICOS: *Pouvoir politique et classes sociales,* François Maspero, Paris, 1966.

PRIMELLES, LEÓN: *Crónica cubana, 1915–1918,* Editorial Lex, Havana, 1955.

————: *Crónica cubana, 1919–1921,* Editorial Lex, Havana, 1958.

QUESADA, GONZALO DE: *Documentos históricos,* Editorial de la Universidad de Havana, 1965.

RAGGI, CARLOS M.: *Condiciones económicas y sociales de la República de Cuba,* Editorial del Ministerio del Trabajo, Havana, 1944.

———: "Contribution to the Study of the Middle Classes in Cuba," *Materiales para el estudio de la clase media en América Latina,* Pan American Union, Washington, D.C., 1950.

RAVENET RAMÍREZ, MARIANA, and JORGE HERNÁNDEZ MARTÍNEZ: *Estructura social y transformaciones agrarias en Cuba,* Editorial de Ciencias Sociales, Havana, 1984.

REGALADO, ANTERO: "Los pequeños agricultores y el plan azucarero para 1970," *Cuba Socialista* 12, 45–48, May–August 1969.

———: *Las luchas campesinas en Cuba,* Comité Central del Partido Comunista de Cuba, Havana, 1973.

Revolución Cubana, 1953–1980: Selección de lecturas, part 1, Editorial Academia de las Fuerzos Armadas Revolucionarias "General Máximo Gómez," Havana, 1983.

RICCARDI, ANTONIO: "Visión económica de Cuba," in Leland Jenks, *Nuestra colonia cubana,* Edición Revolucionaria, Havana, 1966.

RIERA, MARIO: *Cuba política: 1899–1919,* Empreso Modelo, S.A., Havana, 1955.

RIVERO, NICOLÁS: *Actualidades, 1903–1919,* Cultural, S.A., Havana, 1929.

RIVERO MUÑIZ, JOSÉ: *Tabaco: su Historia en Cuba,* Instituto de Historia, Havana, 1965.

ROA, RAÚL: *El fuego de la semilla en el surco,* Editorial Letras Cubanas, Havana, 1982.

ROCA, BLAS: *Los fundamentos del socialismo en Cuba,* Ediciones Populares, Havana, 1960.

ROCHESTER, ANA: "Lenin y el problema agrario," *Dialéctica* 1, 4, November–December 1942.

RODRÍGUEZ, CARLOS RAFAEL: *Letra con filo,* vols. 1 and 2, Editorial de Ciencias Sociales, Havana, 1963.

———: *Cuba en el tránsito al socialismo. 1959–1963,* Editora Política, Havana, 1979.

RODRÍGUEZ, JOSÉ LUIS: "La economía neocolonial cubana," *Cuba Socialista,* no. 37, January–February 1989.

RODRÍGUEZ, PEDRO PABLO: "El pesimismo nacional burgués: el caso de José Comallonga," *Economía y Desarrollo,* Instituto de Economía de la Universidad de Havana, September–October 1981.

RODRÍGUEZ LOECHE, ENRIQUE: *Bajando el Escambray,* Editorial Letras Cubanas, Havana, 1976.

ROIG DE LEUCHSERING, EMILIO: *Los problemas sociales en Cuba,* Havana, 1927.

ROJAS, URSINIO: *Las luchas obreras en el central Tacajó,* Editora Política, Havana, 1979.

ROSSELL, MIRTA: *Luchas sociales contra Machado,* Editorial de Ciencias Sociales, Havana, 1973.

SABBATINI, MARIO: *La formazione della societa neocoliale cubana,* Estratto da Ideologie, Rome, 1967.

———: "Ill crollo dell'ordine neocoloniale a Cuba," *Ideología,* no. 5–6, 1968.

SANABRIA, JOSÉ A.: "El estado de desnutrición en que vive el pueblo de Cuba," *Bohemia*, March 11, 1956.

SÁNCHEZ OTERO, GERMÁN, FRANCISCO LÓPEZ SEGRERA, and RAMÓN DE ARMAS: *Los partidos políticos burgueses en Cuba neocolonial, 1899–1952*, Editorial de Ciencias Sociales, Havana, 1985.

SANTAMARÍA, ANTONIO: "Los ferrocarriles de servicio público cubanos (1837–1959)," *Revista de Indias* 55, 204, May–August 1995.

SARABIA, NYDIA: *Ana Betancourt Agramonte*, Instituto Cubano del Libro, Havana, 1970.

SARRACINO, RODOLFO: "Los asesores yanquis y la Reforma Tributaria en la década del 30," *Revista de la Biblioteca Nacional "José Martí,"* no. 3, September–December 1978.

SARTRE, JEAN-PAUL: *Sartre visita a Cuba, Ideología y revolución; una entrevista con los escritores cubanos; huracán sobre el azúcar*, Ediciones R., Havana, 1961.

SCHMUCKLER, BEATRIZ: "Familia y dominio patriarcal," *Sociedad y subordinación en el capitalismo*, vol. 3, ed. Magdalena León, Bogotá, 1982.

SCHWARTZ, ROSALIE: *Afro-Cuban Mobility in the Republican Era*, a paper presented at the American Historical Association annual meeting, December 1979.

SEERS, DUDLEY: *Cuba: The Economic and Social Revolution*, University of North Carolina Press, Chapel Hill, 1964.

SEIGLIE Y LLATA, OSCAR: *El contrato de Arrendamiento de Finca Rústica, el latifundio y la legislación Azucarera*, Editorial Lex, Havana, 1953.

SELIGMAN, EDWIN R., and CARL SHOUP: *Informa sobre el Sistema Tributario de Cuba*, Talleres Tipográficos de Caras, Havana, 1932.

SEMIONOV, VÍCTOR: *Clases y lucha de clases*, Editora Política, Havana, 1965.

SHANIN, THEODOR: *Campesinos y sociedades campesinas*, Fondo de Cultura Económica, Mexico City, 1979.

SMITH, ROBERT F.: *The United States and Cuba: Business and Diplomacy (1917–1960)*, College and University Press, New Haven, Conn., 1960.

La sociedad neocolonial cubana, corrientes ideológicas y partidos políticos, Editorial de Ciencias Sociales, Havana, 1984.

SOLÁ, JOSÉ SIXTO DE: "El pesimismo cubano," *Cuba Contemporánea*, vol. 3, Havana, 1915–1916.

"Some Aspects of Recent Evolution of Cuba's Economy," *Economic Review for Latin America*, special issue, August 1955.

SOTO, LIONEL: *La Revolución del 33*, 3 vols., Editorial de Ciencias Sociales, Havana, 1977.

STAVENHAGEN, RODOLFO: "Las relaciones entre la estratificación social y la dinámica de clases," in *Social Structure Stratification and Mobility*, ed. Anthony Leeds, Pan American Union, Washington, D.C., 1967.

————: *Sociología y subdesarrollo*, Editorial Nuestro Tiempo, Mexico City, 1984.

STEPHENS, P. S.: *Economic and Commercial Conditions of Cuba*, Her Majesty's Stationery Office, London, 1954.

STONER, K. LYNN: "In Four Languages, but with One Voice: Division and Solidarity of Pan American Feminism (1923–1938)," manuscript, n.d.

————: *From the House to the Streets: The Woman's Movement for Legal Change, 1899–1940*, Duke University Press, Raleigh, N.C., 1991.

————: "On Men Reforming the Rights of Men: The Abrogation of the Cuban Adultery Law, 1930," *Cuban Studies* 27, 1991.

STUBBS, JEAN; *Tobacco on the Periphery*, Cambridge University Press, Cambridge, 1985.

TABARES DEL REAL, JOSÉ A.: *La revolución del 30: sus dos últimos años*, Editorial de Ciencias Sociales, Havana, 1973.

TELLERÍA TOCA, EVELIO: *Los congresos obreros en Cuba*, Editorial Arte y Literatura, Havana, 1973.

THOMAS, HUGH: "Middle Class Politics and the Cuban Revolution," *The Politics of Conformity in Latin America*, ed. Claudio Véliz, Royal Institute of International Affairs, Oxford University Press, London, 1967.

————: *Cuba: The Pursuit of Freedom, 1762–1969*, Harper, London, 1970.

TORRAS, JACINTO: "Lo que antes costaba un peso, hoy precisa para su adquisición, tres," *Hoy*, September 2, 1947.

————: *Obras escogidas*, 3 vols., Editora Política, Havana, 1984–1985.

TRUSLOW, FRANCIS ADAMS: *Report on Cuba*, vols. 1–5, International Bank for Reconstruction and Development, Washington, D.C., 1951.

TUÑÓN DE LARA, MANUEL: *Metodología de la historia social de España*, Editorial Siglo XXI, Mexico City, 1984.

UNIÓN PANAMERICANA, INSTITUTO INTERAMERICANO DE ESTADÍSTICAS: *América en cifras, 7. Estadísticas Sociales y de trabajo*, Washington, D.C., 1956.

UNITED NATIONS: *Estudio económico de América Latina*, Mexico City, 1955.

U.S. DEPARTMENT OF COMMERCE: *Investments in Cuba*, U.S. Government Printing Office, Washington, D.C., 1956.

————: *Investments in the Latin American Economy*, U.S. Goverment Printing Office, Washington, D.C., 1956.

U.S. SENATE, COMMITEE ON FINANCE: *Hearing on Sugar Act Extension*, 84th Congress, Washington, D.C., 1956.

U.S. TARIFF COMMISSION: *Sugar Report to the President of the United States*, GPO, Washington, D.C., 1934.

USEEM, B.: "Peasant Involvement in the Cuban Revolution," *Journal of Peasants Studies* 5, 1, 1977.

VALMAÑA, EUGENIO DE: *Marina mercante cubana*, Havana, 1945.

VILAR, CÉSAR: "Sobre el problema del café en Cuba," *Fundamentos* 9, 39, Havana, 1949.

VILAR, PIERRE: *Crecimiento y desarrollo*, Editorial Ariel S.A., Barcelona, 1983.

VIVÓ, HUGO: *El empleo y la población actual de Cuba*, Editorial Asociación Nacional de Industriales de Cuba, Havana, 1950.

WALLICH, HENRY CHRISTOPHER: *Monetary Problems of an Export Economy: The Cuban Experience, 1914–1947*, Harvard University Press, Cambridge, 1950.

WHITE, BYRON: *Azúcar amargo*, Publicaciones Cultural, Havana, 1954.

WILSON, JAMES H.: *Report of Brigadier General James H. Wilson, Commanding the Department of Matanzas and Santa Clara for the Calendar Year of 1899*, GPO, Matanzas, August 7–September 7, 1899.

WINOCUR, MARCOS: *Las clases olvidadas en la Revolución Cubana*, Editorial Crítica, Barcelona, 1971.

————: *Historia social de la Revolución Cuban, 1952–1959: Las clases olvidadas en el análisis histórico*, Facultad de Economía, UNAM, Mexico City, 1989.

WOLF, ERIC: *Peasant Wars in the Twentieth Century*, Harper and Row, London, 1973.

WOLTER DE RÍO, GERMÁN: *Aportaciones para una política económica*, Havana, 1912.

WOOD, LEONARD: *Civil Report of Brigadier General Leonard Wood, 1901*, n.d.
WRIGHT, P.: *The Cuban Situation and Our Treaty Relations*, Brookings Institution, Washington, D.C., 1931.
XIMENO, ALBERTO DE: *Los ferrocarriles de Cuba*, Havana, 1912.
YGLESIA, TERESITA: *Cuba: primera República, segunda ocupación*, Editorial de Ciencias Sociales, Havana, 1977.
————: *El segundo ensayo de República*, Editorial de Ciencias Sociales, Havana, 1980.
ZANETTI, OSCAR: "El comercio exterior de la República neocolonial," *La República neocolonial*, vol. 1, Editorial de Ciencias Sociales, Havana, 1975.
————: "Las clases de la sociedad cubana en vísperas de la revolución," *Arbor*, March 1993.
ZANETTI, OSCAR, and ALEJANDRO GARCÍA: *United Fruit Co.: un caso de dominio imperialista en Cuba*, Editorial de Ciencias Sociales, Havana, 1976.
————: *Caminos para el azúcar*, Editorial de Ciencias Sociales, Havana, 1987.
ZEITLIN, MAURICE: *Revolutionary Politics and the Cuban Working Class*, Princeton University Press, Princeton, N.J., 1967.
ZUAZNABAR, ISMAEL: *La economía cubana en la década del 50*, Editorial de Ciencias Sociales, Havana, 1986.

Other Sources Consulted

Periodicals

El Acusador, 1952.
Anuario de Estadística Judicial, 1917.
Anuario Estadístico de Cuba, 1957, 1980.
Bohemia, 1945–1958.
Boletín de la Asociación Nacional de Industriales de Cuba (ANIC), 1954–1955.
Boletín de la Cámara de Comercio, 1890–1892.
Boletín de la Junta General de Comercio de Havana, 1881.
Boletín de la Secretaria de Hacienda, 1915, 1918.
Boletín Informativo del Consejo Nacional de Economía, 1953–1958.
Boletín Oficial de Salubridad y Asistencia Social, 1943–1944.
Boletín Oficial del Seguro de Salud y Maternidad Obrera, 1940.
Carteles, 1934–1940.
Casa de las Américas, 1978.
Cuba Económica y Financiera, 1938–1958.
Cuba Importadora e Industrial, 1934–1935, 1937.
La Discusión, 1901–1903.
El Economista, 1903–1909.
Estudios Demográficos, 1975.
Fundamentos, 1938–1952.
Granma, 1970.
Mella, 1957.
El Mercurio, 1919–1921.
El Mundo, 1934–1936.
Panorama Económico Latinoamericano, 1961.
Revista del Banco Nacional de Cuba, 1955–1956.
Revista Interamericana de Ciencias Sociales, 2nd series, 3, special

edition, Unión Panamericana. Secretaría general. Organización de los Estados Americanos, Washington, D.C., 1964.
Santiago (Universidad de Oriente), 1975.
El Tabaco, 1912–1927.
The Times of Cuba, 1926.
El Trimestre Económico, 1963.

Statistical Sources

Anuario Azucarero de Cuba, compiled and edited by *Cuba Económica y Financiera,* 1936–1961.
BANCO NACIONAL DE CUBA: *La economía cubana en 1951–1952,* Havana, 1953.
————: *Memorias,* 1954–1955, 1955–1956, 1957–1958, and 1958–1959.
COMISIÓN NACIONAL DE ESTADÍSTICAS Y REFORMAS ECONÓMICAS, 1927–1933.
CUBA: *Censo de la República de Cuba bajo la administración provisional de los EE:UU., 1907,* Bureau of the Census, Washington, D.C., 1908.
————: *Census of the Republic of Cuba, 1919,* Editorial Maza, Arroyo y Caso, S. en C., Havana, 1921.
————: *Informe General del Censo de 1943,* P. Fernández, Havana, 1945.
————, COMERCIO EXTERIOR: *Anuarios,* 1905–1909, 1925–1929, and 1945–1949.
————, MINISTERIO DE AGRICULTURA: *Memoria del Censo Agrícola Nacional, 1946,* P. Fernández, Havana, 1951.
————, MINISTERIO DE AGRICULTURA, COMISIÓN NACIONAL DE PROPAGANDA Y DEFENSA DEL TABACO HABANO: *Primer Censo de Obreros de la Industria Tabacalera,* Havana, 1947.
————, MINISTERIO DE AGRICULTURA, DIRECCIÓN DE INDUSTRIAS: *Estadística Industrial,* 1945.
————, MINISTERIO DE HACIENDA: *Comercio Exterior, 1945–1958,* P. Fernández, Havana, 1958.
————, SECRETARÍA DE AGRICULTURA, INDUSTRIA Y COMERCIO: *Portafolio de la industria azucarera,* Havana, 1915.
————, TRIBUNAL SUPERIOR ELECTORAL: *Censos de Población, Vivienda y Electoral. Informe General, 1953,* P. Fernández, Havana, 1955.
SECCIÓN DE ESTADÍSTICAS: *El empleo, el subempleo y el desempleo en Cuba, 1958,* Editorial del Consejo Nacional de Economía, Havana, n.d.
U.S. DEPARTMENT OF WAR: *Informa sobre el Censo de Cuba, 1899,* appendix 19, Office of the Director of the Census of Cuba, Government Printing Office, Washington, D.C., 1900.

Index

Abalos, José, 192
Abecedario Party (ABC), 151, 187
Absentee bourgeoisie, 49–52
ACU. *See* Catholic University
    Association
Afro-Cubans. *See* Blacks
Agrarian bourgeoisie, 33–34, 36–37,
    38, 42, 43, 46, 70. *See also*
    Capitalism, in agriculture;
    Landholders; Sugar bourgeoisie
Agrarian reform (1959), 30
Agricultural associations, 73–74
Agricultural cooperatives, 116
Agricultural landholders. *See*
    Agrarian bourgeoisie; Land
    administrators; Land leasehold-
    ers; Land ownership; Land pro-
    prietors; Sharecroppers;
    Squatters; Tenant farmers
Agricultural machinery, 41, 47–48
Agricultural production values,
    43–44, 72. *See also* Subsistence
    farming
Agricultural workers, 40; black, 142,
    144(table); counts of, 110–112,
    123, 162, 163, 178, 187; in dead
    season, 110, 112, 177; displace-
    ment of, 42; income of, 112, 118.
    See also Proletariat, rural
Agriculture, Industry, and
    Commerce, Secretariat of, 75, 108

Alemán, José Manuel, 65
Alonso, Eustaquio, 22
Álvarez de Acevedo, J. M., 88
Aparcería, 71. *See also* Sharecroppers
Arechabala family, 23
Aréchaga, Amado, 192
Arguelles y Busto, Ramón, 22
Arredondo, Alberto, 107
Artisans, 8, 61–62, 83–84, 86, 88, 100,
    143
Aspiraciones, 138
Association of Commission Agents,
    23
Association of Industrialists, 26, 31,
    32
Association of Veterans and Patriots,
    66
Auténtico Party, 59, 66, 68, 82, 96,
    101, 102, 103, 118, 119, 120, 151,
    168, 183, 184, 187
Autonomist Party, 33

Bairoch, Paul, 62
Balcell, José, 22
Baliño, Carlos, 183
Ballegas, Emilio, 150
Bambirra, Vania, 126
BANDES. *See* Bank of Economic and
    Social Development
Bank of Agricultural and Industrial
    Development of Cuba, 74

About the Book

This landmark study traces economic development, social dynamics, and political processes in Cuba from the end of Spanish colonial rule to the triumph of the 1959 revolution.

Ibarra explores the complex and compelling relationship between North American capital investment and the formation—and deformation—of Cuba's national institutions. Focusing especially on class structures, gender roles, race relations, and political change, he brings to life the social and economic circumstances in which most Cubans lived before 1959. He also illuminates the multiple ways in which relations with the United States contributed to shaping the moral and material environment of daily life on the island.

Jorge Ibarra is one of Cuba's most distinguished social and cultural historians. This is the first of his many books to be translated into English.